The Immigrant Next Door

Collected Stories of the American Experience

Praise for *The Immigrant Next Door: Collected Stories of the American Experience*

"James Kenyon assembles a compelling, diverse choir of immigrant voices that deliver a unified song of humanity in his collection of stories, *The Immigrant Next Door*. Kenyon's historical exploration reveals the foundational connecting point for us all, reminding us through the bond of stories that we all have immigrant origins. These stories resonate with a compelling vibrancy that validates the strongest human ties that best happen at the individual level."

    —John Busbee, *The Culture Buzz*, winner of a 2014 Iowa History Award for a feature magazine story

"In *The Immigrant Next Door*, Kenyon shares the stories of individuals from around the globe, who have come to America looking for a new life. Ultimately these are stories not just of hope and freedom, but of love, loss, success, and disappointment. These are stories that need to be told. Their stories are our stories."

    —Lindsey Bartlett, author of *Vacant Childhood*

"Reading this book was an emotional experience for me. As the Director of Special Education and other services in a large urban school district in Texas, I was fortunate to work with many immigrants—special needs children, their parents and fellow educators. One 'immigrant' in particular stands out. This educator and her very affluent family fled Cuba right after the Bay of Pigs. She and her family were terrified and feared for their lives. It certainly made me realize that I had always taken for granted my freedom and safety. She is a lifelong friend and greatly influenced my career. I am grateful she and her family were able to relocate to the United States."

    —Patricia Groda, Ed.D., retired special educator

". . . My mother, aunts, and uncles were first generation Americans who felt they were under the looking glass to demonstrate that they were worthy citizens. Accordingly, each of my uncles served military assignments in World War II. This obligation of duty and integrity was instilled in me and my siblings early in life and I've found this to be a common expectation of immigrant families, no matter their origin . . . I would like to compliment Jim Kenyon for assembling his story collection about these special people who contribute so much to our country and to our social fabric. His set of non-fiction stories truly celebrates the 'Immigrant Next Door.'"

—Wallace Groda

The Immigrant Next Door

Collected Stories of the American Experience

James Kenyon

MEADOWLARK PRESS

established 2014

EMPORIA, KANSAS

Meadowlark Press, LLC
meadowlarkbookstore.com
PO Box 333, Emporia, Kansas 66801

The Immigrant Next Door:
Collected Stories of the American Experience
Copyright © 2024 James Kenyon
www.jamesrkenyon.com

Cover art by Barbara Seward Kenyon
Interior Design by Emilie A. Moll, Meadowlark Press

CULTURE / Immigration / General
HISTORY / Essays & Narratives
BIOGRAPHY & AUTOBIOGRAPHY / Personal Memoirs

ISBN: 978-1-956578-69-0 (paperback)
            978-1-956578-70-6 (ebook)

Library of Congress Control Number: 2025909449

I dedicate this collection of stories from all over the world to my aunt, Dr. Ivanoel Gibbins. She served for thirty-six years as a missionary and medical doctor in India during the world's Great Depression, World War II, India's Independence (and the subsequent partition of the Muslims and Hindus), and the Cold War.

With the Philadelphia Presbyterian Church as her sponsor, she founded a hospital in the city of Ambala where the surgery wing is named after her. She treated all Muslims and Hindus as children of God. She was awarded the King George Medal recognizing her civilian gallantry during wartime.

She sailed around the world six times. She sponsored Indian doctors and nurses to come to America to study and further their education. She brought them to our farm home in remote Western Kansas. Dr. Misera and Lilly Telaram were the first foreigners or immigrants that I ever met.

Lilly was a young, tall and beautiful lady. She wore a stunning full length colorful sari. I sat on her lap at the age of four. I looked into her eyes and face and touched her mahogany-colored cheek and asked, "Lilly, why is your skin so tan?" She smiled and said, "Jimmy, that is the way I was born."

So, wherever on the earth a child is born, each one is a miracle to humanity. To be and become an American is a dream of millions. I believe that Aunt Ivanoel would still be treating the downtrodden, the weak, the poor, and today's immigrants, whether legal or illegal, just as she cared for each of those in her beloved India.

Thank you, Auntie I, for showing me this love for all.

Also by James Kenyon

The Art of Listening to the Heart

A Cow for College and Other Stories of 1950s Farm Life

Golden Rule Days: History and Recollections of

109 Closed Kansas High Schools

Echoes in the Hallway: History and Recollections of

102 Closed Iowa High Schools

A Cat Named Fatima: Tales of 23 Cats & the

People Who Loved Them

Table of Contents

Historical information for this book was gathered through a compilation of research by the author and accounts given by the subjects of the interviews. While historical details are included to add context to the personal stories in this book, we acknowledge that those details may not be factually precise. The historical details from the interviews have been corroborated to the best of our ability.

Introduction

I received an assignment in the fifth grade in my remote rural hometown elementary school. It was to write a biography on a renowned person. Nearly sixty-five years later, I find myself performing the same exercise.

Happenstance. Serendipity. And a fascinating world opened to me.

It started with a coincidental meeting which took place thirty months ago on a Saturday afternoon in Sarasota, Florida. My SUV had been towed to a nearby auto and tire repair shop. I was seated in the front room waiting for the report from the mechanic. In walks a middle-aged man who was wearing a black T-shirt with the word BUDAPEST in large letters across the front. I looked up and our eyes met. I remarked, "You don't see many of those around here." He quipped, "That's exactly why I wear it!" His father, a white-haired gentleman using a walking cane, was accompanying him.

Our conversation started with Budapest and soon moved to the country of Hungary. Celebrated journalistic interviewer, Barbara Walters would have been proud of me as the pages of history unfurled from this older gentleman. For the next hour, I questioned. I listened. He poured out his incredible life story—that of a 1956 Hungarian Revolution refugee who came to America.

Their BMW was finished before my car. I walked them to their vehicle. As they opened the car door, I asked, "Is any of this written down?" Both father and son said, "Oh, it's all in our heads."

I exclaimed incredulously, "This story needs to be told!"

Two days later, I arranged to meet them for coffee at a local restaurant. As the famous radio story commentator, Paul Harvey would say, "And now, this is the rest of the story!"

Thirty months later and I had accumulated more immigrant interviews and completed the research. These thirty-one biographies came to me as word of mouth suggestions from acquaintances. These people left their home countries from five different continents. Whether as refugees, asylum seekers, winners of the immigration lottery, or people hoping for a better life, they all came to America.

Determination, drive, and extremely hard work have assimilated these immigrants into successful lives in their new country.

The battle of public opinion continues about illegal aliens coming unwanted to the United States. As the world's largest and greatest democracy, the melding of people of different skin color, religion, and ethnicity will continue. Man's humanity to man remains active.

James Kenyon

This picture hangs on Ahmed's office wall
and reminds him of his father in Iraq.

Ahmed*

A protected Iraqi survivor of the war in Najaf
immigrated to a midwestern city.

"We were Muslim (Shia), but my family understood that we had a role in the community which was bigger than just being Shia or Sunni . . . We were brought up having an openness to those with other faiths and to see the good that all people have, no matter of religion." —Ahmed

*The name of Ahmed has been changed for protection and anonymity.

Ahmed

The "Cradle of Civilization" is what is known as ancient Meso-potamia, or present-day Iraq. This is the land between the Tigris and Euphrates rivers. The "Fertile Crescent" refers to an arching geographical area from Israel, Palestine, Lebanon, and Syria, north toward the Mediterranean, east toward the Republic of Türkiye (Turkey's official name approved by the United Nations in 2022) and down toward Mesopotamia. Much of present-day Iraq lies within the borders of Mesopotamia. It borders Türkiye to the north, Iran to the east, Kuwait and the Persian Gulf southeast, Saudia Arabia to the south, Jordan to the southwest, and Syria to the west. Most of the people are Arabs, and there also live Kurds, Turkmen, Assyrians, Armenians, Yazidis, Mandaeans, Persians, and Shabaks.

Iraq's land area covers 168,753 sq. mi. (437,000 sq. km.)—about the size of California and slightly larger than Paraguay. Its geography is forty percent rocky desert, and thirty percent mountains. The fertile alluvial plains in the south are conducive to farming. It is mostly a Muslim country, where three-fifths of the Muslims are Shia and about two-fifths of them are Sunni. The languages spoken are Arabic and Kurdish. Two-thirds of the people are Arabs, one-fourth Kurds, and the remainder are small minority groups. Most identify with family more strongly than a national confession.

The history of the region archeologically dates back more than thirteen thousand years. There is evidence of written words recorded three thousand years ago. In the last quarter of the fourth century BC, Alexander the Great conquered the area and the Hellenistic Seleucid Empire (the Greeks) ruled for the next two centuries. This was followed by the Romans' control of the region. Christianity took hold from the first through third centuries AD. Islam, with the prophet Muhammad, took root in the seventh century AD.

The Ottoman Empire ruled Ottoman Iraq from 1534-1918. The British captured Baghdad in 1917. In this Mesopotamian campaign, the British lost 92,000 men. With the fall of the Otto-man Empire and the end of World War I, the British and League of Nations joined three provinces of Mosul, Baghdad, and Basra. The English word for the country changed from Mesopotamia to the endonym, Iraq. Modern Iraq began in 1921 as a British kingdom under Faisal I of Iraq. Independence from the British came in 1932. The monarchy was overthrown in 1958, and the Republic of Iraq was created.

From 1968-2003, the Arab Socialist Ba'ath Party was led by Ahmad Hassan al-Bakr, and later by Saddam Hussein. The Iran-Iraq War from 1980-1988 took an estimated 500 thousand to 1.5 million Iraqi lives.

It was during this war, in 1984, that Ahmed was born in Babylon, about one hundred miles south of Baghdad. His father was a merchant and farmer near the Euphrates River, and his mother cared for the family's seven children. This was considered a small family by Iraqi standards. They grew corn, wheat, rice, cotton, cucumbers, okra, tomatoes, watermelon, eggplant, and dates. They farmed with Massey Ferguson and Fiat tractors. His parents instilled in their children a faith in others and community. Ahmed shared:

> We were Muslim (Shia), but my family understood that we had a role in the community which was bigger than just being Shia or Sunni. We were not brought up in a house that focused on Shia or Sunni. We were brought up having an openness to those with other faiths and to see the good that all people have, no matter of religion.

Many wars impacted Ahmed's life. Ahmed's uncle, his father's brother, was among the nearly one million Iraqi men killed in the hideous Iran-Iraq War. The parties signed a truce after eight years of fighting. There were no land boundaries changed after the war. Saddam Hussein's Ba'ath party had borrowed $14 billion from Kuwait to help fund his war machine.

When Ahmed was six years old, Iraq invaded Kuwait. Iraq found it was not possible to repay the debt, and Saddam's forces invaded the oil-rich Kuwait to make it part of Iraq. A forty-two-country coalition, led by the United States, challenged this occupation. The one hundred-hour war known as Desert Storm pushed the Iraq military back out of Kuwait. Many people fled north through the Babylon area. A faith in others led Ahmed's family to help provide aid and comfort to others in strife. Ahmed vividly remembered the following:

> Both Christians and Muslims stayed at our farm; we provided food and water. We had a lot of fun with everyone swimming in the river [Euphrates] due to the extreme heat. Many in the community were struggling, especially those in the city [Babylon]; daily my mother would pack baskets of food and fruit that my brother and I would deliver to the front doors of people in our area who needed it. We would place the baskets on the ground and run away so they could not see who was delivering the food. Our people are proud and didn't want to accept charity.

The Iraq armies were also headed north, out of Kuwait. Ahmed said:

> Our country was under constant propaganda of the dictator Saddam Hussein and the Ba'ath government. People were forced to join the Ba'ath party or be jailed. My father learned to keep his head down. There were images from that time showing how great Saddam's family and regime were posted on billboards and signs throughout Iraq.

Ahmed started school at the age of seven, delayed due to the war. "Our family believed in education," he proudly shared. During the summers on the farm, he played with and investigated the engines of the farm equipment. He wanted to be an engineer. His education continued through high school in Babylon. The teachers were very dedicated, but most of them had second jobs to help support their families. He was able to go directly to Najaf University because of his grade point average. He studied engineering and graduated with a degree in mechanical engineering.

Ahmed was still at Najaf University when the Americans declared the War on Terror in 2003. Najaf became a focal point in the war. The Valley of Death, the world's largest cemetery, is located in Najaf. The six-square-mile hillside has over five million graves. This was a hiding area for Muqtada al-Sadr and his Mahdi militia, weapons, and ordnance. Shelling, mortar fire, and rocket-propelled grenades (RPGs) were fired continually from this cemetery. The gold-domed Imam Ali mosque became a refuge for the militia. This is a sacred site for the Shia. Al-Sadr was protected near the mosque. The Americans and allies made every effort to avoid damage to the mosque and cemetery. For three weeks, street and building-to-building fighting came to a poorly honored truce, which allowed al-Sadr to leave Najaf. Many weapons which were meant to have been turned over to the Americans ended back in the militia's hands. Al-Sadr reemerged in Iran.

During this time, Ahmed was in his final year at the university. The militia came to the school and all over the city to recruit men for their forces. Ahmed described the worst point for him:

> We were scared and did not want to be taken away. Two of my classmates were shot and killed that were standing beside me. The Kalashnikov [Soviet AK-47 assault rifle] was pointed at me. It made repeated clicking sounds as the shell did not fire. So, the man instead took the butt of the gun and started hitting me. At this very moment, Apache helicopters, fighter jets, and troops came toward us. The militia all started running and fled. There is no sound as loud and distinct as an Apache. It is the most terrible sound ever. Ultimately this saved my life. Tanks were patrolling the streets less than a quarter of a mile from the university. The Americans were everywhere. We were just students, but we all looked like we could be militia too. I had to hold my ears every time an F-16 jet flew over because they were flying so low. The US was able to attack

at night because they had night vision equipment. These were the worst years of my life.

There were no cell phones. There was very limited food available at the university. The students were not able to go home or leave the area for many weeks. Ahmed remembered:

> Some hard bread was offered which had green mold on it. We dipped it into water and the green dissolved and we ate it. Another time a dead mouse was in my soup. I picked it out and ate the soup anyway. We all thought we were going to die. We had no freedom. We had said "no" so often to those in power. I spent a lot of time reading and spoke with a friend often about wanting to build a better country.

After graduation, in hopes of making things better, Ahmed started working as a consultant for a company operated by the Americans. He assisted in setting up a telecommunications system in Iraq. Ahmed told this story:

> We were constantly under threat. By working for a USA-affiliated company, we were thought of as betraying our country. I received phone calls and texts with threats saying, "How dare you!" We were all the time trying to stay under the radar. I was lucky because my family had a second house in Baghdad.

By 2010, the American forces were withdrawing and those that had assisted them in trying to help Iraq became even more vulnerable. "I did not want to leave, but felt I had no choice. I took an eighteen-hour bus trip to Syria," remembered Ahmed. There were checkpoints all along the highway. At each one of them, the driver had to pay a bribe to the guards who threatened to turn them all over to Al Qaeda. Once in Syria, Ahmed was confronted with the ISIS threat, which was escalating. He had money back in Iraq, but only four hundred dollars in his pocket.

At an internet café, he contacted his former boss in Iraq, who was now in Belgium, by email. Twenty-four hours later he returned to the café to find a reply. This man directed him to get out of Syria immediately, go to Lebanon, and ask for asylum. Through channels in Lebanon, Ahmed flew to Turkey, then Chicago, and then to Minneapolis.

He had only a small bag with all of his belongings. By this time, the shirt he was wearing had holes in the elbows. He knew very little English. At Catholic Charities, he was given two hundred dollars in food stamps and two hundred dollars in cash. He told the woman there, in very broken English, "I do not want charity. Don't just feed me a fish every day—teach me how to fish."

The lady at Catholic Charities was amazed at this honest man's introduction. She said to Ahmed, "Okay, I will share with you the best advice that I can give you. First you need to find a job. You must learn English through the English as a Second Language [ESL] program at our local community college. You need a different jacket." She gave him an ill-fitting, extra-large North Face coat from the racks and told him to wear this from now on. Ahmed refers to this as the "recipe" that got him started in America.

Although Ahmed was an engineer in his country, he had to start all over. He found a job at a gas station in what was considered a rough neighborhood. Since his English was limited, his initial jobs were lawn mowing, shoveling snow, stocking shelves, and making sure the buckets for window washing were full. The owner was a Palestinian Christian. His co-workers were Moroccan, Mexican, and Somalian. It was a dangerous neighborhood, so the register was behind a glass window. There was often stealing from the cash drawer by the workers. "The boss had a camera set up to watch the station. He saw me give change and put the money in the cash drawer. My boss commended me and gave me more hours to work. Nothing was easy," said Ahmed. He took all the hours that he could get. There were times when someone would yell, "Go back to your country!"

He took the bus to and from work. Ahmed detailed his progress:

> I was waiting on my asylum papers, so there was no green card. One night when returning to my apartment in Saint Paul, I tried to put the key in the lock, and it was like it was jammed. I was scared and got back on a bus and rode it all night until the next morning, changing buses when they stopped at terminals. I had a second job cleaning houses to make more money. All the time I was thinking of the lady who had given me the "recipe." I prayed to God every day to keep me going.

Ahmed completed the English proficiency test at the community college. In addition to the ESL class, he read newspapers, highlighting and looking up words he did not know to enhance his knowledge of the English language. He also loved listening to Minnesota Public Radio (his favorite show was *Car Talk*) and watching the sitcom *Friends*. A Moroccan friend, who often saw him reading and knew how much education meant to him, suggested he investigate St. Thomas University in Saint Paul. To get credit for his mechanical engineering degree, he was able to test out of college classes and was ready to pursue more schooling in the United States. His English was better, though he admitted, "I don't know how I passed the test. It was all about faith."

At St. Thomas he interviewed with admissions to study in the Computer Science Software Engineering master's program. Ahmed described the interview:

> The interview was with a man who reminded me of an image of Albert Einstein who had books everywhere. He asked if I had a green card, and I was happy to finally say "Yes, yes, I have one." I would be the only Iraqi in the master's program. There was an application fee and of course I had no checking account. My friend who had started me on this path put in his own check, and I was accepted into the school.

Ahmed rented a basement apartment near the school. He worked days at the station and attended classes each night from 5:45 to 9:00 before boarding the bus to go back and work night hours at the station.

> I still did not know the system here well. I had no knowledge of post-traumatic stress syndrome, but I had many nightmares of my life in the war in Iraq. I got a driver's license and a car. I spent many nights in the school library studying until 2:30 in the morning.

One of his classes was on Saturday mornings. He often worked the night shift at the station and sometimes nodded off in class. The student sitting beside him couldn't believe it and said, "You worked at a gas station all night?" Ahmed shared, "It was a very difficult class. I went to the professor and asked for some help. He asked, 'Isn't there someone else from your country that could help you?'" Ahmed told him that he was the only one from Iraq at the school. "'In order for me to get better in the class, could you give me two assignments for every class to get better in doing coding?'"

The point was I needed to get better," admitted Ahmed.

Ahmed graduated with a master's in computer software engineering. He often thanks God. "I visited a lot of churches in the [Twin] Cities, God was everywhere. Sometimes I cried when thinking of my life in Iraq and how far I had been blessed in my new country. Amazing blessings continued to surface in different forms and people."

A classmate referred Ahmed for a job interview for an information analyst position at a financial services company. He was hired. He stayed with the company for two years.

At his second job, he was interviewed by a former army man who had been in Iraq. Ahmed was sent to a conference on money laundering prevention. It was just before the Super Bowl, and this meeting led him down another interesting path. An attractive woman seated at his table noticed Ahmed making an origami paper horse.

"She pulled out her phone and showed me the cover photo of her horse. I did the same on my phone and, well, the rest is history. She is now living with me in our beautiful home," Ahmed said with a happy smile.

Epilogue

Ahmed has a second master's degree from New York University in cyber security. He is enjoying his current job in cyber security working for a large retail company.

He became a citizen of the United States in 2019. During the immigration interviews, it happened that the immigration officer had spent time in Iraq. "When he was telling me the event, I would tell him the details. As we shook hands, it felt like a good sign on my path to establishing my new life in the US," he reflected.

Ahmed made an anxious trip back to Iraq during Covid to visit his father who had just had a stroke. Wearing the Covid mask felt like an added layer of security—he felt that it provided anonymity and maintained his safety. The water level in the Euphrates was very low, but the family still had the farm from his youth.

Ahmed and his partner enjoy spending their free time at the barn where she has her horse in America. Ahmed loves doing odd jobs around the farm with the barn owners. He can be found smiling while driving the Massey Ferguson tractor. Time there brings back happy memories spent on the family farm in Iraq.

Massey Ferguson Tractor

Andre (top left), sister Milica, Friend,
(bottom row) Cyril, Rosa, Joseph, John

Andre Sadl

A Slovenian immigrated to Missouri with
his family to escape communism.

*". . . We were hiding behind a tree as the German Shepherds came on
patrol. Sure enough, they turned away as they had lost our scent. That was
a close call. Freedom is very, very, very precious, and important for people
to live."* —Andre

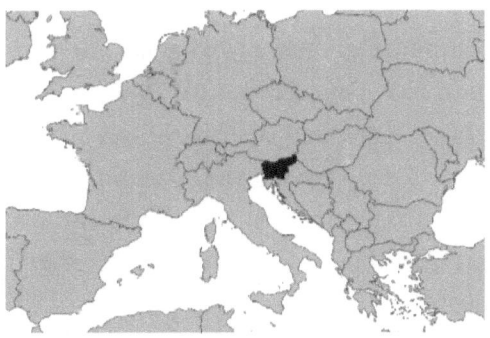

Andre

Slovenia has been ruled by Eurasian empires for much of the last two thousand years. Geographically, it is located at the northernmost part of the Balkan Peninsula near the center of Europe. Its borders are shaped like a chicken with its head extended into Hungary and its tail into the Adriatic Sea. Its land size is identical to the state of Massachusetts' at 7,827 sq. mi. (20,271 sq. km.). It borders Croatia to the east and southeast, Hungary to the northeast, Austria to the north, Italy to the west, and it shares twenty-five miles of shoreline with the Adriatic Sea to the southwest.

The people of this area, sometimes referred to as Southern Slavs, were part of the Roman Empire for one thousand years. This was followed by the reigns of the Byzantine Empire, Bulgarians, the Ottomans, and the Habsburg Empire (Austro-Hungarian Empire) for three hundred years, up until the end of World War I. In 1918, Slovenes joined the Croats, Serbs, and few Italians to form the State of Slovenes, Croats, and Serbs. It was renamed The Kingdom of Yugoslavia in 1929.

During World War II, in the year 1941, Nazi Germany invaded Yugoslavia. For the duration of the war, the region was forced into the conflict by Germany and Hungary. By March 1945, the Russians had overrun all of Eastern Europe as well as the Slovenian region. Yugoslavia became the Socialist Federal Republic of Yugoslavia under communist rule of the dictator Josip Broz "Tito." Joseph Stalin proclaimed his anathema against Yugoslavia. The Soviet Union under Stalin had close ties with Yugoslavia until 1948, when Tito declared his own brand of communist doctrine. Businesses were nationalized and there was contempt for anyone showing capitalist endeavors. People were imprisoned and sentenced to lengthy terms without charges or any hearings. These prisoners were used for forced labor, and many were shot and killed.

On June 12, 1987, at the Brandenburg Gate in Berlin, the United States President Ronald Reagan spoke the immortal words, "Mr. Gorbachev, tear down this wall." This marked the beginning of freedom for Central Europe and the end of the Iron Curtain. Within thirty months, the Berlin Wall was taken down and freedom came after more than forty-five years of communist rule. Yugoslavia was divided back into the six countries which comprised the federation: Slovenia, Croatia, Serbia, Bosnia-Herzegovina, Montenegro, and Macedonia.

The State of Slovene, or Slovenia, had been created in 1945. Slovenia is the farthest north of these regions that made up the former Yugoslavia. Western Slovene was influenced in the sixteenth and seventeenth centuries by the battles between the Habsburg monarchy and the Venetian Republic to the west (which is now Italy). Late in the seventeenth century, its intellectual, architectural, and cultural activities were influenced by the Baroque artists who settled in the Slovene lands. The Age of Enlightenment brought a period of peace in the mid-eighteenth century. By the end of the nineteenth century, a strong standardized language of Slovene was established. At the turn of the twentieth century, as many as three hundred thousand Slovenes immigrated to the United States, specifically to the areas of Cleveland, Chicago, and Pittsburgh. They worked in steel mills and factories. Others came to work in the mines and forestry. Some Slovenes immigrated to Argentina and Australia.

One half of Slovenia takes the form of forests, mountains, and parks, putting Slovenia in the lead of all other European countries in natural preservation of the land. There is one vineyard for every seventy people in the country.

Joseph Sadl (pronounced "saddle") left his home in Slovenia when he was sixteen years old and lived and worked for a farmer in France for five years. When he returned to Slovenia in 1939, he had enough money saved to build a house. Upon his return home, he went directly into the military. Since he was the only son in his family, Joseph had to serve just nine months. He married Rosa Puhan. They first lived at Ivanci near Rosa's parents in a house that Joseph built. Joseph operated a mill for grinding wheat into flour for himself and the neighbors. The family had a ten-acre farm and vineyard, which Joseph and Rosa worked to grow grapes, potatoes, and hay. All the farm work was done by hand. The soil was tilled using a Clydesdale horse and their four cows to pull a plow. The hay was cut with a scythe and laid flat to dry. A pitchfork was used to pile the hay into thirty to forty piles for additional drying before being stacked on a wagon, taken to the barn, and stored in the hay loft.

Andre Sadl, son of Joseph and Rosa, was born on February 15, 1944, at Martjanci, Slovenia (then part of Yugoslavia). At a young age, Andre began working in the fields with the family. Andre started school in 1949, the same year his father, Joseph, was sentenced and put in prison for three years. Since Joseph had a small milling business, he was suspected of being an enemy of the state. There were thirty-eight millers from Prekmurje (a region in northeast Slovenia) imprisoned in Yugoslavia at the same time. They were marched in chains to the railway station, and brought to a prison in Murska Sobota. Joseph told later:

> The line was accompanied by thirty policemen on each side. We had never done any harm to anybody, none of us even thought of anything like that. In the people who were gathered along the road, our suffering provoked bitter tears, pity, and pain. The people did not believe the communist rulers. Men and women were aware of the truth, and they cried in pain on witnessing what the new power had done to the honest and innocent men, their fellow citizens.

He was later transferred to Goli Otok, also known as Naked Island or Barren Island. This prison was on an island off the coast of Croatia, where prisoners of the communist government were tortured and forced into the labor of breaking rocks by hand, making gravel for roads.

Andre's school was a one-room classroom for all grades. He helped in the fields in the absence of his father and worked for the neighboring farms. By the time he was fourteen years old, he was able to purchase a special wagon and two horses. His wagon was in demand for weddings and special occasions. He once took a lady who was in labor seven miles to the town of Murska Sobota to get to a doctor for the delivery.

Joseph was put into prison for a second time for another five years. Since he had gone to France to earn money to build a house for the family, it was seen by the Communists as an activity which forbade any advancement in the socialist system.

On November 2, 1960, a mailman brought a letter from the government. Andre remembered:

> We were working in the fields with the fall harvests. The letter demanded that Father was to report to the police station. He said he was never going back to prison again and did not report to the police. He sent me on the bicycle to find people who would help us get across the border into Austria which was twenty kilometers [fifteen miles] to the north. By the third day, after Father had not reported to the police, our German Shepherd started barking at the police who were approaching our house at night. Father jumped out the window and started running. He ran for seven miles to a town where his sister lived.

At his sister's place, Joseph met Franz Gamoc, who went back to get a message to Rosa and the family that he was safe, and they were to join him. Franz got the message to a neighbor three houses away from the family home, who then relayed the message to Rosa and family. There were spies and informants in all neighborhoods, so trusting a neighbor with this word was dangerous, yet vital for the family to escape. Franz's message described their escape route town-by-town, and explained which woods to take. The family all got into a wagon in the afternoon with their rakes and scythes like they were heading to the fields. Andre was following them on his bike on the dirt road. He described the day sixty-three years before as vividly as if it were yesterday:

Grandma dropped us off. We met Father in the woods just like clockwork. We started walking at night to another town where Father's other sister lived. We walked behind the house and barn and knocked on the door. She gave us some food and we stayed in the barn with the pigs and chickens. I remember being thirsty. We stayed away from the roads. We stopped and prayed along the way. Our aunt had given us some sausage. We used a blanket to cover our heads while Father used the flashlight to study our map. Father had learned in prison to put pepper on our shoes and feet. It was used to confuse the tracking German Shepherd dogs if they were tracking us. Of course, the communist had shot and killed our dog the night that Father jumped out the window at our house. One time, we were hiding behind a tree as the German Shepherds came on patrol. Sure enough, they turned away as they had lost our scent. That was a close call. Freedom is very, very, very precious, and important for people to live.

Joseph, Rosa, and the three boys spent that night inside stacked corn shocks shaped like tepees, with a hollow center just big enough for the five to crowd inside to hide. A farmer and a lady came the next morning to start loading the bundles onto a wagon. "The farmer started poking the stack with a pitchfork and dad jumped out and said, 'No wait!'" The farmer said it was okay to stay. Dad gave him a little money. We waited there during the daytime and started walking to the closest town, where we found another barn and a lady said, 'No problem, you stay.'"

"We slept that day in the hay loft," said Andre.

They walked the next night to an area close to the border. The Communists were shooting flares to lighten the skies at night. Andre continued:

Example of a corn stack, where the family hid.

We waited until there was a changing of the guards and
headed for the river. There was no moon that night. Dad
knew the Mur River was the border. We tried three times
to cross the river. It was chest deep and the current was
swift. It was cold in the November night air, but we were
exhilarated. When we reached the other side of the river,
Dad sent me to ask a boy if this was Austria. I returned
with a piece of a newspaper written in German which
proved that we were indeed in Austria.

The family walked to a town and stayed again in a barn. A lady
greeted them the next morning and told them to start walking and that
the police would pick them up and take them to a camp. The police
did find them walking and took them to the police station. "They gave
us nice food. Freedom was everywhere. We were told to stay there to
warm up. They took us to a camp where the men and women were
separated," explained Andre.

In the camp at Traiskirchen, Joseph was able to get a message to
Viktor Herzl, a man who had been in prison with him at Maribor and
Ljubljana. When Viktor and his wife were released from prison in
Yugoslavia, they left the country for Graz, Austria, and established a

candy shop. He came to see Joseph through the fence at the camp and was so elated that he and the family had escaped the Communists. He brought the family all kinds of goods and food. The KGB came to this camp one day and took away two Yugoslavian pilots who had escaped the country. "Dad said we will not be safe until we reach America and freedom," said Andre.

At the town of Drskirhea, Austria, which is fifteen miles from Vienna, Joseph received a card giving him permission to work for an Austrian farmer, while Rosa worked for a bakery. Andre and Joseph then worked for a construction group for three months, digging trenches by hand to lay waterlines.

They applied for papers and asylum as political prisoners at the United States Embassy in Salzburg. After three or four visits to the embassy, they received papers to come to America. Coordinated through Catholic Charities, the stipulation was that Joseph and the family would work on a farm and repay Catholic Charities the cost of their transportation to America. Another month passed until the five Sadl's boarded a flight from Salzburg to London, and from there to New York City. At Grand Central Station, they obtained train tickets to St. Louis, Missouri. They were greeted there by Wenzel Herman. He escorted the family to his farm in Fenton, Missouri. He provided a farmhouse for the family to live in, while all five worked on the farm. Joseph, Rosa, Andre (17), James (12), and Cyril (9) were paid a total of three hundred dollars per month.

> As I recall, Mr. Herman also provided us with a whole beef each fall. It was such a strange meat which we found not very appealing. We only had chicken back home in Slovenia and occasionally pork. The farm was one hundred sixty acres and dad took care of the cows. The pay was horrible.

Andre and his dad raised pheasants and quail, which were released for Wenzel's hunting friends. Wenzel trusted Andre and gave him the keys to his truck. Andre shared:

He told me if the hunting dogs were ever sick, I was to take them to the vet. If a horse was ever sick, I was to call the vet to come care for them. It was just his hobby farm, but it was a foothold for us in America. I learned to drive a tractor and then a truck. We at first felt like prisoners again because we had no car and even had to get a ride to go to church. Dad and Mom lived there for eighteen years. I lived there for twelve years to help Dad on the farm. In 1969, I got a job at Chrysler [car assembly plant] working the second shift. This allowed me to help on the farm in the daytime. After one year, the plant shut down and was retooled for a new model. I was asked if I would come back and be a supervisor. I told them I would fire eighty percent of the workers because they were lazy and even sabotaged the product lines.

In 1965, a letter arrived at the farm from the Selective Service Administration. It ordered Andre to report for a military physical in downtown St. Louis. At the age of twenty-one, not yet an American citizen in his new country, Andre drove himself to the location for the physical. He was asked to go to the restroom changing area to get into his underwear for the lineup physical. He accidentally started to go into the women's room where a guy grabbed him by the neck and sent him into the proper restroom locker. He passed his physical with flying colors. A month later, the bus was lined up at the induction center for the new draftees to be sent to Fort Leonard Wood, Missouri. Andre remembered:

I was standing in line waiting for my name to be called. When the sergeant came to my name, I was stunned when he said, "Sadl, you have been removed—drop out." It was explained that my language was not good enough. I always have wondered if Wenzel had something to do with getting me out of the army. I was very willing to go into the army

for my new country, which had given me freedom and an
opportunity to work and make a life for myself. I tell people
that I would have either become a general or be dead
because of my passion for leadership.

In a public swimming pool, Andre's life would change again.

"Excuse me, madam," said Andre to the girl whose leg he had accidentally touched with his foot under water. The girl was Roberta, a high school girl from the St. Anthony's of Padula High School. At the time, she was thinking of maybe becoming a nun, but Andre asked her for a date. The nuns at the school were skeptical of this Andre who she was seeing and requested that he come by the school so they could meet him. They approved of Roberta's boyfriend. Two years later Andre and Roberta were married, just three weeks after she graduated from high school in 1966. Andre said, "She gave me my first-ever birthday party with a cake and ice cream and the works. In my old country it was called 'name day,' but was never celebrated quite like this."

Andre moved his new bride into another of Wenzel's farmhouses on fifty acres. By this time, he was making $225 each month for working the farm. Andre learned English from the other farmworkers.

On a spring day in 1969, Andre was at the Fenton Feed Mill picking up supplies for the farm. The owner asked him if he would be willing to drive a delivery truck for him to deliver some washing machines. When he returned that afternoon with the truck, he was told to come to the office.

"I wondered just what I had done wrong. As it happened, the manager was so impressed with my abilities that I was asked if I would be willing to drive a truck to Iowa to deliver Speed Queens to many small-town stores around the state," remembered Andre. This was the first time Andre had ever been out of Missouri in the United States. Three days later upon returning the truck to the business, Andre was once again summoned to the manager's office. Again, he worried ahead about what he may have done wrong. On the contrary, the company had heard back from the customers in Iowa. They reported how this new driver had helped not only to unload and uncrate the machines, but to help set up the machines. They had never had such great service and were impressed with this new driver's work ethic. "I was still working two jobs, but when they asked me to work for them full time, I accepted," reflected Andre.

For the next nine years, from 1969-1978, Andre was employed at Gateway Coin and Equipment until it went bankrupt. It had over thirty employees at that time. He worked as a delivery driver to the surrounding states of Iowa, Illinois, Indiana, and Arkansas. His many contacts and service to these customers became a problem with the sales representative who was also covering this region of the country. The sales representative accused Andre of not being honest with the customers he was delivering to. An Indiana customer came to Andre's defense and reported to the Gateway Coin management, "Andre wouldn't steal a candy bar if he was starving." The sales rep was fired, and Andre became the sales representative serving the same area.

During the gas shortage, the oil embargo, and the long gas lines crisis of the mid 1970s, Andre would strap extra five-gallon containers to the truck to give himself extra gas storage, as the lines at the pumps gave him problems delivering the products to the customers on time. "I tell people today these energy stories. We should never rely on our enemies for oil and energy. America is truly the last frontier in the world; if we lose this, Jesus Christ himself must come down to save us," Andre proclaimed.

Following the bankruptcy, without a job, Andre started putting his contacts with the former customers of Gateway to use. They began calling on him for new and used washing machines. "I pulled my brother John into our business, and we became a distributorship of equipment," he explained.

His former boss at Gateway had a laundromat that was offered to Andre. He borrowed against his house. "I started doing this for other people, loaning them money to help them get started in their laundromats. Our company was National Laundry Equipment International, Inc. We later changed it to an LLC [Limited Liability Company] for tax purposes," he proudly remembered.

Andre and his dad bought a farm twenty miles away from the Wenzel farm, paying fifty dollars per acre. They built a pond with a sandy beach on the property. Joseph and Rosa moved into the house after eighteen years of operating the Wenzel farm. Many family and social gatherings were held at the farm. "For a number of years after church on Sunday, we all went to the farm and shared the beauty with all the family together," said Andre.

In 1984, at the age of forty, Andre and Roberta bought a new Cadillac DeVille. Their oldest son Jayme and a family friend drove the car to New York, where it was placed on a ship to Bremerhaven, Germany. The five Sadl's flew to Frankfurt and took a train to the port just as their car was unloaded from the ship. They proudly drove this automobile through Germany and Austria on the Autobahns, stopping at a US military base for directions and gasoline. As luck would have it, they were befriended by a sergeant and even spent the night with his family. This sergeant was able to get the Sadl's directions to Berchtesgaden Castle in Germany to spend the night there.

At the border into Yugoslavia, their Cadillac, with USA plates and two USA flags on the front fenders, was waved on through the checkpoint by the guards. Andre chuckled as he shared:

> They must have thought we were important people. I had not wanted to go back to Slovenia until I was forty years old for fear that I may be drafted yet again into their military. The people stared at the car. It was still very communist. There were guards everywhere and it just felt like communism. Roberta worried continually that they were going to take me away. I think they thought I was a "big shot." Here I was, back in my old homeland and a free man. We met my sister, Milica, who had been left behind when we escaped twenty-three years before. She was away at college the night we escaped. When she came home two weeks later, she was informed by our grandparents that we were gone. Milica was standing

waiting for us beside a bend in the road near the church.
Our hugs and kisses with her were unbelievable.

The Cadillac came back to America minus the two flags and the front hood ornament which had been stolen in Yugoslavia. This trip was such a walk back through time for Andre, and was particularly important for him to show his family the beauty of his homeland but also the destruction of lives through the cruelty of communism. The word "freedom" was mentioned over and over.

A return trip with his parents in 1987 took them back to their village. They saw the old mill, the house Joseph had built, and the vineyard they had cherished and cultivated. Words cannot explain their memories of a lifetime and the scenes with old friends, their church, and community. "Dad gave away something like fifteen thousand dollars in cash to the guards and old friends that we met to show them what freedom can bring," reflected Andre.

Epilogue

At the age of seventy-nine, Andre Sadl continues with his ownership of several laundromats. Andre still calls his brother John, who he brought into business with him, "Janez," which is Slovenian for John. Both of his brothers John and Cyril, who escaped Slovenia with the family, served in the United States Navy.

He and Roberta have two sons and a daughter who have all been successful in their endeavors in business. Their son, Jayme, also has two sons. He is a college graduate, soccer player, and owns a dry-cleaning business. Matthew is a ski instructor and nearly made the Olympic ski team. He has a concrete contractor business. Their daughter, Andrea, works with her brother Jayme in one of his businesses.

Andre's eyes dance when he says he always challenges people to a mile race. He says, "I will give them two hundred dollars cash if they beat me." To date, he has had no takers. Only in America.

Christiane Śemirot Edmondson

A French educator immigrated to the
United States following World War II.

*"We heard the heavy German boots marching on the street outside. They
stopped at our front door. We were all scared as there was a knock at our
door. They had a map with pins on it marking our location. They said,
'France is kaput!'"* —Christiane

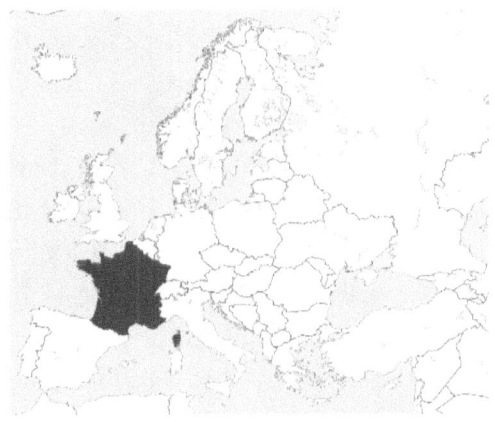

Christiane

In early January 1939, a baby was born near Bordeaux, France. Her father was one of over five million citizens in the French armed forces. Her mother was a schoolteacher.

Bordeaux is three hundred miles from Paris in southwestern France. The eighteenth century was considered one of the "golden ages" of Bordeaux. This port city's traffic volume along the end of the Garonne River was second only to London in Europe. This port was also called the Port of Moon and supplied coffee, sugar, cotton, and indigo to Europe. From this port, 150 thousand slaves were sent in five hundred expeditions to the Americas.

The Romans occupied the region in 60 BC. By the first century, they introduced wine to the area. The Kingdom of England claimed the region from 1214-1453, when their empire stretched from Ireland to the Pyrenees. France reclaimed the region when Louis XIV entered the city in 1653.

The Armistice of 1918 was signed in the Compiègne Forest on November 11, 1918, officially ending the "War to End all Wars," World War I. This agreement came several months before the Treaty of Versailles was signed on June 28, 1919. In the years following this event, from 1918 through 1935, France spent a large percentage of its Gross Domestic Product (GDP) on its military. This was the largest amount spent by any of the great powers and governments at the time.

France established the Maginot Line along the eastern and northeastern borders, separating themselves from Germany and protecting themselves from invasion. France made large investments in armaments for their borders. About one-third of the male population between eighteen and forty-five years of age were in uniform. This brought the strength of its armed forces to five million. Nearly 240 thousand of these served in the Army of the North.

When Germany declared war and invaded Poland on September 1, 1939, the dominos were in place. The Maginot Line proved to be ineffective in protecting French borders. Germany circumvented it from the north with eight armored divisions that had four hundred tanks in each division. Germany invaded through the Netherlands and then into Belgium. The Blitzkrieg started rolling. The Netherlands surrendered after six days of invasion on May 17, 1940. The rout of the Allies was so fast that more than 1.75 million men were captured by the Germans in one month. Losses, including captured, killed, missing, and injured, totaled more than two million.

Winston Churchill flew from London to Paris on May 16, 1940, to rally the French. He was welcomed, and witnessed a defeated country. The Germans had surrounded the Allies in northern France. The miracle evacuation at Dunkirk known as Operation Dynamo occurred from May 26 to June 4, 1940. France's First Army defended, fighting a rear defense against seven German divisions, which made the evacuation possible. The evacuation on the French coastal town of Dunkirk was carried out for 338 thousand Allied soldiers in over 550 light amphibious warships and 650 other vessels across the English Channel to the coasts along Dover, England. Churchill addressed parliament on the final day of the evacuation on June 4. It was called the "Miracle of Deliverance Speech," where he remarked:

> We shall go on to the end.
> We shall fight in France.
> We shall fight on the seas and oceans.
> We shall fight with growing confidence and growing
>   strength in the air.
> We shall defend our island, whatever the cost may be.
> We shall fight on the beaches.
> We shall fight on the landing grounds.
> We shall fight in the fields and the streets.
> We shall fight in the hills.
> We shall never surrender.

The next day, on June 5, the Germans started a second offensive into the Somme and Aisne departments. Paris fell on June 14. Hitler visited the city nine days later and his entourage drove around the Arc de Triomphe and down the Champs-Élysées.

The surrender of France occurred on June 22 at the exact same setting as the Armistice of 1918. Negotiations for France's surrender were held at the Forest of Compiègne. Hitler viewed this as a supreme moment of revenge. He sat in the same exact seat as French General Ferdinand Foch had twenty-two years earlier when he faced the defeated German representatives at the Armistice signing prior to the Treaty of Versailles.

On January 11, 1939, into this war-torn world, Christiane Sémirot was born. Her parents were Pierre and Fermande Sémirot. Pierre was in the army, and Christiane did not remember seeing him until the age of seven. She lived in a two-story house in a suburban area of Bordeaux with her mother, sister, and two grandmothers.

It was a common characteristic that soldiers involved in wars did not tell of their experiences. This was true of Christiane's father, Pierre. She elaborated:

> He graduated with two PhDs. He was an officer in the army. He was a leader of a company of Senegalese African troops. He had requested to go to northern France to help in the fight at Dunkirk. His army commanders laughed and denied his requests and told him his African troops could not stand the cold weather. He was not happy. Instead, he resided in a mansion along the French Riviera. It was never known to the family at the time, but he wanted to cross the Mediterranean Sea to support the French in North Africa. What is known is that the Germans occupied all of France by the end of 1940.

> Our house was two stories, and we lived on the second floor; It was the last of three houses on our rural setting outside of Bordeaux. We heard the heavy German boots marching on the street outside. They stopped at our front door. We were all scared as there was a knock at our door. They had a map with pins on it marking our location. They said, 'France is kaput!' There were about ninety of them

and they camped in the woods across from our house. We
had a well which was our water source. My grandmother
was carrying two pails to fetch us water from the well. One
of the officers volunteered his German soldiers to carry the
heavy pails to the house for my grandmother. In my
memory as a little girl, the German soldiers were very
polite and nice to us.

France was divided by the Germans into three zones. They were
the North, West, and *zone libre* (free zone) in the South. At the age of
eighty-four, French General Philippe Pétain, who had been called the
Lion of Verdun and hero of the First World War, replaced the Third
Republic as the leader. Under his sovereignty, the country became
known as Vichy France.

Four years later, on June 6, 1944, with the D-Day invasion along
the Normandy coast, the German forces were defeated. Paris was
liberated on August 25, 1944. By the end of September most of the
country was liberated.

Christiane explained, "Our Bordeaux fell under the German
occupation . . . The Italian Royal Navy established a submarine base
here [BETASOM]. It was also a port for the German U-boats."

During the war years, Christiane went to school a long distance
from their home. Her grandmother took her to school. It was in a very
poor neighborhood. The teachers lived on the second floor and the
school classrooms were on the first level. Classes were taught by a
husband and wife. The woman taught grades one through four. She
was a strict disciplinarian. The man taught the upper grades. There
were around forty-five students in each of the two classes at the
school.

Christiane remembered:

They really emphasized math and reading. Every student
knew how to read. This was such a wonderful start for me,
as I studied physics in college. None of the other students
had dads, either. My mother was also a teacher at another

school, which gave our family enough money to get food
and provisions. My grandmother did all the shopping,
though the shelves and available goods were very sparse.

Pierre, Christiane's father, returned to Bordeaux after he was
released from the army in 1946. He resumed his career as a leading
scientist with the French observatory. He became the president of the
Bordeaux Agnostic Society. There is a street in the city named after
him. When he was working at the Observatory in Paris, he, his wife,
and their oldest daughter moved to Paris. They lived in his office as
there was no available housing following the war. When they were able
to find and afford an apartment, Christiane and her younger sister also
moved to Paris.

Christiane attended public schools in Paris in the fifth grade. She
learned English at the age of ten. She attended Bordeaux University,
majoring in physics and chemistry. Her father invited his wife and
Christiane to join him at an International Astronomical Union
conference in Saint Petersburg (Leningrad at the time) and Moscow in
Russia in 1958. She met a young man there from Indiana in the United
States who was also accompanying his father to the same conference.
They fell in love. A long trans-Atlantic romance followed. A year later
she married Frank Edmondson in 1959 in the United States. He was in
the Air Force ROTC at the University of Indiana. After graduation, he
started his active-duty pilot training with a six-month assignment at
Malden, Missouri. Christiane remembered:

> It was a very unhappy time for me. It was hot and the bugs
> were big, and I mean really big! We had no air
> conditioning. I thought it had to get better when we were
> reassigned to Big Springs, Texas, for the next six months. It
> was somewhat better, but it was hot. Again, it was really,
> really hot! I was often asked if I was a war bride. I would
> answer, which war? Some of the young wives would look
> at me confused.

Life of a military wife is not easy. I am in a new country
with a new baby, and a husband who is gone all the time.
The next air force assignment was to Évreux, France, for
four years. My daughter Mylene was born in Texas. The
twins, Yvonne and Catherine, were born in France. I was
twenty-three years old with three babies and all alone. It
was not great to be back in France with a husband who
was gone all the time.

Frank was next stationed at Lockbourne Air Force Base near
Columbus, Ohio. Christiane and the girls moved to Columbus, where
she attended and graduated from Ohio State University in physics with
a French minor. Frank was sent to Okinawa, Japan, and flew sorties
into Vietnam. With this separation, the marriage did not last. When
the girls were nine and seven in 1969, Christiane and Frank divorced.
Christiane was adamant that he agreed to pay for half of the girls'
college education.

Christiane started her first teaching job at East High School in
Columbus which was an all-black high school.

I had a wonderful principal, Jack Gibbs, who was also
black. The students were respectful of a first-year teacher
and we both learned from the experience.

To increase my salary, I needed to get more education. At
the time, the public schools encouraged teachers to get
additional college training. I took classes at Ohio State
University and received a Master of Arts degree. Another
art that I learned in between classes was the game of
Bridge. A man there taught eight of these teachers how to
play the game. I was hooked. The competitive bidding and
the offense and defense were a great challenge for me.

She became a United States citizen in 1972. She remarried in 1976
to an uncle of her first husband. She and the girls moved to New

Jersey to live with him and his daughters. One month after the marriage, she awoke and was alarmed to find that her husband had not come home the night before. She awakened his daughter to tell her, and she said, "Get used to it. He's big enough to take care of himself."

The girls all graduated from Shawnee High School. "These New Jersey schools were great, and we all loved our New Jersey years," Christiane remembered.

Christiane was unable to find a job teaching French but there was a great need for Spanish teachers. She inquired at a branch of Rutgers University about getting a degree in Spanish. She was told there was no way she could do it in one year. This hurdle did not deter her, and one year later she did have the endorsement in Spanish.

She taught French and Spanish at Cherry Hills High School. She continued:

> The student mix was one-half Christian and one-half Jewish. Oh, what an experience! They were good students and I had sweet classes. I tried to teach them Christmas songs in French. One student said this was not a good idea because his father was a Rabbi. We all learned them anyway. My principal was amazed. That is why we use all methods of teaching. All my classes loved this.

When the second marriage deteriorated, Christiane moved back to Columbus. The girls were already attending college at Miami University in Oxford, Ohio. Each daughter graduated in four years. Mylene became a math teacher and loved teaching for thirty years. Yvonne student-taught in a very rough Cincinnati school and decided teaching was not for her. She went to work for the Limited store chain. Following graduation, Catherine started a career in retail with a job at Victoria's Secret. Christiane was able to send all three girls to college and they graduated with no debt.

Coming back to the Columbus School District was not an easy transition, even for a former district teacher. Christiane found a job in a middle school. She taught six classes. One Spanish, one French, and four classes of illiterate students. She shared the experience:

> These kids were tough. Most of them were bussed to this school in an attempt at racial balancing. Because of the bussing I could not keep them after school. I told them, "I will teach you to read, and it will open the world to you." I could not have them in my classroom over the lunch periods. One said, "I have the right to not want to read and write!" I was assigned to a job to supervise the parking lot because the kids had been slashing tires. Another job was to supervise the free breakfast in the lunchroom. I was shocked when trying to tell them, "You need to pick up because this is a mess." The response was "F. . . you." So, after this year, I found a job at a private girls' school.

For the next fourteen years, Christiane taught French and Spanish at Columbus Girls School (CGS). The pay was less but the students wanted to learn and were achievers. Christiane related, "There were about fifty to sixty girls per grade level. I took numerous trips to France and Spain on summer education trips with my students. So much fun teaching students who wanted to learn."

With three girls in college, Christiane took on a night teaching position at Ohio State University to supplement her income.

> These were incredibly challenging and discouraging experiences as a teacher. Many of the attitudes were appalling. They did not care what grade they obtained. Getting a D average was just fine for some. I asked a hockey player if he was satisfied with a D? He said, "So? It's passing isn't it!" They were lazy and remarked they had no time to study. Another time, a cheerleader begged to take a test later because her grandmother was sick. They did not care but had to take the required course to graduate.

So much for a college degree from what some think is a great university of higher learning.

Christiane gave up the great position to go back into the public schools. "The retirement benefits were to be based on the last years of salaries. I needed to get the highest level of salary possible," remembered Christiane. She went back to a wonderful Granville High School. She taught French for the next four years. She resumed taking students to Europe in the summers for this experience in the countries of the languages they were learning.

Epilogue

Christiane retired after teaching for thirty-three years. In her new country she had given all of herself to educate students at the middle school, high school, and college levels. None of these students could completely relate to this immigrant teacher who had lived through a dark period in France's history.

Her presence was much taller than her barely five-foot physical height. Her wit and beautiful personality will be remembered by her students. Even an illiterate student, a privileged cheerleader, or college hockey player might have learned some character from their teacher.

She spends some of her winter months in Florida. Christiane is the lady with a physics degree, who possesses a great math brain, and frequently wins the pot at the ladies' Bridge table. This charming octogenarian smiles and says, "I've had a wonderful life in America!"

Daniel and Carmen Torres

Two Mexicans fled during the Mexican Revolution and
created a life for themselves in Colorado.

*"Life is like a quarter. Tail is the negative of life and head is the positive.
Both are needed."*   —Daniel

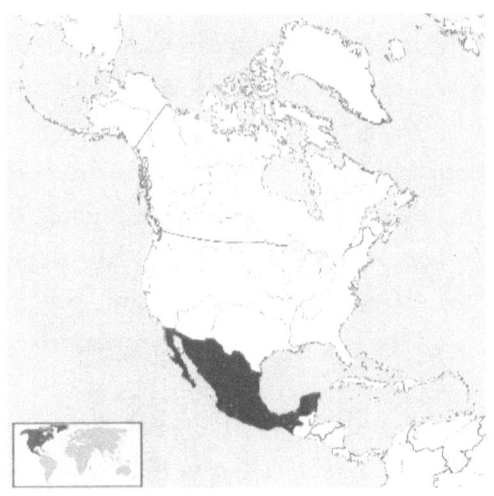

Daniel and Carmen

Daniel and Carmen were a product of their Mexican lives during the Mexican Revolution of 1910-1920. These teenagers, one from poverty, and the other from wealth, were influenced by guerrilla warfare and the Mexican revolutionary, Francisco "Pancho" Villa.

The Revolution, spurred by President Porfirio Díaz's jailing of his opponent during his eighth reelection in 1910, ignited a series of government overthrows and a succession of leaders during this ten-year revolution. Francisco Madero, from his base in San Antonio, Texas, became the first to evolve as president after the revolution.

Two militants, Pancho Villa and Venustiano Carranza, amassed a guerrilla force of between twenty thousand and forty thousand men. Villa had been imprisoned by General Victoriano Huerta and condemned to death. President Madero stayed the execution. After Madero's own execution, Villa escaped and fled north. He returned to Mexico and became the Governor of the State of Chihuahua. Together with Carranza, they won a decisive victory over General Huerta in June 1914 and entered Mexico City as victorious leaders of the revolution.

Distrust between Villa and Carranza forced Villa again to flee Mexico City to the mountains in northern Mexico with Emiliano Zapata in 1914. They executed seventeen Americans at Santa Isabel, Chihuahua, in 1916. In March that year, they crossed the border into the United States and executed another seventeen in Columbus, New Mexico.

President Woodrow Wilson directed a military expedition in 1917 led by Gen. John "Blackjack" Pershing in pursuit of Pancho Villa. Villa was never captured or defeated, and evaporated into the mountains. Pershing crossed back into the United States. Just fourteen months later, he was the commander of American forces in France during World War I.

Through this upheaval, in 1920 Daniel Torres crossed the Rio Grande at the age of seventeen. He was the only one from his family to leave his home area of Romita in the state of Guanajuato, which is about one hundred miles from Mexico City. Little is known about how he moved north nearly five-hundred miles to cross the Rio Grande. The most likely explanation was that he made it by walking through Nuevo Laredo into Texas.

He worked in Pennsylvania and California. He traversed the region, and he may have come to Colorado because he had heard of prospects for work.

Upon reaching Colorado, Daniel Torres worked at various jobs in coal, gold, and silver mining, in addition to working on the railroads in the Rocky Mountain area. While on a railroad crew, he met John Romero, who worked on a farm in northeastern Colorado and said there was a need for farm workers. Daniel rode the train to Logan County and lived there with John Romero and his mother. The northeastern Colorado county borders the Nebraska panhandle. The Platte River traverses the county, which sits on the largest underground water source in the world, the Ogallala Aquifer. In this semi-arid region, he found that a special tuber, a sugar beet, was growing in many fields. He had picked up some English words and was able to communicate with the landowners and stewards. Lloyd and Raymond Ramey had five farms in the northeast corner of Logan County near Padroni, Colorado. They approached Daniel while he was working for Bill McNear and asked him to rent their farm. Dan rented one after another until he had all five farms as well as Lester Smith's place by the mid-1960s.

John Romero was killed in an automobile accident in 1948. Daniel felt the need to step in. He arranged for John's mother to live on one of the rented farm places near Padroni. She lived there until Daniel purchased a home for her in Sterling after he retired from farming and sold his machinery in 1966. Meanwhile, Daniel became a guardian to John's two daughters and his mother upon John's death, even giving each of the girls away upon their marriages.

Daniel continued to learn English by using the dictionary to select words and learning their pronunciation and meaning. This became a ritual. "Every Sunday night, my dad would pick ten words at random from the dictionary and try to use them during the next week," recalled his youngest son, Dan Jr.

Carmen Prado fled the town of Torreón in the center of Mexico in the state of Coahuila, about two hundred miles west of Monterrey. Torreón was the crossroads for railroads, and all travel had to pass through this city. Carmen was raised by her mother and grandmother. Her family had been wealthy land and property owners before the revolution. They regularly attended the opera and galas. They owned many of the businesses and restaurants around the town square. Carmen's father, Tomás Prado, had died when she was two years old while he was in the Mexican Army. Their lives were soon changed; without the protection of the government, the revolutionaries started attacking the wealthy. Carmen's cousin was in the funeral business and a supply of wooden caskets was available. The three women— Carmen, her mother Dorotea, and grandmother Celedonia—hid the family's young children in the caskets as they headed north some five hundred miles to El Paso, Texas. Traveling by carts pulled by donkeys, these caskets were used as a ruse, since the guerrillas would not open them out of respect to the family. The women were also able to hide a few of their families' belongings this way and eventually reached America. They had heard there were job opportunities in Colorado. These three women came to Pueblo, Colorado, before yet another two hundred-mile journey to the northeast to Logan County. Carmen's brother, John, worked for the Pueblo steel mill. All the legal documents laying claim to property in Mexico were destroyed when the Arkansas River flooded. Relatives in Mexico took over the property, refusing to relinquish it without evidence of a deed formerly held by Celedonia.

Daniel and Carmen Torres were both twenty-six years old when they married in 1930 at the St. Anthony's Catholic Church in Sterling. They farmed together for the next thirty-six years near Padroni. Twelve children were born to the union. Nine children survived. Having a big family of nine children certainly helped the Torres family with the field work. The tedious hand work gave way to more mechan-

From the left back row:
Daniel, Max, Tom, Ben.
Bottom row: Danny and Joe.

ization. The horses gave way to the tractor on the land that Dan and Carmen cultivated. The hoe gave way to the field cultivator.

All but the oldest three of the nine Torres children attended St. Anthony's Catholic Elementary School in Sterling; eight graduated from Padroni High School, while Ben graduated from Sterling. It was not until the ninth child started elementary school that the St. Anthony connection ended. Dan Jr. was quite a talker, which also got him into fights at school. He was dismissed, or rather "kicked out" of school in March of his first year in school.

Dan Jr. recalled the incident and the story of his father taking him to the public school in Padroni the next week. "My dad dropped me off and told the principal, 'This is my son. I want you to teach him. If he gets into trouble, discipline him. Let me know, and I promise you, he will never do it again.'"

It did not take long for trouble to find Dan Jr. Two days later, a second grader popped off to him, "Are you pretty tough?"

Dan said, "Yes."

The challenger shot back, "Well, I'm the toughest kid in the second grade."

Dan spouted back, "Not anymore!"

"I punched his lights out," he remembered with a smile. "That was the last fight I was ever in."

All nine of the Torres children attended college. Each of the five boys served in the military. Max, the oldest, received an appointment to the first class at the United States Air Force Academy in Colorado Springs, although he chose not to accept it. Max's youngest brother Dan said, "In 1971, brother Max and I farmed at Iliff in southeast Colorado. In 1974, we partnered and farmed over one thousand acres in Morgan County, Colorado." In 1978, Dan sold the Morgan County land and bought seven circle irrigation farms in Phillips County. Max once said to his partner and younger brother Dan, "Little brother, why did I ever turn down that appointment to the Air Force Academy?"

The first sugar beets grown in Colorado were reported to have been brought back from Germany by a Leadville banker in his suitcase. The silver mines were beginning to dwindle in their productivity. The sugar beet thrived in the semi-arid climate. The beet, or tuber, grows beneath the soil. Its long roots extend deep in the soil in search of moisture. The German and German-Russian immigrants had come to Colorado to farm and ranch. The sugar from the beet proved to be of great quality when processed. Since much of the work in cultivating and harvesting was labor intensive, field workers were needed for the sugar beet farms. Mexicans, Spanish-Americans, Japanese, and even German POWs during World War II were employed in the fields. Many of the Mexicans became farmers and landowners as well. The peak production year was 1930 when 3.3 million tons of beets were processed in the twenty beet plants in Colorado. Irrigation made it possible to raise from eight thousand to twenty thousand pounds of beets on an acre of land.

By 1941, Daniel started leasing the Ramey farms one at a time. Farm number two came in 1958, until he leased all five farms in the 1960s.

"My father was renowned for his analytical sayings and adages and passed them down to all of us children," Dan remembered. Some of them were:

> Kids are like dogs; they will do just what you let them do.

> Do you want to work from the neck up, or the neck down?

> Profanity is the crutch of the ignorant.

> Life is like a quarter. Tail is the negative of life and head is the positive. Both are needed.

Then there was the saying Dan Jr. remembered his mother using about people who live by a double standard, meaning they only know you when they need something:

> Only when it is convenient—you come here.

At the height of the Great Depression, in 1936, came the first of three paper treasures which were kept for the rest of Daniel and Carmen's lives.

The first was a voucher from the Bill McNear Farm that Daniel had a job, so that he could retrieve Carmen and the children after a job in Colorado. The second was the first lease agreement to have his own land. The third came sixteen years later when Daniel became a citizen of the United States.

Daniel never spanked any of the children. He relied on taking away something as a form of punishment, believing it was far more painful. Mother Carmen inflected her motherly discipline with a wooden spoon, often finding its mark not on the bottom, but on the top of the head.

Their son Dan Jr. remembered in 2021:

> My dad was very mild-tempered. He was humble, quiet,
> loyal, and did not curse. He remembered the kindness
> that had been extended to him when he first came to
> Logan County. We called him Chief, or El Jefe, as he was
> such a great father to us. Holidays were family get-
> togethers for all the children and our families. Every
> Easter, everyone piled into two cars to drive to Estes Park
> for a picnic.

After Daniel and Carmen married, Carmen cooked and cleaned chickens to sell. Three of the Torres boys became farmers. Dan Jr. served in the Army in Vietnam, flying in one hundred seventeen helicopter missions and surviving during the horrific thirteen months from August 1967 to September 1968. His parents did not know where he was during this time. When he returned home on leave from the army, he was astonished to find that his parents had moved and now lived in Padroni where his father had retired from farming, in a house purchased from Lloyd Ramey.

Epilogue

The Torres legacy in Logan County, Colorado, lives on today. Their son Dan Jr. proudly served as the mayor of the county seat for the city of Sterling. He is married to Karen, the granddaughter of Raymond Ramey, whose place his father Daniel started farming over ninety years before in Padroni.

Siblings: Harald, Renate, and Dieter Nickel

Dieter Nickel

A German mother escaped with her children from
East Germany during World War II. Her sons became
successful engineers who settled in Iowa.

*"I was seven at the time. We were all separated to be interrogated about
our intentions for moving. I remember the bright lights in my face as the
Communist authorities carrying guns interrogated me . . ."* —Dieter

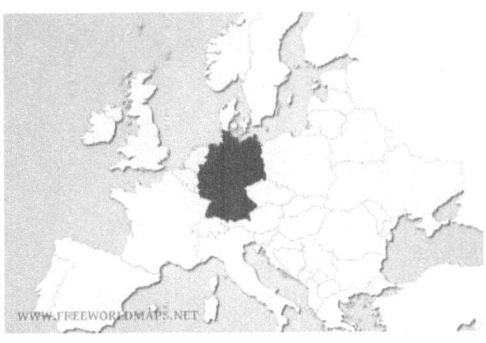

Dieter

With a mischievous twinkle in his eighty-year-old eyes, Dieter unfolded his story. Two German boys set sail for America—sent on a mission by their mother to check up on their sister. Imagine Dieter and Harald Nickel at the ages of nineteen and twenty on an ocean liner. They had limited English in their schooling. These were short courses which they may have not taken seriously. Their vocabulary was only "thank you" and "please" in English. Fortunately, the boys did not have to buy anything but beer, and they enjoyed the excellent meals included with the fare. With limited funds at sea, they managed to find cheap beer, cigarettes, and snacks. They enjoyed movies, swimming, and had nine days of adventure, which included flirting and chasing girls around the clock for the nine-day journey. This brought them to the Hudson River in New York City. While standing on the observation deck, there it emerged from the foggy morning: the "Lady." "The Statue of Liberty was fantastic! It was a euphoric and unbelievable welcome to America," were Dieter's words while remembering the sight. "Every time I hear the song 'Coming to America,' sung by Neil Diamond, I choke up, and it is so true these sixty-plus years later," said Dieter.

This boy, Dieter Nickel, born in Werder, Germany in 1941, was about to step ashore in America in the year 1960. How he came and immigrated is a miraculous journey of a wartime family and their escape from communism in East Germany. His father and mother, Ervin and Maly Nickel, lived in the beautiful village of Werder. It was about an hour southwest of the capital, and Germany's largest city, Berlin. The word "Werder" means river peninsula or river island. And it truly is located on an island in the Havel River which is a tributary of the Elbe River. About eight hundred people lived in that portion of the city.

Dieter remembered:

> Werder was a tourist destination when I was little. The
> cherry and plum tree blossoms brought tourists and

sightseers to this beautiful scene. It was like a *Tom Sawyer* life for a little boy. We had our own soccer fields and a swimming area. We were allowed to play and roam all day. Only once did I remember getting in big trouble. That was when six of us took canoes and paddled all the way around the island. It seems it had taken much longer than we had thought as kids, and we got a good beating when we got home. We had no babysitters at this time, and our neighborhood was our playland and security.

Ervin was an aircraft mechanic at the airport. The Nickel's had three children: Renate born in early 1939, Harald born in late 1940, and Dieter born in 1941. Throughout the maniacal Hitler regime's invasion of Poland in September 1939, France in 1940, and the Soviet Union (USSR) in 1941, Ervin continued to work in the vital position of mechanic. A father to three children, he was not forced into the army until drafted in 1944.

In June 1944, the D-Day Allied invasion of the continent and the liberation of France resulted in a very fortunate Ervin ending up in a POW Camp in France. Dieter remembered his father sharing:

My dad told us he was one of the very lucky. The Americans oversaw the POW camp. We had never been fed so well and treated so well. When the French took over the POW camp, things changed dramatically. The French were determined to take out their retributions for all the five years of the German hostilities and occupation of France.

With this new treatment, Ervin was able to escape from the camp close to the Belgium and Holland border. He walked east to reach Frankfurt in extreme Western Germany. When Ervin reached Frankfurt, he contacted the authorities, and they negotiated for him to return to Werder to join his family, which was in what had become part of East Germany.

When the Germans surrendered in May 1945, there were refugees everywhere. The Soviets had pushed westward to Berlin. The Potsdam meeting in August 1945 between US President Harry Truman, Soviet Joseph Stalin, and British Winston Churchill was an attempt to avoid the mistakes of the Paris Peace Conference in 1919 at the end of the First World War. The priorities were: the administration of Germany, establishing the demarcation of Polish boundaries, occupying Austria, defining the USSR's role in Eastern Europe, determining reparations, and confirming the USSR's agreement to join in defeating the Japanese.

Ervin was reunited with the family in Werder in late 1946. He was able to find work as a mechanic. One Friday night after work, and after multiple beers at a local pub, Ervin expressed his outrage and disgust for the miserable Russian occupation and the gall of their division of Germany into an East and West. With Berlin only an hour away, the unbelievable division of the city into the American, British, French, and Russian zones was condemned as the men loudly talked.

On Monday morning, one of his friends came to Ervin and warned him not to come to work as "they were looking for him." They were not only the Russians but also the turncoat Germans who now were part of the new East Germany, or the German Democratic Republic. Once again, Ervin set off by foot to travel the 120 miles west to get out of East Germany. He hid during the day and sneaked across at night. He landed alive in Frankfurt.

His wife, Maly, was interrogated about the disappearance of her wanted husband. She was able to convince the police that she had no knowledge of his disappearance. Months later, when letters started coming, they had obviously been opened and resealed. Words of love and encouragement were shared. By some subtle wording, Ervin was able to say he was at his former location near Frankfurt in the west. Maly decided to try to defect, but she had to convince the East German authorities that she was leaving Werder to go live with her parents in Spremberg, East Germany, near the Polish border.

In East Germany everyone was given a passport. Following an interrogation of her wanted husband, Maly's passport was taken away. She was only known by an official paper with her name on it. Children did not get passports until they were fifteen years old. Maly dressed the three children; Renate, Harald, and Dieter, then ages nine, eight, and seven years old. They knew nothing of her plans to defect, only that they were going to live with her parents in Spremberg. They packed their clothing and all the household goods and items they could carry on the train trip, leaving all else behind. They boarded a packed train where all the passengers stood. There were no friendly smiles, and all their faces were fixed.

To get to Spremberg, the train had to go into Berlin through two exit sectors. The first exit was into the American zone, and the second exit was in the Soviet zone. The train had a stop at Potsdam, where all the passengers had to show their passports and intent for travel. Dieter recalled:

> I was seven at the time. We were all separated to be
> interrogated about our intentions for moving. I remember
> the bright lights in my face as the Communist authorities
> carrying guns interrogated me. Since we knew nothing
> different, Harald, Renate, and I each innocently confirmed
> we were going to our grandparents in Spremberg.

Following the interrogations in Potsdam, Maly's only instructions were, when back on the train, the children were to stay very close to the door with all of their belongings and be ready to exit the train. When the train slowed to a stop, the children were to push themselves up against the glass doors and jump off onto the platform at the first stop. When the train slowed for the American exit in Berlin, she quickly pushed the children through the crowd and up against the glass exit doors. The moment it opened, they exited the train. "It was only then that Mom told us we were not going to Grandma and Grandpa's, but that we were defecting from East Germany and going to join our dad. We had all of our luggage and bags, so the exit was rather hurried, and once on the platform in West Berlin, we immediately felt safe," said Dieter.

They had made it to West Berlin. The four Nickels were now refugees, but far from safe. A policeman directed Maly and the children to the authorities where the refugees were sent. For the next fourteen months, they lived in four or five different camps. Maly had to prove that she was a legitimate refugee and not a spy. The first camp was at an abandoned manufacturing plant which somehow had survived unscathed through the war bombing. The family and other refugees separated themselves with clotheslines with blankets thrown over them. Quasi schooling for the children was available but any continuity was disrupted because of the frequent changing of the camps and instructors.

Letters to Ervin in Frankfurt let him know of their successful escape. After fourteen months in the American sector of West Berlin, the family was airlifted to Frankfurt and bused to Wiesbaden into yet another camp. They met up with their dad and still had no permanent housing. Ervin had his own apartment, but Maly and the children had to stay in the refugee camp until family housing was available.

After six months, the whole family was able to move into an apartment. Ervin worked as a mechanic for the Hoechst AG chemical company, and Maly found employment as a housekeeper. There were few jobs available. The West Germans had some resentment toward the refugees getting these jobs. There are many different dialects in Germany. "Coming from outside the area, I remember being shouted at, saying, 'Hey you refugee!' So, we always tried to stay very low-key. Berlin and the surrounding area had a much different dialect."

Schooling for the children became more consistent. After grammar school, there were two different tracks available. The three-and-a-half-year program with an apprenticeship for multiple trades was the track for most of the students. That was because most families did not have the financial ability to support kids who chose to attend universities, the second track for advanced schooling. The Nickel children attended the trade school. The morning classes were in world geography, history, science, and math, much like high schools in America. In the afternoon, the classes consisted of trade training and trade-specific work. There was very little English grammar exposure.

"I believe there was an emphasis on geography and history to educate us about the past and help us understand the world outside of our own borders," added Dieter. Harald and Dieter both had excellent training in tool and die classes and apprenticeships.

In 1956, at the age of seventeen, Renate met an American GI who was stationed in Frankfurt. They were married the next year. In 1958, when her husband's army tour was up, Renate left her family and came to America to his hometown of Shell Rock, Iowa.

By 1960, Harald and Dieter had finished trade school and had jobs in the tool and die trade. Their mother had saved enough money to send them to America, most importantly to check up on their sister, Renate. Dieter recalled, "At the US Consulate, we were given green cards, all paperwork, and possibly some vaccinations. We took a train to Bremerhaven on the coast and boarded the USS *America*."

The USS *America* was a new ship and of the same design as the USS *United States*, which at the time was the fastest ship to cross the Atlantic. Dieter reminisced:

> It was really decked out and a much nicer ship than the USS *United States*. It had chandeliers and big hallways, but boy, did I get seasick! The voyage docked in England, back across the English Channel to France, and then across the Irish Sea to Ireland. The last five days in the open sea, the sickness subsided.

Off the island of Nantucket, the ship slowed to a minimal speed. The passengers were told that they were slowing so as not to dock at New York on a Sunday. It seems that the unloading fees were double what they would be if landing on a Monday.

Waiting in New York to meet the boys were Renate, her husband, and a brother-in-law and his wife. As thrilled as they were to see New York, they were even more excited to find they would be traveling in a 1956 two-door hardtop Ford Galaxie. None of the Nickel's owned cars in Germany. The six of them left New York, traveling on many two-lane roads for the 1,200-mile trip west to Shell Rock, Iowa. The rolling topography of Pennsylvania reminded them much of Germany. They only stopped to gas up, grab snacks, and maybe take an hour nap in the car, before reaching the sleepy village in Iowa. Shell Rock was more like "Shell Shock" to the Nickel boys coming from the huge metropolitan city of Frankfurt. They were overwhelmed by the isolation and quiet country. They shared an upstairs bedroom. Every immigrant had to be sponsored by someone. Their sponsors were Clair and Crystal Bohan from Waverly, Iowa. (Crystal had been a war bride.) Clair was a friend of Renate's husband, who was stationed in Germany at the same time. The sponsor was responsible for the immigrant until they became a citizen.

During their first year in America, Harald and Dieter sent money—as much as five-hundred dollars each month—in an envelope by USPS to their parents so that they could come to America. Ervin and Maly immigrated to Iowa in 1962. Ervin became a mechanic at Volkswagen in Waterloo and then at H&H Tool and Die (H&H).

Three years later, Harald and Dieter became United States citizens in Cedar Rapids, Iowa, at the Federal Courthouse. Accompanied by their sponsors, they were asked to read in English. There were questions about the country that they had to know. Dieter smiled as he said, "The questions about history and geography were so easy, as I had learned in Germany more than most Americans could have answered about their history."

Within six weeks of arrival in Iowa, both Harald and Dieter had jobs at Progressive Tool and Die in Waterloo. This job opened the door for them to both move to H&H in Cedar Falls. The new company was impressed by their great skills, intellect, and training in tooling and die making. Three years later, Harald became the chief engineering manager in the engineering department. Dieter was named a project manager for all John Deere Waterloo projects. They designed, and H&H built, primarily for the agriculture industry for specific tractors and machinery. The sophisticated tooling's purpose was to design machines, run off and test these machines at a site, and get approval from the customer. Quotes were given on a client's particular project. If approved, a purchase order was submitted, and the work began. There were no royalties unless there was a patent involved. There were quotas from each station, seven through one, at which point a purchase order was placed, and the customer could come in and inspect. That was when H&H would get paid. At that time there were between seventy and eighty employees at H&H.

In 1979, both Harald and Dieter went to the owner, Roy Miller, to discuss the business. It was a Friday night, and Mr. Miller gave them his blessing to leave H&H and start their own company. It was an interesting time, as Harald was married to Roy's daughter. Roy Miller even helped them get a bank loan for a startup for Dynamic Tool Company in 1979. Dieter recalled, "We each asked for twenty-five thousand dollars for a total loan of fifty thousand dollars." Financing had incredible interest rates. With the inflation of the seventies and the beginning of the agriculture crises, beginning rates for a loan started at eleven percent. Within a few quarters it had risen to fourteen percent and escalated to sixteen percent for borrowing money.

Dynamic Tool was doing the same tooling as the Nickel brothers had been doing at H&H. The company started with six employees and grew to sixteen men by 1984. They did business with Magna International, an equipment company in Canada, building transfer dies and metal fabrication. Magna had five manufacturing sites in Iowa at Montezuma, Victor, Belle Plane, Williamsburg, and Traer. Dieter reminisced:

> Dynamic Tool was a contractor to Magna, it was slow paying us. I met with them and said "Guys, we've got to have the money." Magna was doing well at the time. I met with them and said, "We have to be paid on time to deliver on time." In 1984, they asked, "How would you like to sell to us?" I went to Toronto. They wanted our business, but they especially indicated they wanted our management and knowledge and experience in tool and die. By the mid 80s, hard times and a national recession was affecting the United States. I ended up going to Toronto three times to work out the deal. They were five

thousand dollars short and I said I can't sell at that price. The negotiator said, "Let me call the president," and he said, "Sure, buy it now."

After buying Dynamic Tool Company, Magna received a contract from GM Indianapolis Truck and Bus. Magna approved of building a plant at Traer, Iowa, just twenty-five miles from Cedar Falls, home of Dynamic Tool Company. Dieter shared:

> Magna did not want Harald and I to split up until the new plant was up and going. Production at the new plant in Traer Manufacturing started in 1985. They received a contract with GM Indianapolis which required Traer Manufacturing to make stamped-out door frames for small GM trucks. This was completed and delivered in five months.

This contract included a door frame for both sides, all to be made from scratch. The Traer plant had to add an addition to the already new building, import six presses, with five coming from Geary, Indiana, and another double action press from Indiana, which they paid one dollar to purchase. Voss Equipment company was hired to transport the presses. GM could not believe that such a deadline could be met, but the product was out the door at the designated time and met specifications.

Magna's Montezuma plant was having management problems. Dieter was asked to go there for at least six months as manager and to reorganize the company. When things were corrected at Montezuma, the company sent him to Clinton, Tennessee, in 1987 to renovate an existing building and manage another new Magna plant. He recalled:

> The Tennessee contractors and architects still called us "Yankees," and they did not like the Magna architects. At a contentious meeting with the Tennessee architects I said, "You lost to the Yankees once, but my former

country lost to them twice." I winked with a smile. After a
bit of silence, this drew laughter and eased tensions.

After two years in Tennessee, Magna gave Dieter the next challenge: a move to St. Louis to build and manage another Magna site. "Have management skills, will travel," was the motto for the new challenge. This new site was to build all the seats for the Chrysler minivan. He said to the Magna president, "But I know nothing about building seats for a minivan." The company headquarters in Toronto replied, "You can learn about building seats. What we need is a manager, and you are well qualified for that." The facility had two 125,000 sq. ft. buildings and stretched over an area equivalent to eleven football fields.

In the week between Christmas and New Year's in 1989, the delivery method for the seats had to be changed. The first seats had to be installed starting on January 1, 1990. Dieter had to make a design between Chrysler's style of delivery and their own style. In fifteen minutes—from off the truck and into the vehicles—the precision of delivery had to be perfect. The blue seat had to match to the exact green vehicle every time it hit the assembly point. Again, Dieter met with his managers weekly. "Their bonuses would come later, but if the seat designs and shipping details did not meet the specifications there would be 'penalties' and I am not going to be the one in trouble," Dieter grinned in reflection.

By 1991, Magna was almost bankrupt and declared Chapter 11 (reorganization). The plants in St. Louis, Missouri and Windsor, Canada were the only ones making money. A four million dollar loan to the St. Louis operation was frozen. Dieter called the President, Fred Gingle in Toronto, and urged, "We have to pay this. We don't want Chrysler to be worried about delivery." He got the go ahead to pay the bank from the profits at the St. Louis plant in Pacific, Missouri. Within six months, Magna had worked itself out of bankruptcy. Today, Magna International is a billion-dollar Fortune 500 company. Dieter shared:

Working at Magna was almost like family. Magna was very decentralized, and all decisions were made locally except for the Human Relations department. All financial decisions were also made locally. There was only one criterion: your division had to make a profit!

Epilogue

In 1995, Dieter retired from Magna International while still manager of the St. Louis Seating Company. This was exactly fifty years after the catastrophic end of World War II, where family had been caught behind the Iron Curtain in East Germany as refugees. After retirement, Dieter and his wife moved back to Cedar Falls, Iowa.

Elisabeth Drummond Hempfling

An Englishwoman followed a "help
wanted" ad to New Hampshire.

" . . . It was a great feeling to now officially be a citizen." —Elisabeth

Elisabeth

Just sixteen months after the end of World War II, England in 1947 had transformed from being a country under siege. There were many changes in government: there was the marriage of Princess Elizabeth to Prince Philip at Westminster Abbey, and Clement Attlee replaced Winston Churchill as prime minister of the UK. The Labor Party swept the elections and held the majority in Parliament for the first time. King George was still the monarch.

On January 1, 1947, the coal industry was nationalized. It would be the first industry taken over by the government but many more were to follow. February brought the coldest month in recorded history (records dating back to 1878). The mandatory age of fifteen was set as the standard for children to attend school. Foreign travel bans which had been enacted before the war were lifted. The University of Cambridge began awarding degrees to women for the first time. Soft toilet paper was first sold at Harrods. Rock star David Bowie (David Robert Jones) and musical legend Elton John (Reginald Kenneth Dwight) were born.

This same year on January 1, 1947, Elisabeth Drummond was born at a hospital in Salisbury, a city 125 km. (eighty mi.) southwest of London and only twelve km. (eight mi.) from Stonehenge. The population of Salisbury was twenty-five thousand.

Her father, James, was a general medical practitioner in Salisbury. He had entered the Royal Navy in 1939 as a doctor. He served upon ships in the Mediterranean throughout the war. He had shared only that the experience was both boring and horrifying. Boring when there was no action. Horrifying when they were under attack and taking casualties onto the hospital ship, racing to save lives.

Her mother Neilma had been sent north into Scotland during the war for a safer location away from the German aerial bombardments and away from the English Channel. She had shared, "The food supply was very limited and erratic, but we lived with a family who were hunters and fishermen. Much less typical than the other wartime families, we lived on pheasant and lobster." James apparently made it back to his family on leave during the war because two sons were born in this Scotland farmhouse in 1941 and 1944.

After the war, James returned and reunited with his wife and sons in Salisbury, the "Cathedral City." In his medical practice, Neilma answered the phone during the off hours and at night. Near the end of 1947, doctors had to vote if they would be accepting and making their services free to patients through the National Health Service starting in 1948. Neilma often laughed and told, "It was a lot easier getting the sleeping doctor out of bed in the middle of the night knowing he would be actually getting paid by the government for his services. Before that, getting paid had not always been guaranteed by his clientele, friends, and neighbors." The practice prospered and grew to six doctors.

Elisabeth attended Godolphin, a private girls' school with fifty girls per grade level. She was an excellent student. In England, students who were hoping to attend college needed a grade of A, or ninety percent, and had to pass an assessment test. She received a certificate of completion of her classwork in secondary school. She was a very sociable girl and loved to dance. She took ballet and attended balls. Her father was rather disappointed that she had no interest in going to college. He said, "What are you going to do? You can't just party all the time." She explained, "No Papa, I'm going to get a job." Elisabeth began waitressing at a tea room in nearby Wilson. While perusing the want ads in the *London Times*, her eyes lit up when she saw the ad:

WANTED
**American family looking for English Girl
to be a nanny in New Hampshire, USA
Send application to . . .**

Elisabeth had long wanted to come to the United States. At the age of ten, she had fallen in love with Elvis Presley and his rock 'n' roll songs. "I thought surely I could be a nanny because I was bigger than the kids," she remembered. She wrote a letter to the address in the advertisement, and within a week, a phone call came to her parents' number. It was an agency in London inviting her for an interview. They had been hired by John McLane from New Hampshire to interview applicants for the position. They had been drawn to Elisabeth's letter of application and her way with words. They made the offer over the phone and sent arrangements for flying over the Atlantic via mail.

The year was 1965 and in England, Sir Winston Churchill had just died at the age of ninety. The Rolling Stones performed "(I Can't Get No) Satisfaction." The Beatles released back-to-back hits with "Yesterday," and "Help." The Beatles visited Elvis at Bel Air. At seventeen, Elisabeth boarded a flight from Heathrow to Boston, Massachusetts, arriving on January 18, 1965. It was much colder than her home in England. John and Betsy McLane met her at Logan International Airport. They were holding a sign with their names on it for Elisabeth to find them. John was an attorney and Betsy worked as a professional photographer. It was an hour's drive from Boston to Manchester, New Hampshire. Elisabeth remembered:

> I had been on an airplane before but now we were driving
> on the other side of the road. The driver was on the left
> side of the seat. Everything was so big: the roads, the cars,
> the houses, the buildings, and even the robins. When we
> arrived at their home, the children were already in bed. It
> was so warm inside. I had never known of central heating. I
> was shown my room which also had its own bathroom.
> This house was not as big as our home in England. The fact
> that it was warm and not drafty was wonderful. I had never
> seen a shower before, only bath tubs at home. When I got
> into the shower and finally figured how to turn on the

water, it was actually hot. I could have stood there for
hours. This was heaven

Nannying three-year-old twins and an infant was a challenge. She
said, "The famous book on parenting by Dr. Benjamin Spock had just
become the bible on raising children. There were few boundaries and
the twins had never heard the word 'no.'" Just three months after
taking the job, she was shocked when reading a letter from her mother
announcing she was pregnant. Elisabeth was stunned; she had always
asked for a younger sibling, but this baby brother was to be eighteen
years younger than his big sister. Her mother was forty-eight years old
when the baby was born.

She made it through the year fulfilling her contract. She recalled:

> I had wanted to see the rest of the United States. I planned
> to purchase a ninety-nine-day Greyhound bus ticket for
> ninety-nine dollars. I had loved watching Western movies
> and shows on the telly back as a youth. I wanted to meet a
> real-life cowboy. Just as I was about to purchase the ticket,
> an urgent plea came from a recent divorcée. Barbara
> needed help and a nanny for her two young children. I
> accepted the job and had to postpone meeting a cowboy
> for thirty years.

Elisabeth fell in love with Robert Fontaine, who was a student at
Saint Anselm College in Manchester. They were married in the Saint
Raphael Catholic Church in Manchester in May 1967. Both of her
parents, a bridesmaid, and another friend from England, as well as her
godfather from Canada came for the wedding. "I'm sure my mama
was happy for me, but the thing she was most elated about was the
fact that Robert was Catholic. Mama was a Catholic and Papa was
Church of England, but they made their marriage very successful. I
had gone to Sunday school at All Saints Church."

Robert graduated in May 1967. He knew that he would be drafted
into the military. He chose to enlist and applied for officer candidate

school. The lives of so many men and their spouses were affected by the Vietnam conflict. Robert advanced quickly through basic training and Advanced Infantry Training. He applied for and was accepted into the Officers Candidate School (OCS) at Fort Belvoir, Virginia. Elisabeth joined him there, living with two other army wives. She and Robert were able to see each other only on Tuesday nights for church services and on Sundays. Robert was sent to Vietnam in 1968, where he was a Green Beret. He was wounded in combat three times. The last time was the most critical, and he carried a bullet in his chest for the rest of his life. He was hospitalized for a month in Germany and was discharged from the army in 1969 after his two-year obligation was served.

That summer, Americans were transfixed by televised images of the Moon Landing, and the younger generation celebrated rock and roll and free love at a music festival on a farm in upstate New York. But the news that rocked New Hampshire was the deaths of five Manchester National Guardsmen, whose truck hit a land mine one week before they were to come home from Vietnam. The city convulsed with grief.

A son, Christopher "Kit," was born in 1969. A daughter, Jennifer, was born in 1971. Like so many service couples, Elisabeth and Robert had to endure the difficulties of being separated and the yet undiagnosed term Post Traumatic Stress Disorder (PTSD). When Robert returned from Vietnam, he had become a different man and husband. He started working for an insurance company as a claims adjuster.

Elisabeth became a United States citizen in 1975. She had studied the citizenship booklet and thought she had a good knowledge of the content.

> I stood before a judge whose only question for me was, "Can you name any of the Supreme Court Justices?" This was sure not in the booklet, but I thought and carefully said, "That would be Hamilton Burger." The judge chuckled and said, "That's close enough." This was the name that I

had come up with, though obviously it was not exactly correct but a close call for the then Chief Justice Warren Burger. It was a great feeling to now officially be a citizen.

Manchester along the Merrimack River was noted as "The Manchester of America," in reference to Manchester, England, during the Industrial Revolution. The river and canals were a source of power for its many manufacturing businesses. It was home to the world's largest cotton mill containing four thousand looms. That mill stretched 900 feet, or the length of nine football fields, by 103 feet wide. At one time in 1912, woven cloth in the mill yard had reached fifty miles of cloth per hour. The decline of the textile industry, strikes, the Great Depression, and floods led to the closing of the mills. The textile mills had moved overseas. Many of the mill yard buildings were abandoned, the canals filled, and the Mall of New Hampshire was built on the site in 1977. That year, Elisabeth started working at the Jordan Marsh department store while the children were at school.

In her early thirties, Elisabeth surely pleased her father as she went to college at the University of New Hampshire at Manchester. She said, "I relished every class. It was me! It was not the wife or the mother—it was me."

The Fontaine's separated in 1986 after nineteen years of marriage. Elisabeth was working at an engineering firm along the Merrimack River. She was a single mother with two teenaged children. Kit went off to Boston College. Elisabeth often drove to Boston to see him and delivered care packages of food to him.

In her early forties she met Charlie Hempfling. He was fifty-six years old when they married. He was a banker at Pioneer Bank in Boston. When Charlie retired, the couple moved to Florida and lived one year on Longboat Key and built a house in nearby Palmetto, Florida. When Kit graduated from Boston College, he was unable to find a teaching job in the area, so he enrolled at the University of New Hampshire to get a master's degree. He saw a flyer about a job fair in Florida. He flew to Sarasota and was picked up at the airport by

Elisabeth and Charlie. Kit changed clothes in the back seat as they hurried to his teaching interviews. Before the day was over, he had three job offers. He did not want to live in Miami, so he took the job teaching immigrant children in Wimauma, Florida. He is presently an elementary school principal at Citrus Elementary in Tampa.

In Florida, Elisabeth started working for Kelly Services. What an experience working for a temp service. Her first job was at the Manatee County Hospital. "It was huge, crazy, and overwhelming. It was like working in a labyrinth for two weeks. I was afraid I could not find my way out," she said emphatically. Next, she worked for an architectural firm for two weeks. She found nirvana at her third assigned employer. Sun Trust Bank needed a short-term temp in the mortgage department. Elisabeth smiled as she shared:

> I worked for a wonderful woman, Gloria Mangual, in the mortgage department. I became a numbers cruncher doing analysis work and spreadsheets. You must remember that those were the days of the first computer programs, so there needed to be a written copy prepared also to compare it to the computer-generated material. The woman must have seen something in me and asked me to stay on permanently. So, this short-term temp lasted for the next eighteen years.

Elisabeth's dream of meeting a cowboy became reality when she visited a friend for her fiftieth birthday in Florida. "We stayed at the Flying G Ranch. I learned the Texas Two-Step and met enough handsome cowboys with their Stetson hats to fill a lifetime," she remarked.

Elisabeth had often told Charlie that when she retired, she would like to raise dogs.

Epilogue

The rest of the story unfolds in Elisabeth's words:

> In 2012, I retired and started raising puppies for Southeastern Guide Dog school (SEGD). My job is to bring home a ten-week-old puppy and teach her/him how to behave in the house, something they cannot learn living in a kennel. After several kindergarten classes, the puppy is rewarded with a coat that states this puppy is a Guide Dog in Training. The coat is the passport to stores, banks, churches, schools, or any other place the puppy raiser needs to go, and is essential for teaching the puppy how to behave appropriately wherever she goes.
>
> It takes a village to raise a puppy. The school does not just give you the puppy with a manual and expect you to give it back twelve months later with perfect house manners. Puppy raisers belong to a group that meets twice a month and is overseen by an area coordinator. A trainer comes to the meetings to give tips on how to teach the behavior they expect and give advice if any raiser is having a problem. In addition, there are other training sessions that raisers can attend if they wish to do so. Some members of the group are "puppy sitters," and they are invaluable. They take a puppy in an emergency, or if the raiser wishes to take a vacation without their pup.
>
> I was a full-time raiser for some of my puppies, but for others I had a co-raiser to share the experience. This works really well when a first-time raiser is paired with an experienced one. People often ask us how we can bear to give up a puppy after having them for twelve or thirteen months. Of course, we all fall in love with the puppy that is in our care for a year, but we know from the beginning that

this dog belongs to SEGD. When our dog is matched with a blind person or a wounded veteran, and we see them working together, it makes our job utterly worthwhile. Also, when I give up my dog, she is young and healthy and is going to make a difference in someone else's life. As long as I keep doing this, I will never have to take an old dog to the vet to be put down. Raising puppies has brought me great pleasure and it gives my life purpose.

Elisabeth came to America for a one-year nannying job. Her dreams brought her from England and its post-war reconstruction period to a quiet New England manufacturing town. America's involvement in the Vietnam War changed this country, as well as millions of men and women who were thrown into this quagmire. The crystal ball spins in circles for young people, and can lead them to completely different careers and family circumstances.

This immigrant was a lovely addition to her new country. Her father's hopes for her education were fulfilled. She shares her love for others by training guide dogs, and through this, she brings security to people who are visually impaired.

Enfys McMurry

A Welsh woman moved to America seeking education, and created a
life for herself as a historian, writer, and humanitarian.

*". . . At the conclusion in front of the whole class, he pointed to me and
said, 'Hasn't anyone told you that you can write?' The rest of the students
in the class all clapped. This support, this instinctive response from those
students is something so distinctly American."* —Enfys

Enfys

In Llwynypia, a village in the Rhondda Valley of South Wales, Enfys was born on September 20, 1936. That same year, on December 10, 1936, another major event aroused all the attention in the United Kingdom. King Edward VIII abdicated the throne because of his marriage to a twice-divorced American socialite, Wallis Simpson. Sixty years later, there would be a timely connection.

Thus, this immigrant's story begins. A grandfather who was a poet insisted on Welsh as the primary language of the home. Welsh is the oldest spoken language in Europe. His girls' names reflected this influence: Enfys, meaning "rainbow" in Welsh, and her sister's name, Mair Eluned, meaning "beloved image." They did not speak any English until they went to school. The family lived within Cowbridge to the Vale of Glamorgan in southern Wales, where their father worked as an electrical engineer. Coincidentally, William Randolph Hearst purchased St Donat's Castle seven miles away from their home on the coast. Enfys's father planned the castle's electrical work, including connecting the castle to the South Wales grid. When Hearst purchased the castle, there were three bathrooms, but after the Hearst renovations, there were fifty-seven bathrooms, all with gold taps. Enfys's first book, published over sixty-five years later in the year 1999, was titled *Hearst's Other Castle*. She wrote that Hearst's last act at the castle was interviewing King Edward VIII, then telephoning the story back to his New York paper. Hearst's *New York Journal-American* was the first newspaper to break the story of the impending royal marriage to the world. The headlines of the *New York Journal* read, *"King Will Wed Wally."*

Enfys's sister, Mair, was five years older. She was very smart and academically gifted, winning national awards. "She had explosions at home and showed defiant actions. I learned from witnessing these episodes to avoid such actions and to self-control my emotions," remembered Enfys.

At the age of eleven, Enfys took the famed British Eleven Plus Test, currently used only by select schools. This test was given in the last year a student was in primary school, upon turning eleven. Those who passed the test were accepted into "grammar schools." This test and selection process was given to working and middle-class families for a chance to get a better education for their children. The wealthy families' children were then taught in exclusive private schools as they are today, thus perpetuating the British class system. With this system, cognitive abilities, verbal reasoning, mathematics, and English were more important than financial resources in determining what kind of schooling a child would receive. Those not selected to these grammar schools continued their education at secondary schools or technical schools, directing them into the trades. Enfys became one of a small group who passed the test, which is based on intelligence rather than knowledge. She entered Cowbridge Grammar School in 1947, and for the next six years, she excelled with her studies. However, Enfys remembers being intensely disliked by the head mistress, Enid Walker, who tried to intimidate and ridicule Enfys in front of the class and the whole school. Using the self-control learned at home, Enfys took any teasing and attempts at humiliation without retaliating. She tried to tell her parents about this treatment, but they did not support her and thought she was exaggerating. "I kept as my guide: If you depart from the truth, you are on your way to mental illness," Enfys said.

Following graduation, Enfys wanted to go to London and become an actress. Her mother prohibited it, saying, "Actresses just sleep with the directors and get abortions." She did go to London and took an intense two-year course at a constituent teacher's college of the University of London. Shockingly, having learned that Enfys was doing well in London, Miss Walker (head mistress) committed suicide and left a note on her desk blaming Enfys for her action.

Enfys taught elementary grades at Friars on Webber Street (near the Old Vic Theatre) and the Robert Browning School on East Street. She excelled as a teacher. Her students loved her, and she immersed herself in their education.

Her weekends and social life centered around political events. She met Peter Jackson at a political rally. He was immediately attracted to this little five-foot two beauty. He admitted that his goal was to become a member of parliament (MP). Knowing that his status was important, he convinced Enfys that this unworldly Welsh schoolteacher may not be up to his standards. "He told me if I was ever to accompany him as an MP, I needed more credentials," Enfys told. He arranged for her to enroll at the University of Arizona in Tucson and found her an unlikely scholarship in Latin American studies. So, at the age of twenty-two, Enfys made her first trip to America.

At first, Enfys was desperately homesick. However, two people changed her life. She met Tom Bahti, an anthropologist who remains an icon in America's Southwest, although he died in 1972. He ran a Native American art store near the campus in Tucson with his trademark "hand" symbol. His passion for the social plight of American Indians and for their art and culture made a huge and lasting impression on this young graduate student, one she still celebrates with visits to the Southwest, particularly Santa Fe, New Mexico. The second major influence at that time was physicist Earl William McMurry who worked at the University's Institute of Atmospheric Physics and spent some time seeding clouds with iodine crystals to bring rain to the arid Southwest. Soon, Enfys and Earl became romantically involved.

One day while sitting in a lecture class at the University of Arizona, a secretary tapped Enfys on the shoulder and handed her a note. She cautiously opened it. "Please come to the President's office at ten o'clock to receive an international phone call." She was awestruck that she had been identified in her classroom and immediately thought the call was about her mother who had been previously diagnosed with breast cancer. At the appointed time, Enfys took the call, only to hear Peter Jackson request in a begging manner that she come back to London to marry him. Enfys recalled:

> There were three such calls. The first time, a ticket accompanied the call—a paid airline ticket from Tucson to London. I returned the ticket. The second call was followed by a job offer from Liverpool City Council to begin teaching in response to "my application," though I had never sent

an application. After the third time, I received a form from
the British Income Tax to support Peter's claim of me on
his income tax return. Then came the amethyst
engagement ring in the mail, and I returned that, too.

Eventually, Enfys did return home—this time in response to family warnings of her mother's ailing condition. She found a teaching job near her parents in Wales to help care for her mother. Peter married someone else within three weeks of her return. He became a Member of the British Parliament, representing the High Peak Constituency in Derbyshire.

In the next twist of fate, Earl McMurry came to England in 1963 to work on his doctorate. He and Enfys were married on October 4, 1963, in Westminster. Exactly four years later to the day, their son John was born at Westminster Hospital. Earl earned his PhD in 1968 from the Imperial College at the University of London. The dissertation was: *A Paleomagnetic Study of Tertiary and Devonian Igneous Rocks in Britain*. With this background and doctorate in hand, Earl moved the family to Canada and taught at the University of Alberta in Edmonton. Continual criticism of America's involvement in Vietnam resulted in Earl's decision to leave. He told Enfys, "Let's go back to America."

He brought Enfys and John back to America to a small town in Iowa. It was not a happy move. There was no job. There was no money. There was no home. The former home of Earl's parents was deeded to their only son and grandson. It was like a museum full of Earl's parents' memories; their possessions and even their clothes had not been used for forty years. Any change evoked threatened nervous breakdowns and what appeared to be catatonic depressions from Earl's mother. With the death of Earl's father, the situation deteriorated further. Earl and his mother became one. After his mother's heart bypass surgery, he moved in with her. A school bus collected young John for the local public school, and Enfys faced complete physical and emotional isolation.

Earl's family had an excellent community reputation. Both of his parents were teachers, and his uncle was an attorney, state senator, and former brigadier general. Enfys, with no family on this side of the Atlantic, feared to speak out. She was warned that there could be consequences, even legal ones. Addressing her situation with her husband and his mother, Enfys was presented with what the consequence would be should she continue: Clarinda, an Iowa mental health institution.

She worked out a solution. It was London! She had always loved the place. She would research it and dream of walks through each district. The books came at reduced postal rates by the box load from Iowa's state library at first, and then from anywhere she placed a request. And Enfys read. She took notes. And she wrote. She put a large map of London on the floor, divided it into sections, and its people and its citizens came alive to her. Charles Darwin and Oscar Wilde and Annie Besant. Then she read E. L. Doctorow's *Ragtime*, and his fictional characters imposed on American history. This book gave her the idea to write.

After languishing without a job, a break happened for Earl when he was hired at Northeast Missouri State University (now Truman State University) in Kirksville, just ninety minutes south into the state of Missouri. Enfys yearned to continue her studies and questioned if she could be enrolled as a junior and be admitted into a class called Creative Writing taught by Jim Thomas. She shared:

> The first day of class, he asked us to write a ballad and be prepared to read it to the class the next day. I had no idea what a ballad was, but went home and researched the word and wrote that ballad. I wrote verses on the victims of Jack the Ripper. Each verse was separated into two repeating lines in Cockney. The next day, we read our ballads. Some in the class had attempted the assignment. I read mine out loud and I noticed Jim Thomas raising his eyebrows in a way which seemed to indicate his approval. My verse went as such:

"O'ave you seen the shadow luv go slippin' past the wall?
O'ave you seen the shadow luv?
Like you they say 'es tall
O'ave you seen the shadow luv?
'Cos murder is 'is game
And Albert Duke of Clarence is 'is Royal Bloody name."

That day's assignment was to write a *terza rima,* which I
again had no clue what that was. That night I read Dante's
Divine Comedy again and studied the arrangement of the
lines. I wrote my terza rima, and again the next day we all
read aloud our writing. For some reason, Jim had me read
mine last. At the conclusion in front of the whole class, he
pointed to me and said, "Hasn't anyone told you that you
can write?" The rest of the students in the class all
clapped. This support, this instinctive response from those
students is something so distinctly American.

Enfys completed her bachelor's degree in elementary education
and a master's in aesthetics from Northeast Missouri State in 1978 and
1979. She joined her husband Earl on the faculty at Indian Hills
Community College based in Ottumwa, but on the Centerville
Campus. She was to teach a class in the course of study, Aesthetics
and Civilization. The aesthetics degree meant she was knowledgeable
in the history of arts, music, and literature. Her creativity and intense
skills in researching and detailing any subject led her to create three
courses in a historic timeline. The Aesthetics and Civilization
curriculum emerged into three classes at Indian Hills, titled, I. From
the Lascaux Caves of France to the Renaissance; II. Renaissance to the
Reformation; III. Reformation to the Twentieth Century. She also
taught World Literature and College Writing Skills. She retired after
twenty-three years in 2001 to continue her research and writing.

Enfys's teaching evaluations reflected nothing but the highest of
marks. Her speaking and her historical grasp on the importance of

accuracy and research became a hallmark in southern Iowa. She became captivated by the history of Appanoose County and Iowa immigration. Many of the immigrants from over forty nationalities had come in the 1880s and into the twentieth century to work in the coal mines. Her book, *Centerville: A Mid-American Saga,* published in 2013, was a ten-year endeavor with six hundred pages and over seven thousand references in this classic story. This should be a must-read for any Iowan or historian of America of the last 150 years. It personifies the word "aesthetics."

Her marriage ended after twenty-seven years. Earl moved to a house adjacent to Enfys. When Alzheimer's affected his life, Enfys took care of him for three years, their son John taking the last three years. Earl died of Alzheimer's disease in 2013.

Epilogue

At eighty-nine years old (in 2025), Enfys continues to write and speak (at no charge) to audiences in southern Iowa and northern Missouri. She has published two books, plus articles in the *Western Mail* (UK); *Ninnau;* the *Centerville Iowegian,* the *Des Moines Register,* the *Christian Science Monitor,* and the *San Francisco Examiner.* She has just completed the story of Continental Airlines Flight 11—the first bombing of a jet liner on American soil. It occurred May 22, 1962, over southern Iowa and northern Missouri. She brings her intense creativity and keen Welsh wit and humor to every endeavor.

This immigrant has concerns about her adopted country. She believes, "Social media inundation where ignorance is spread has led to the idiocy of groups evangelizing about their Second Amendment rights and their rights about themselves and not others. During the pandemic of 2020 and 2021, the larger pandemic is one of misinformation." The wisdom which guided her as a youth, that, "If you depart from the truth, you are on your way to mental illness," continues to be her steadfast belief.

Creativity, ingenuity, and a zest for humanity comes into every endeavor of Enfys's life. How could the last attempted invasion of

Britain ever become a historical movement in Iowa in the United States? The invasion happened in 1797 during the French Revolution when a French landing of 1,200 troops set foot in Fishguard, Wales. The mission was to invade the British Isles. The Battle of Fishguard is commemorated in a 100-foot tapestry which was unveiled in 1997 on the two-hundredth anniversary of the invasion by the French. And just who would attend this exhibit? None other than this Welsh American who was visiting a cousin in her native Wales. Enfys was so moved that the community of Fishguard had preserved this rich history that she dreamed of a similar idea for her home in Centerville, Iowa. Having written the accomplished book, *Centerville: A Mid-American Saga,* could the first 150 years of its history be preserved in a tapestry in similar fashion?

Enfys gathered a group of historians, quilters, and weavers together. With her zeal for this idea, she proposed an embroidered tapestry for Centerville. As with most ideas, it takes a leader, not just a dreamer, to set the wheels in motion. The citizens of Indianola, the county seat north in Warren County, jumped at the idea. A group of doers at Promise City, likewise, were very interested. Enfys returned to the Centerville community particularly because of its rich history of coal mining, immigration, and the saga of the Mid-American city. And as Paul Harvey would have said, "And now the rest of the story." Working together with more than thirty women embroiderers, thirty feet have been completed of the longest tapestry in America (as of 2022). It tells the story of fifty-seven historical events in one tapestry in what will be a one-hundred-foot masterpiece.

Jeremy McElvain, a former student at Indian Hills Community College, shared his relationship and admiration for Enfys:

> I took World Literature, Speech and Communications, Aesthetics and Civilization, and Art History, all which Enfys taught. She was very popular and an outstanding lecturer. She taught with such high energy and was a performer. Her charismatic concerns and deep care for her students were emblematic every day. Her speeches to this day are

in a performance mode. She knows the history of this area like the back of her hand. Truly a local treasure! She can connect the history of Centerville with every audience. She has a specific affinity for World War II veterans, as she lived the events in England at the time. She can process the knowledge of the dates and tell each veteran where they were at that time of the war. Enfys influenced my studies, and we remain friends as I am now working on my doctorate. She encourages everyone that they can move up with their ability from our station in life, and it is all based on education. This is opposed to the British system where it is much more difficult to rise above your class. When I talk with her frequently and share my doubts of the next endeavor, her line to me is always, "Oh, yes you can get that next degree!" I give her the same message when she questions her next accomplishment.

Enfys McMurry's grasp of the Constitution should be a course which every American needs to enroll and study. Since eleven of the original fifty-five signees of the Constitution came from Welsh ancestry, this Welsh scholar and immigrant should be the one who speaks to America.

Enfys's story is still being told. Her book, *Disaster at 39,000 Feet: How Small Town America Came Together at a Time of Crisis,* about the first domestic airline bombing was published in 2024. From the Eleven Plus Test, London, Tucson, Edmonton, Canada, and eventually to Iowa, this dynamic lady continues to leave her footprint on mankind.

A lasting conclusion of our interview was that if you are ever in Santa Fe at the St. Francis Hotel, order a Burned Sage Margarita from the mixologist in Enfys's and Tom Bahti's memory.

Gustav Verheul

A Dutch boy wandered Europe during World War II,
and came to America to find education and success.

"Mother ordered us to no longer speak Dutch, not a single word . . . After all, we have only reached the bottom rung of life's ladder in a new country." —Gustav

Gustav

Gustaaf Wilhelm Verheul was born in Amsterdam, Netherlands, on March 12, 1931. He was the third child of Adrianus and Thea Verheul. His mother had immigrated from Germany to the Netherlands in 1925 at the age of twenty-two. Thea had planned to immigrate to America where her brother, Herbert, and her sister had gone with their families during the great surge of Europeans leaving their countries because of the difficult times after World War I. She married Adrianus in 1926, followed by four children, thus ending any plans for coming to America.

The name Netherlands means "low countries." The Netherlands is smaller than the state of West Virginia. More than half of its land is below sea level. The country borders Germany to the east, Belgium to the south, and the North Sea to the west and north.

The Verheul family story was just one of millions who endured and survived World War I. His mother Thea's parents lived in Kiel-Pries, Germany, over 425 miles from Amsterdam. At the age of four, Gustaaf was sent to live with his grandparents, Otto and Minna Kubisch. They were known as Opa and Oma to the grandchildren. Opa had been a German military officer and was the mayor of Kiel-Pries. With Opa's instruction, Gustaaf learned to speak German and to garden. He learned world geography by studying his grandfather's stamp collection, while Oma tutored him in German and basic schooling. Gustaaf returned to Amsterdam the next year on a train by himself at the age of five.

The Netherlands remained neutral during World War I. Over one million Belgians streamed north as refugees. Neutrality was not possible during the next world conflict. World War II brought the country into havoc with a five-year occupation from May 15, 1940, through May 1945.

When Gustaaf was nine, his parents separated, and he and his brother Aries went to live with his father. Because of his father's neglect, he was rescued by the Salvation Army, where he attended church and loved the music. His Aunt Truus fetched him and put him in a home for boys in Amsterdam.

This all changed on May 15, 1940, with the German invasion of the Netherlands, which resulted in an eighty-eight-hour battle with Germany. His mother, being of German heritage, was drafted by the Germans to work at a hospital treating German soldiers. She arranged to send Gustaaf and his sister, Hildegaard, to Bern, Switzerland.

They left on Gustaaf's tenth birthday, May 12, 1941. This ten-year-old and his sister, then age six, were on their own to get across a war-torn area to reach neutral Switzerland. They went by water on a vender boat, which was safer than traveling on land. They got lucky, and were speaking Dutch on the shores of the Rhine Canal (German: *Rhein Kanal*), when a couple asked if they spoke German. Gustaaf, having learned German from Opa, replied, "*Ja.*" Hildegaard spoke some French and this couple just happened to be French. This was the beginning of an incredible four years of survival through Europe during the war. The couple, Monsieur Marcel and Madame Nadien invited them on board—in exchange for help with the language and doing some chores, Marcel and Nadien would take the children as far as Cologne (German: *Köln*), Germany. They were delivering the vender boat to Cologne for a friend. Marcel and Nadien were part of the Strassburger Circus, which was headquartered in Metz, France, at the time.

At Cologne, Madame Nadien bought the children a ticket on the train for Bern, Switzerland. They had to change trains at Strasbourg, France, before the next two-hour train ride to Bern. Upon arrival, arrangements had been made for Hildegaard to go to a house for girls. Gustaaf walked to a YMCA hostel that helped traveling male students needing IDs. He was able to get an ID with claims that he was a German and a relative of his Opa Otto, who apparently was an influential person. After staying there a few days, Gustaaf was off on foot and crossed the Austrian border. Homeless, young, and at a high altitude, he became ill and stopped for a few days. He was found by some nuns who were picking berries.

Sister Teresa brought Gustaaf to their manse, a refurbished castle for religious purposes, and gave him a blanket, food, and medication. The nuns spoke Latin. There were nearly forty boys staying at the manse. Among them, they spoke nearly eighty languages. The boys were required to learn language, math, and how to tell time. After three months, Gustaaf once again left on foot to go to a German army post in Innsbruck, Austria. He met some German officers who allowed him to tag along and ride on their truck if he would polish their shoes. The truck took him to Regensburg, Germany, on the Danube River, where he stayed at a youth hostel for two days.

Another officer offered to take him to Treblinka, Poland. Gustaaf had no idea Treblinka was not an army post, but an extermination camp. He stayed with the officer and his wife in exchange for food by doing chores. Fortunately for Gustaaf, the officer was transferred, so Gustaaf was able to leave and head west on a bicycle.

With the bicycle having flat tires, he was again picked up by two officers and rode on a military truck to Rosenheim, Germany, a transportation hub that connected to Prague, Czechoslovakia. He cleaned in exchange for food, and caught a ride to Metz, France, which was under German occupation. He found the Strassburger Circus, but Monsieur Marcel and Madame Nadien were not there because they had returned to Belgium. He was directed to their concessioner wagon. He slept under the wagon until they returned. Gustaaf was able to get food in exchange for teaching the highwire boys his language skills. When Marcel and Nadien returned, they gave him a key to the wagon.

After four months at Metz, Gustaaf traveled back north to Amsterdam with Marcel and Nadien. Just before Easter 1943 at their hotel, they said their goodbyes, and he left with his duffle bag and backpack. He boarded the train, and he cried all the way to the hospital to see if he could find his mother, Thea. It had been three years since he had seen his mother when he left for Bern with Hildegaard on his tenth birthday. At the hospital in Amsterdam, he was told that his mother lived just two blocks away. When he rang the bell, he saw his mother at her fourth-floor window crying out his nickname, "Koosie!" They met and were both very emotional. They talked of their family one at a time. Opa had died just before the war. His mother's two brothers had gone down with the Bismarck battleship off the southern tip of England in 1941. His brother Arie was a member of the Hitler Youth, or *Hitlerjugend*, worker program, and was working in a submarine factory. Thea told Gustaaf there were eighty thousand Amsterdam Jews who were rounded up and taken by train to the northern tip of Ukraine and to Treblinka in nineteen trainloads. The first four trains were passenger trains. The last fifteen trains were made up of cattle cars.

Gustaaf met his father, Adrianus, and spoke to him in Dutch. He found that his father was involved in the underground smuggling of downed Allied airmen back to England via Brussels, Belgium, along the Comet Line. This was a Resistance organization in occupied Belgium and France during World War II.

It was now December 1943. With his backpack in hand, Gustaaf left notes for his parents and headed north toward the densely populated area of North Holland (Dutch: *Noord-Holland*), then south toward the town of Zaandam, Netherlands. German soldiers gave him coins to get food and drink along the way. At one point, Gustaaf found a YMCA that lent him a pup tent for the night, which had to be returned by nine the following morning. At another point, he found a Salvation Army site, which allowed him two nights plus one meal with a proper ID. Gustaaf made a sign which read, "Work for Food." After struggling for over two weeks to locate a safe place to stay, he went back to Amsterdam. At the tram station, Gustaaf met a man, Erik von Houten, who fed him. During conversation, he was impressed with Gustaaf's wanderings during the war. So, Gustaaf was encouraged during the journey to write down, in German, his story of the last four years. Upon arriving back in Amsterdam, Gustaaf was introduced by Mr. von Houten to his wife, Helga von Houten, who offered Gustaaf a place to sleep in the small garden house. This was in exchange for him working in the eighty-plot gardens. The owner of the gardens was a German-born doctor, Dr. Frieberg, who had been drafted by the Germans. Dr. Frieberg's wife, Mevrouw Frieberg, was a nurse at his clinic, and too busy to see to all the garden work. Fortuitously for Gustaaf, she was Helga von Houten's sister. When Gustaaf was asked if he would help with whatever needed to be taken care of for food and lodging, he eagerly, enthusiastically, and gratefully accepted.

In the spring of 1944, while Gustaaf was working in the gardens, he was hit by a stray shrapnel from aerial combat planes. A tourniquet placed above the knee saved his life. Erik von Houten carried Gustaaf to the medical clinic where nurse Frieberg removed the shrapnel. He was lucky that it did not break the bone. Following suture, it left an eight-inch scar. Helga von Houten started homeschooling work for Gustaaf. Mevrouw Frieberg gave him much homework over history, biology, earth sciences, and the Bible, all in German.

Gustaaf remembered, "The news of the Allied invasion on the beaches in France on D-Day gave us all immense jubilation."

When Gustaaf left at the end of the war, Mevrouw Frieberg gave him five twenty-five Gulden (gold coins) and bought him a bicycle. He said, "I arrived in Amsterdam on May 5, 1945, and went to church for a special end-of-war celebration."

A letter came from Uncle Herbert from Michigan with money enclosed for food, clothing, and tickets. The letter said he would sponsor the whole Verheul family to come to America. Since so many Europeans were applying for immigration, the quota system limited the number allowed from Holland. Gustaaf's earlier relationship with the von Houten's became extremely important once again. In addition to all the support they had provided him, Helga von Houten now was able to streamline the immigration papers for the entire Verheul family to come to America four years later. She worked at a government agency, and thus knew how to guide the process. She had the Verheul's first get visas and passports. They next applied to get on the immigration list. Birth certificates, medical records, and legal information were all documented. Then they waited for over two years, until they were informed that in July 1947, their request to immigrate would be granted. Brother Arie received his draft notice to report on the first of July 1947. Holland was at war in the Dutch West Indies, and all available men were needed in the military. With some luck, Helga von Houten was able to find a couple who would trade their June exit date for Arie and his older sister, Thea, to leave for America two weeks earlier in late June, thus missing the draft into the Dutch Army. Gustaaf, his mother, and younger sister, Hildegaard, left as scheduled two weeks later in July. They were on the first airplane KLM DC-4 flight, with immigrants from twelve different countries, to America from Holland. All previous immigrants had had to travel by sea.

As the plane lowered and circled New York to land at Idlewild, they saw the Statue of Liberty out the side window. At the airport, the Verheul's were gratified to see a sign in their native language directing them where to go next. Passports in hand, Gustaaf and his mother were processed by two agents. With the envelope which Helga von Houten had completed, their documents and bags were inspected and stamped. The agents returned the passports and informed them of their new name changes. Gustav remembered:

> My new name was Gustav, Hildegard now only had one "a," and Mother's middle name, Klara, was eliminated. With luggage in hand and placed on a dolly, we followed the rope path to the exit. The agents shook hands and wished us good luck. Thea pointed to a sign where Uncle Heinrich and Aunt Lieschen met us. They had immigrated in 1926. We all hugged and made our introductions. A taxi ride took us to their place on East 40th Street.

Gustav stayed in New York for three weeks, and his cousin Billy showed him the city. Subways, buses, ferries, horse and buggies, and rented bicycles helped in the exploration. Learning English was a vital part of the day. Gustav wrote new words on three-by-five index cards. Billy helped him conjugate the verbs.

Aunt Lieschen purchased tickets for them for the train to Michigan, which brought the Verheul's to Uncle Herbert's farm near Port Huron. Billy came along to help work on the farm for the rest of the summer. Gustav continued reviewing his index cards and reading Tom Mix Western books in English. Billy had said that Uncle Herbert's farm was the most beautiful and best equipped farm in Michigan. Gustav told this story as if it were yesterday:

> Uncle Herbert had bought a small rundown house without indoor plumbing and water for us to stay in and remodel. Finally, all four of us children and mother were alone and together. Mother ordered us to no longer speak Dutch, not a single word. She reamed out Arie and said, "Do you understand?" After all, we have only reached the bottom rung of life's ladder in a new country.

After Labor Day in 1947, Gustav and Hildegard registered for school in Port Huron fifteen miles away. They were placed in several classes together as seventh graders, though they were sixteen and fourteen years old respectively. After several weeks, the administrators wanted to move Gustav straight to tenth grade. He asked to stay in the seventh until Christmas to help Hildegard adjust with her English. His mother had started singing and humming, which she had not done for years.

Gustav's mother had started seeing Fritz. He was one of Uncle Herbert's friends, who had helped the Verheul's remodel their house. An opportunity had come for the couple to buy a farm. The gold coins given to Gustav became part of the down payment for the farm. He gave the coins, by then with a net worth of three thousand dollars, as part of the required five thousand dollar down payment. The farm owner, Mr. Scheiterlein, suggested, "So, tell you what. I'll take Gussie to Florida and let him work for me for the other two thousand dollars of the down payment, and I'll teach him a trade." The deal was made. Legal documents were signed. And Gustav was once again on the road to an unknown place with a near-servitude working situation.

This was less than one year after Gustav started school in his first ever formal educational setting in Port Huron. His parting words for Fritz were, "You have a lifelong opportunity to show your thanks by taking care of my little sister, Hildegard. She wants to learn to play the piano."

Gustav knew how to read maps and found himself leading a man and his family on a 1,400-mile, three-day trip to Sarasota, Florida. By Christmas 1948, they had built a cottage for the family and four more houses in just four months. Gustav was paid fifty cents per hour, given five dollars per week spending money, and charged an unannounced fee for room and board.

Life took a big turn on Gustav's eighteenth birthday on May 12, 1949. He informed Mr. Scheiterlein that he was taking the day off. Mr. Scheiterlein was not happy and became quite mad. The lady at a nearby gas station whom Gustav had helped in the evenings had told him, "Go to the beach, see the girls, swim, and be happy in the sun." He said, "My life changed on that day. I had always been independent, but not self-reliant. I had become more assertive."

In May when school was out in Sarasota for the Scheiterlein daughters, they all headed back to Michigan to build houses for the summer. In the fall it was back to Florida. For the second time, things became much different and improved. Gustav asked for a raise to seventy cents per hour, asked for and received weekends off, and bought a motorcycle. He found a place to stay which eliminated the deductions from his pay for boarding. He made friends, had a few dates, and went to church. "Though I was still a bashful blond with wavy hair, I signed up for GED classes and got a night job at a bowling alley setting pins, which also gave good tips," Gustav remembered.

In the summer of 1950, it was back to Michigan, with the GED books in hand, to build more houses.

Once back in Florida in the fall, Gustav started his own business laying asphalt shingles. His fee was seven dollars per square, and he could set eight squares in a day. Within two weeks, he was able to pay off his debt to Mr. Scheiterlein. An attorney at church helped him get the legal documents related to the payoff settlement.

A draft notice came to him in the mail. Gustav was again caught up in a war. This time it would be as a soldier in Korea. From Columbia, South Carolina, to Fort Leonard Wood, Missouri, Gustav became an explosives expert. In January 1952, he left Seattle on a ship for Tokyo and onto Incheon, Korea. It was snowing, and no lights were allowed, not even cigarette lighting. The unit marched all night, and the snow became worse. They were thrown into a major assault where twelve men were lost, including the squad leader. Gustav was to replace him. He was later borrowed to help blow up bridges on the 38th parallel on very dark nights. "As a boy in Europe, it was survival. In Korea, it was 'kill or get killed,'" he told. He was wounded in both wars. In Korea he was evacuated by a helicopter with a concussion, and taken to a MASH unit.

Gustav received his honorable discharge on August 21, 1953. At the request of Colonel White, Gustav next had a most solemn assignment. He was flown from Fort Jackson, South Carolina, to Detroit, where he expressed condolences and gratitude for the ultimate sacrifice on behalf of the US Army. Being the "grief officer," he delivered a flag and commendation letter to the families of three soldiers. All three of the men had been in his platoon. The military then flew him back to Florida where he went back to evening classes at Sarasota High School. He passed the citizenship class just before Christmas. He had to go to Tampa to be sworn in as a citizen of the United States of America.

Gustav shared:

> I was spending a lot of time at church with my girlfriend who later became my wife. The attorney friend from church again helped me by telling me, "With that GED and as a veteran you can get financial help for college." The closest college was St. Petersburg Junior College, which happened to be the first junior college in Florida. I applied and started school the next fall. My major was music. I was

inspired by a Dr. Ridley, who was Russian and educated at the Vienna Conservatory, where she received her doctorate. She had immigrated the same year we had in 1947. She had a beautiful contralto voice, was very attractive, and had an extraordinary and frequent smile. This opened my world to education, and the opportunities were endless. With the help and understanding of my wife and my three children, I was able to reach unbelievable accomplishments.

Gustav received an associate's degree from St. Petersburg Junior College in two years and started teaching at the same Sarasota High School where he had taken the GED classes. He taught German and algebra. It was 1960 and the school had not been integrated yet. He was the only first-year teacher that year. The next year, the principal announced in a reluctant voice that the school would be integrated, and asked in an assembly for a show of hands of those teachers who would be willing to take Black students. Gustav reflected, "Of course, my hand went high into the air. I did not see if there were others who did so also. My first Black student in my German class was a very bright and charming girl named Wilhelmina."

When asked to become an assistant football coach, a reluctant Gustav claimed he had no experience or knowledge of the sport. Following a summer workshop course at Florida State University under coach Bobby Bowden, Gustav became an assistant coach for the next twelve years. His German class of twenty-five students were led to Salzburg, Austria, in 1962 by Gustav and his wife.

A Fulbright scholarship as awarded to Gustav the next summer to study in Germany and Austria. It was awarded for a music composition he had written, and he was one of forty chosen. It was his first time back to Germany in sixteen years. He attempted to visit the many friends who had helped him survive during the five years he was on the move during the war.

He earned a master's degree and finally a PhD from Florida State University in 1971.

Gustav applied and received sabbatical leave for the 1972-73 school year. He indeed used the trade he was taught by his Uncle Herbert and Mr. Scheiterlein and built the first of eight duplexes on one block zoned for multiple residences. "The owner of the concrete company had come over to remind me to always have something formed so I can get leftover concrete for half price at the end of the day when a less than full load was still on the truck. The concrete company was only two blocks away and was on its way home from the other construction sites," said Gustav with a smile.

Gustav retired after thirty years from teaching at Sarasota High School in June 1988. He and his wife had separated. He bought a Suburban and a twenty-four-foot camper. His goal was to visit national parks, historical monuments, seashores, and state parks. During the next ten years, he traveled to over two hundred national and state parks in the United States and Canada. He periodically was hired at several parks for his building skills. "I had worked in several national parks. There were jobs at Death Valley, Yosemite, Grand Teton, and Glacier. My work consisted mostly of replacing badly rusted screws in walkways or rotted wood. I used mostly pneumatic tools."

Gustav continued:

> Two places became very special to me. Rincon Country West in Tucson, Arizona, was the most beautiful park I had ever seen. It is completely enclosed with a steel-staked fence, wide paved streets, large-graveled lots, with picnic tables, a huge pool with submerged benches along the sides, a recreational complex including all kinds of craft rooms, game areas, and a huge bulletin board. I stayed there three times, a month at a time. The other one was Twentynine Palms RV Resort in Southern California. It was by far my favorite place. I had my first hip replacement there in Palm Springs only forty-five miles south. Also, my second knee replacement occurred the following year. The

RV resort had its own golf course. The lady pro and club-house manager taught me how to play. I was then sixty-five years old and had stayed there five winters for five months, December through April. I never had to pay rent, and I had been paid $2,500 each year for the work that I performed around the camp.

Epilogue

The time had finally come for Gustav to give up his nomadic travel life. He purchased a fixer-upper—a $1,300 mobile home park in Bradenton, Florida, called Trailer Estates. The park was featured on CBS's *60 Minutes* in the 1990s. He became very active socially, including frequent ballroom dancing, playing golf, daily swimming, potluck dinners, Saturday park breakfasts, periodic stage shows, and holiday parties. He joined Park Church and became a frequent soloist.

He made his last visit to Holland, Germany, and Austria on his seventieth birthday. It was truly a walk down memory lane for Gustav. He walked in the footsteps of those unbelievable people who had helped save his life as a boy. Rosa, a sweet and musically talented girl from the village of Edam, Netherlands, with whom he had studied and played, had been the last to pass away one year earlier. She had become a physician. Her son was also a physician and continued her medical practice. Rosa had named him Gustaf.

For his ninetieth birthday in 2021, Gustav presented his daughters Denise and Suzanne with a seventy-page memoir from which much of this story has also been written. From the Netherlands to America, this brilliant man continues to share his talents and incredible life with others.

Heinrich, Frieda, Klaus and Heike
on a ship to America

Heinrich and
Frieda von Allworden Goedecke

A German POW returned to Kansas to join his
family and became a metallurgist businessman.

*"My mother, Frieda, gave birth to Klaus on October 4, 1943, just three
months after the massive bombing of Hamburg ceased. Can you imagine
the horrific explosions and fire storms, much less being so near term to
deliver her first baby at just the age of twenty-three?"*

—Heike Goedecke Daily, Heinrich and Frieda's daughter

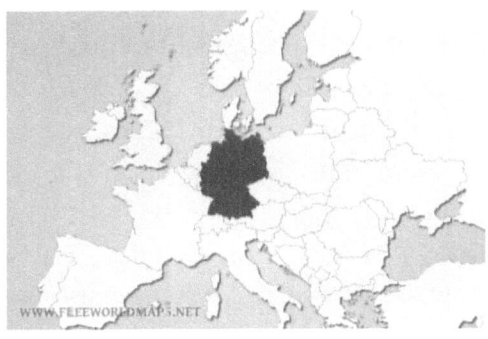

Heinrich and Frieda

Man's inhumanity to man.* With the War to End All Wars dimly in the rear-view mirror and the ink barely dry on the armistice signed on November 11, 1918, another even more horrific world cataclysmic debacle unfolded. Historians have suggested that the Treaty of Versailles placed stringent reparations and restrictions on Germany, carved up the Habsburg Empire, and provided little guidance for how countries of Europe were to survive. With the worldwide 1930s depression, the stage was perfectly set for a little mustached artist and former army sergeant to rise to German leadership and create the Third Reich.

More than six million Jews were killed in the Holocaust. Man's inhumanity to man! Estimates of human losses during WWII in Europe include: Soviets—20 million, Germans—6 million, Italians—470,000, Czechoslovakians—46,000, Estonians—34,000, Finnish—95,000, French—210,000, Greeks—35,000, Hungarians—200,000, Latvians—30,000, Lithuanians—25,000, Luxembourgers—3,000, Dutch—6,000, Norwegians—200,000, Polish—5.7 million (including Jews), Portuguese—50,000, Romanians—200,000, Yugoslavians—400,000, and British—383,000.

The war at sea was no less tragic than that on land. From 1820 to 1940 and during European colonialization of Africa, South America, and southern Asia, the British Navy was the power of the high seas. Even though the Treaty of Versailles limited Germany's navy to one-third of the British navy, these well-intended measures were ignored.

With the emergence of the Third Reich, the German *Kriegsmarine* (Navy) dominated the North Sea, Baltic Sea, and Mediterranean Sea until the Allies turned the war by late 1943. With the surrender of 240,000 Germans and Italians in North Africa, the invasion of Crete became the turning point in this hideous war in Europe.

"Man's inhumanity to man," is a line from the poem "Man Was Made to Mourn" by Scottish poet Robert Burns, originally published in 1784.

The thirteen largest German ships sunk by the Allies in the nineteen months from October 1943 until Victory in Europe Day (V-E Day) on May 8, 1945, included thirty-eight thousand Germans, Italian POWs, Greek POWs, and Jews that drowned in the sea.

Minensuchboot, or minesweepers, built by the Germans starting in 1940 in Dutch shipyards were coal fired and much less dependent on fuel supplies. They were used for escort duties for the *Kriegsmarine*. Heinrich Goedecke may have been aboard such a minesweeper.

Heinrich Goedecke was born January 31, 1913, in Hamburg, Germany. He was the son of Karl and Dora Goedecke. He had one sister, Elfida, who died at the age of twenty-one. Frieda Von Allworden (Heinrich's wife) was born on August 30, 1920. Frieda's father had died when she was one year old aboard a non-combat ship. Heinrich and Frieda were married on August 16, 1942, in Hamburg.

Hamburg was Europe's largest seaport and industrial center. On July 24, 1943, Operation Gomorrah started, lasting eight days and seven nights with the largest Royal Air Force (RAF) and United States Air Force (USAF) aerial bombing mission of the war. Over three thousand planes dropped bombs on Hamburg, destroying shipyards, U-boat pens, and oil refineries. Most of the city was flattened and burned. Over one million people were evacuated and over sixty percent of the housing was destroyed. Hamburg was struck sixty-nine more times in the next twenty-one months until the end of the war. In January 1946, Major Cortez F. Enloe, a surgeon in the USAF who worked on the US Strategic Bombing Survey, said that the fire effects of the atomic bomb dropped on Nagasaki, "were not nearly as bad as the RAF raids on Hamburg. It was estimated that 40,000 died in Hamburg."

Heike Goedecke Daily, Heinrich and Frieda's daughter, related in 2021:

> My mother, Frieda, gave birth to Klaus on October 4, 1943, just three months after the massive bombing of Hamburg ceased. Can you imagine the horrific explosions and fire storms, much less being so near term to deliver her first

baby at just the age of twenty-three? Her stories of this event were never shared with our family. Whether she had been evacuated from Hamburg or was living with her mother and stepfather was never revealed to her children. She talked a few times of the ordeals of protecting my brother, Klaus, in what seemed like continuous air raid shelters for two years. Her only constant companion was infant Klaus. With *Vatti* [Father] away in the war, *Mutti* [Mother] had no idea of his whereabouts or if he was even alive. A letter written by *Vatti* arrived somehow in late 1943, verifying that he was indeed alive and was a POW in America. It was the only letter she ever received until many months after the war ended officially on May 7, 1945. War time for Frieda and Klaus was devastating. Her main resolve was to protect and nourish her baby any way she could. The aftermath of the end of the war was equally terrifying, with finding food, shelter, water, coal, and rations a constant worry.

Heinrich Goedecke was aboard three German minesweepers that were sunk in the Mediterranean. With each sinking, he was rescued either by another ship or washed ashore. When the third ship was sunk, he was picked up and captured in Tunisia in 1943. Records of the event and any knowledge from military files or family stories do not reveal the particulars of Heinrich's capture, surrender, or imprisonment as a German POW in North Africa.

By 1943, the British were overwhelmed with POWs, and called upon America to take over 435 thousand German and Italian POWs. These POWs were transported and escorted across the Atlantic Ocean to forty-six of the then forty-eight United States. Being imprisoned by the Americans was considered a much better option than being imprisoned by the Soviets.

The 640-acre prison camp at Concordia, Kansas, opened in May 1943. The first Germans arrived on July 15. They were soon followed by three thousand enlisted men and two thousand officers. Many were from the Afrika Korps who were part of Rommel's tank divisions and armies in North Africa. Some were strong Nazis and were belligerent captives. The camp had a six ward, 177-bed hospital, library, dental office, theatre, and a newspaper called *Der Stacheldraht* (*The Barbed Wire*). Most of the POWs at Concordia were in the army but three hundred were naval personnel. Heinrich had been a lieutenant naval officer, and he arrived at Concordia. On New Year's Eve 1944, a letter from Frieda arrived, telling him that baby Klaus had been born on October 4, and weighed twelve pounds at birth. Nineteen years later in 1963, Heinrich told the *Salina (Kansas) Journal*, "Boy, did I celebrate! Even though Klaus was now over a year old!" Just three months after his arrival at Concordia, all the navy POWs were relocated and sent to Phoenix, Arizona.

Heinrich in the German Navy

Camp Papago Park in eastern Phoenix confined 3,100 POWs. There were four compounds for the enlisted men and one for the officers. The prisoners, mostly U-boat internees, called the camp *Schlaraffenland*—the land of milk and honey. There was a theatre where two films were shown each week. It also provided a place for the camp choir to practice. The camp newspaper was called the *Papago Rundschau*. Heinrich was assigned as the officer in charge of recreation.

Each morning he would meet with American officers to plan the day. They became good friends. As he told the *Salina Journal* on June 17, 1979, "I used to meet each morning with the American officers to get things organized. We used to sit around and drink coffee, and they would offer me cigars, though I never smoked once in my life, and we would talk. At the end of the war, I think I had more close American friends than German friends." The most famous escape from American camps happened at Papago Park. Twenty-five men dug a 175-foot tunnel, which was three feet high and half as wide to escape into the desert. They were all apprehended within two weeks. One turned himself in because he became aware of the Christmas menu to be served. This treatment was quite different from the POW camps of the Axis powers—Italy, Japan, Germany, and others who opposed the Allied powers. Man's HUMANITY to man *was* possible, and friendships after the war and reunions continued long after the last shot was fired. Most escapes happened out of boredom as few had any hopes of ever being able to get back to Germany.

A total of 2,220 German POWs escaped from the camps in America which was .5% of the 425 thousand prisoners. Nearly twice that of the Italian POWs escaped. This rate was still less than the nearly two percent escape rate from American prisons and jails at the time.

Though many of the German POWs were released from the American camps in 1945, Heinrich was not released until the next year on May 13, 1946. Heinrich was returned to Virginia where he was one of twenty thousand POWs selected to be part of a training group to reorganize and rebuild Germany. The Special Projects Division (SPD), directed by university professors, was a program which provided classes on democracy. 2,500 graduate POWs returned directly to Germany instead of being used for additional labor in Europe. They were employed in areas to rebuild the country and society. "My one regret was that I did not stay and take the SPD education class but opted for going back to my country to help in the rebuilding," Heinrich told his daughter, Heike, years later. "I just wanted to get home to my wife and son that I had never seen, and to my Hamburg. I had no idea what Hamburg would look like. The letters from Freida had been sketchy about what was left of Hamburg or any of the circumstances of daily life."

Upon release from Papago Park, Heinrich was transported by train across the United States to the east coast along with other released naval personnel. He befriended a guard who accompanied the train ride. Chatting casually, the guard learned that Heinrich was anxious to return home to his wife and three-year-old son. The guard gave Heinrich a chocolate bar which he promised to give to his son when he saw him. This chocolate bar was the only thing that Heinrich had to give to his son, Klaus. Heinrich later wrote a letter from Germany to the guard, thanking him for his kind gesture and telling him this was the first time his son had ever seen or tasted chocolate. A half century later, this guard's son came upon the letter and traced Klaus from Germany to Salina and eventually to Huntington Beach, California, to give him the letter written by his father in 1946. Man's humanity to man!

In Germany, Heinrich found his wife and son living in the small village of Klein Rönnau. Even though the war had been over for nearly a year, their conditions were very bleak. Heinrich told the *Salina Journal*:

> It was the worst of times in the history of Germany, a terrible time; no . . . more than terrible. No food, no clothes, no factories, or work, no gas or electricity. There were so many refugees—we lived in a small house by American standards, too small for one family, along with two other families. We were fortunate to survive.

They were able to subsist by trading for food. Heinrich climbed trees to find wood to heat their stove. He had been allowed to bring 150 pounds of baggage home from the States. This included soap, cigarettes, wood carvings, and clothes, which helped the family trade for food and survive. He found a job at a filling station and was willing to do anything to provide for his family. As a boy, he had wanted to be an engineer, but his alcoholic father consumed all the family's resources. Joining the navy had been his only way of getting an education. He later found work in a milling shop and learned to craft metal designs.

A daughter, Heike, was born at home on March 20, 1947, weighing eleven pounds. Heike related:

> My *Mutti* always said it was a beautiful sunny day. Can you imagine remembering this after just delivering such a large baby? My grandmother was able to help. *Mutti* made all our clothes for Klaus and me. When I was born, the family was allotted one cloth diaper by the local authorities.

For some reason, their camera was either confiscated, or film was not available, but there are no pictures of baby Heike for the first three years of her life.

Heinrich's friend, Gary Borck, worked in a bakery north of Hamburg. The flour used in the bakery came from the Robinson Milling Company in Salina, Kansas, with the gold emblem and wheat symbol printed on the white flour bag. Heinrich had told his friend of the wealth and opportunities and the vast spaces in America. Gary wrote a letter to the company in Kansas, telling of his experience in the bakery and asking if they would sponsor him to come to America. With the flour mill's help, Gary and Ursula Borck immigrated to Salina in 1950. Gary worked at the Salina Dillon's grocery store in the bakery.

Gary found Don Dieter, a surgeon and a friend of the Morgenstern's (who had sponsored and brought Gary Borck to Salina) in the grain business, who would put up one thousand dollars to bring Heinrich Goedecke and his family to America. They were co-sponsored by the Trinity Lutheran Church. What an irony that just nine years before, Heinrich's first American experience—the Concordia POW camp—had been only sixty miles north of Salina.

Frieda did not speak a word of English and carried her English-German dictionary everywhere. In 1952, the ship docked at Charleston, South Carolina. The harbor was lined with warehouses.

A picture of the shoreline on the horizon shows Frieda standing at the railing of the ship bringing the Goedecke's to the States.

Stepping onto the cobblestone docks, the children were drawn to the vending machines. Five-year-old Heike saw a picture of ice cream on a machine. She remembered nearly seventy years later:

> I can still see that ice cream picture on the vending machine. Ice cream was the first English word that I learned. *Vatti* told us that the train would take us all the way across the United States to a place called Kansas. We were met in Newton, Kansas, by *Vatti's* friend, Gary Borck, and his wife and other members of the Trinity Lutheran Church. They took us by auto to Salina, about an hour's drive away. We moved into a dark basement apartment owned by a church member. *Mutti* always said it reminded her of the years in bomb shelters. We lived in this basement for about three months until *Vatti* had earned enough for us to move out to a three-room apartment up the street.

Klaus and Heike were immediately enrolled in school. Heike started in kindergarten and Klaus was gradually moved up to the third grade as he learned the English language. It did not take long to learn English, as both children were fully immersed in school. They learned English along with the other normal studies.

Several times a week, all four Goedecke's walked to Dr. Dieter's office. Indeed, they had to walk everywhere, as they had no car. They cleaned their sponsor's office for a year to pay him back the one thousand dollars that he had paid to bring them to America. Frieda once said, "Cars would stop and we would be asked if we wanted a ride, but since we did not speak English, we declined or did not look up. It just made us walk faster."

Kristine was born in 1954 and was always told she was a surprise baby. Heinrich laughed and said, "Kristine is the only one of you kids who can be president of the United States because she was born here."

A job was waiting for Heinrich at a machine manufacturing company. He worked at Salina Manufacturing for nearly eleven years. Salina was booming in the 1950s. The population in that decade increased sixty-five percent, from twenty-five thousand to forty-seven thousand. Schilling Air Force Base in southwest Salina was built and occupied in 1942. When it was closed in 1965, there were approximately 5,300 personnel at Schilling, including 4,244 airmen. The Strategic Air Command planes flew all over the world. Many of the pilots brought back marble and artwork from Europe. They became acquainted with Heinrich who had started working in iron works in the area. In his garage, Heinrich started artistically designing those pieces of marble into tables and mountings for the pilots.

In 1963, eleven years after immigrating to America, Heinrich opened Heinrich's Metal Arts shop on Cloud Street, and eventually on Elm Street, in Salina. He was a blacksmith and artist. A friend of the family and Salina native Diana Ashton Warren says, "There is not a piece of iron works in Salina to this day that does not have Heinrich's hands behind it." His daughter Heike said, "*Vatti* never charged enough for his talents, but he provided a good living for our family."

An article in the *Crosswinds* magazine dated May 1979 reported:

> *Heinrich's Fireside and Patio is an iron craft business known for quality craftmanship throughout the nation. Hand-wrought railings, chandeliers, tables, patio furniture, fireplaces, plant stands, and they adorn the rustic showroom on South Broadway. Recipient of eight national*

awards for his work, Heinrich said, "We have many friends here. It is home to us now." Heinrich was recently awarded first and third place awards at the National Ornamental [& Miscellaneous Metals] Association in the category of metal in the home.

Frieda, in addition to raising three children, was incredibly involved with the arts community of Salina. She was a leader in the German American club. Heike remembered, "My, did they love to dance! *Vatti* loved his beer as well. They were a fixture at the dance halls in the area."

The whole Goedecke family sat together at Ahearn Field House in Manhattan, Kansas, in June 1964 to see Klaus's graduation. The pride in having their son graduate from college was cherished by Heinrich and Frieda. It was mandatory at the time that all freshman males had to enroll in Reserve Officers Training Corps (ROTC). Klaus was in the US Army ROTC for four years and graduated as a second lieutenant with his degree in geography. He went on active duty and was soon sent to Vietnam. Heike remembered, "My *Mutti* was distraught at the thought that her little Klaus, who she had saved and protected during the horrific World War, was now in another war for his new country. *Mutti's* worries caused her to have a nervous breakdown. This may have been part of the reason that Klaus was reassigned stateside." After Klaus retired from his career in the army, he worked for the insurance company AAA.

Epilogue

All three of Heinrich and Frieda Goedecke's children attended Kansas State University. Heike became a teacher. After raising her four children, she taught elementary school for twenty-four years. All four of *her* children also attended Kansas State University: Jeff is a fire inspector in Salina, and two of his three boys are at K-State. Aaron is an architect with his KSU graduate wife, Leslie, in Atlanta, and their twins are now attending K-State. Bradley is an orthopedic surgeon in Salina. He and Kristina are parents of four girls. The eldest has received numerous scholarships and will be a freshman at K-State, majoring in pre-med. Megan is a teacher in Salina, and her husband Paul (another KSU graduate, originally from South Dakota) works in agriculture and in finance. Their mother, Heike, was happily able to be a long-term substitute teacher when Megan gave birth to their daughter, Bristol.

The city of Salina, along with the state of Kansas and Kansas State University, have been blessed with these two amazing and industrious immigrants. Heinrich and Frieda Goedecke left their imprint on all as they found their way in their new country of America. *Man's humanity to man.*

Henry Yurk
(Heinrich Jurk)

A Volga German man escaped Stalin Russia and joined the German Army in WWII. He became a POW before escaping and making a family, then making good on his deal with God.

"Even Jesus Christ had been asked to suffer horribly. So why not a simple sinner, Henry Yurk. I have been a lucky man. God had saved me. If it was now my time to go, then so be it. It could have happened years ago in the snows of Russia." —Henry

Henry

Catherine the Great, the German princess who would become the last Czarina ever to rule Russia, had just deposed her husband, Peter III, in 1762. She published a manifesto inviting non-Jewish Europeans to immigrate and become Russian subjects if they would farm Russian lands east of the Volga River. The Volga River flows through central Russia to the south and drains into the Caspian Sea. Some German immigrants who were fleeing religious persecution at the time, came and were allowed to maintain their culture, language, traditions, and churches (Lutheran, Catholic, Reformed, Moravian, and Mennonite).

Thousands of peasants immigrated to Russia and became known as Volga Germans. They were promised no military service. They were also promised autonomy—freedom of speech, freedom of religion, and freedom of the press. They did not have to learn the Russian language unless they hoped to go to college.

Under the rule of Alexander II in 1871, the military exemption was lifted, and the Volga Germans' privileged status of autonomy was canceled. For those reasons, as well as the lure to American lands offering homesteading in the Midwest, nearly 100 thousand Volga Germans left Russia for America. Others also immigrated to Canada, Argentina, and Brazil.

At the turn of the twentieth century, Alexander III declared that "Russia must belong to Russians." The names of German towns were replaced with Russian names. The Russian language became compulsory in schools. Freedom of the press and speech were canceled.

During World War I, 300 thousand Germans served in the Russian Army. At the same time, their land holdings were being seized by the government. Pogroms (military-sanctioned riots) ordered the plunder of many German shops. Some were beaten and murdered. Though their farms were in the richest valley of Russia, there was starvation.

With the Bolshevik Revolution in 1917, things went from bad to worse. In 1919, the government of Vladimir Lenin requisitioned the entire harvest. Under communist rule, the lives of the Volga Germans became ever more difficult. As many as one-fourth of the population starved or died of disease and suffered brutal repression in the 1920s. All the churches were desecrated. All the ministers and professors were detained and deported to Siberia. According to government figures, over 105 thousand of the 1.2 million ethnic Germans were arrested in the new Union of Soviet Socialist Republics (USSR).

The Volga German Autonomous Soviet Socialist Republic (ASSR) was established. Engels, named after the German Communist philosopher Friedrich Engels, was the capital from 1918 to 1941. At the outbreak of WWII, Stalin disbanded the ASSR and deported the entire Volga German population. The area was combined into the Saratov and Stalingrad oblasts. Saratov Oblast was a larger region nearly as large the state of Kentucky in the United States at 38,700 sq. mi. (100,700 sq. km.) The NKVD, or the secret police, separated the men from the women and children and sent them all to Siberia, Kazakhstan, and other camps in September 1941. The Volga Germans were put into forced labor in the forests and mines. According to the USSR, 950 thousand were forcibly deported. It is estimated that between thirty and fifty percent of deportees perished due to inhumane conditions.

In 1941, the NKVD barred ethnic Germans from serving in the military and sent tens of thousands of those Volga German soldiers to the *Trudarmee*, the NKVD labor army.

Into these times, Heinrich Jurk was born on May 9, 1920, in Reinwald, Russia, today named Staritskoye. His parents were Heinrich and Sophia Jurk. His father was a peasant farmer. His mother was a housewife who helped with the farming. They were simple, devout Lutherans. Heinrich learned to ski before he could walk. In good weather, he ran barefoot, fished, and laid on his back watching clouds while chewing on a stem of wheat. Heinrich thought of himself as a scientist. He loved sports, gymnastics, swimming, and soccer. He believed he had an idyllic childhood.

Another failed harvest in 1932 was even worse than the ones in the 1920s. There was mass starvation among the Volga Germans.

Farmers were shot, and their food was taken. Heinrich was thirteen years old when his father died in 1933.

Heinrich earned a scholarship to the University of Saratov. He received a PhD in botany in the summer of 1941, hoping for the position of the People's Commissar of Agriculture.

At 0315 hours on June 22, 1941, Hitler's Army invaded Russia some one thousand miles west of the Volga. Within a week, Heinrich was drafted into Stalin's Red Army. He went to artillery and machine gun school. He failed a loyalty test by the NKVD when he failed to inform on a fellow roommate soldier. As a result, he was placed in a rifle company and sent to the front. The rifle company was mostly Mongolians, but by the luck of the draw, he found his brother was in the same rifle company.

After one week at the front, the rifle company was cut off by the Germans. He and his brother considered why they should stay and fight for Communism while shooting at ethnic Germans. At night, they slipped away from their company and dove into an icy river separating the two armies. A Russian sentry spotted them and started shooting. Heinrich's brother was hit in the head and died in his arms. He swam the rest of the way underwater, reaching the German side. He reported that he was seeking asylum but was taken prisoner. He had never been in Germany. He had never met a German before. Volga was his home. He knew nothing of the German aims which were filled with hatred and irrational ideas. He thought *Mein Kampf,* the ideological program Hitler established for the Holocaust, was very mediocre. The NKVD executed Heinrich's uncle. His mother, sister, and cousins were never seen again.

Within a week of his capture and defection, Heinrich was released as a prisoner and given a German uniform. He was in "no man's land." If captured by the Russians, he would be treated as a traitor and hanged. He was determined to stay alive. He could never go back home again. He was assigned to the 322nd Infantry Division, a security division which covered the entire German Army. It was the backbone of the 285th *Sicherungs-Divisionen* (Security Division). Since he could speak and read Russian, he was often called to the headquarters. One of the unwritten rules of warfare is that a captured officer is not allowed to be interrogated by an inferior ranking officer. A general is not to be interrogated by a lesser ranking general. A colonel is not allowed to be interrogated by a major. Heinrich often dressed up in brass as a general for interrogations, although he was only a corporal.

He never forgot the personal friendships he made as a translator with his lieutenant and his regimental company commander. Heinrich emphatically stated: "I knew if captured as a traitor it would be death by hanging. I always armed myself with at least one extra bullet to spare to use on myself."

Heinrich took a shrapnel in his leg. He crawled back to the German lines. The doctors wanted to amputate his leg, but he begged them not to. He feared if he went to sleep that he would wake up without his leg. He always said, "My leg was a present from the Russians." From 1941 to 1944, the Germans' advance into Russia was mired into a stalemate. Heinrich continued, "At first, when liberating villages, the Russian attitudes greeted Berlin as liberators. If Berlin had only offered these people some autonomous freedom and promise of a better life, the Russians would have kicked Stalin out themselves. Yet, the Russian girls kissed the German soldiers."

German girls sent anonymous letters to the army soldiers. They were laced with encouragement and words of pride for the soldiers' bravery. The letters were often of a flirtatious nature. Heinrich knew he would never receive any such mail from home. George Schulz felt sorry for him and handed him the letter from his niece, Hildegard Schulz from Miastko, Pomerania (German: *Rummelsburg*), which is now a part of Poland. The letter sent to her uncle's unit surrounding Leningrad and was delivered at the mail call. It was perfumed and only addressed to the "unknown German soldier." Heinrich opened the letter to find flirtatious sentences and pictures. Heinrich was given his first and only leave from action near Leningrad. Since he could obviously never return to his village on the Volga, he accepted George's invitation to come home with him. George introduced Heinrich to Hildegard. Heinrich was twenty-three and Hildegard was sixteen. She wanted nothing to do with him. She had three other sisters, and her mother liked the idea of a college man in the family. He didn't see Hildegard again until after the war five years later.

By 1944, the Germans were outnumbered approximately twenty-to-one by the Russians. On the Eastern Front, the German and Soviet deaths were horrendous. There were twenty thousand deaths *each day* during those four years. In comparison, on the two bloodiest days of Pearl Harbor and D-Day, there were a total of ten thousand American deaths. Outnumbered, out-armed, and suffering from the winter supply line deficiencies, the German Army was in full retreat. Heinrich's unit of one thousand men was being annihilated. There were only six survivors following an all-night artillery bombardment. When morning came, Heinrich could not believe he was still alive. He had fallen asleep during the bombardment. He prayed and promised to God if he lived, he would serve him for the rest of his life. That morning, the six survivors, two being badly wounded, collected all the remaining machine guns and ammunition. They placed them along the barricades and foxholes. When the Russians advanced that morning, they were led to believe that there could be no German survivors. Instead, they were greeted by heavy machine gun fire along the line. When firing from one position, the six men would hurry to another awaiting machine gun to commence shooting at the next location. Down the lines, back and forth the German guns confused the advancing Russians, and they retreated. The six Germans then also retreated to their lines. Heinrich carried one of the wounded men on his back all the way back to safety, only to find him dead when he laid him down. The officer in charge offered him a medal. Instead of a medal, Heinrich requested a transfer to France. Knowing of his previous defection, the officer immediately wrote a transfer note. Again, Heinrich was reminded of his promise to God.

Upon arrival at the garrison at Lorient, France, Heinrich found it was the largest base and fortress along the Atlantic coast. It was a submarine post. Heinrich told his son Klaus, "It was like war on a vacation. The Western Front was little more than a sideshow. The Americans and Western Allies think they won the war. World War II was won by the Russians with the aid of American weapons and supplies and Russian blood."

On May 7, 1945, the Germans unconditionally surrendered, and World War II ended after six years. Two days later, on the eve of Heinrich's twenty-fifth birthday, he and the entire Lorient garrison walked out with their hands up and surrendered to the British. He was placed in POW Depot #114 in Lannion, France, for the next two and a half years. Only one-third of the German POWs survived. They starved and were allowed to die. Heinrich said, "Depot 114 was one of the bad ones. The French were retaliating for their wartime occupation and their own suffering."

Heinrich escaped in 1948 and rode a train toward Germany. He walked all night and reached the German border. At a Red Cross Missing and Displaced Persons Service, he inquired about Hildegard Schulz and her family. They were living at Kolbermoor in Bavaria. They had escaped the Soviets when Pomerania had been encircled. He walked the next day; on January 6, 1948, Heinrich found the Schulz family. He was arrested by an American MP and sent to a local internment camp. Hildegard's mother, Berta, intervened and went to the *Bürgermeister* (mayor). He suggested that the Allies were not sending married men back to "voluntary servitude." Though there was "red tape" involved, Heinrich married Hildegard on January 30, 1948.

He could not get a teaching job because the town was ninety percent Roman Catholic, which was not his faith. Heinrich's God was Lutheran. He did get a job selling insurance to people who had no money. At International Services, Berta found a coat at the Lutheran World Relief Box. She grabbed it for Heinrich. Upon trying on the coat, he found a note in the pocket from Carl Yurk of Hastings, Nebraska, asking the recipient of the donated coat to contact him. Heinrich sent him a letter to Nebraska, and they found that they were distant relatives.

Baby Renate was born in 1949. This was the year of the Berlin blockade and airlift, which caused Heinrich to worry. He still knew the NKVD had his name on a list and it would be channeled through to the KGB.

By 1950, the insurance business was finally picking up. After the third time Carl in Nebraska suggested that Heinrich and his family immigrate, Heinrich and Hildegard said, "yes." They were going to come to America where the streets were paved with gold. There would be no hunger, no cold, and it was the home of the free and the brave. Carl Yurk would be their sponsor, and the St. Paul Lutheran Church in Hastings, Nebraska, sent money for their travel. Their third child, Helmut, was born in the fall of that year.

The family of five left Germany in January 1952, headed for America. Since the baby was less than six months old, he was not allowed to travel on a steamship. They flew instead on the Flying Tigers airline from Frankfurt, to Azores, to Toronto, then to the Idlewild Airport in New York City. They passed through customs and immigration. They boarded a train to travel for the next three days to Nebraska on the Burlington Zephyr. Heinrich and the family arrived on January 31, 1952. He had $1.56 in his pocket with his wife and three hungry children.

Carl Yurk had a house lined up for them. Heinrich washed dishes for the next year at Carl's mom and pop restaurant. The St. Paul's Lutheran Church welcomed them with open arms. At that time, they still held a service in German.

Heinrich's second job was with Hal Lainson and Sons, who owned a plastics manufacturing company in Hastings. He was hired first as a gardener, and his botanical skills were raved about. He saved and bought a house in 1953. Their fourth child, Harry, was born in Hastings. However, all was not good for the family. Hildegard and her son Klaus were confronted once at a grocery store and spat upon. The words were shouted, "Get on the God damned airplane that you came on and go back to Germany."

Heinrich and Hildegard became United States citizens at the Federal Building in Lincoln, Nebraska, in 1957. They had waited the required five years before they could become citizens. At the suggestion of Mr. Lainson, Heinrich, born in Russia, Americanized his official name to Henry and changed the spelling of his last name from Jurk to Yurk.

At the age of thirty-eight, Henry went back to school. He heard God saying to him, "Have you forgotten your promise to me?" In the fall of 1958, he entered the Central Lutheran Theological Seminary in Fremont, Nebraska. The family all moved into cramped quarters at a student dormitory designed for two, not six. The kids all slept in the bedroom and Henry and Hildegard traded places sleeping on the couch and a chair. That year, Linda was born, so now there were five kids in the dorm room.

The next year, Henry got an internship at a country church and moved six miles north of Platte Center, Nebraska. They moved into a parsonage. Within months of becoming a student pastor, Henry was driving the sixty-five miles to Fremont to finish seminary for the next two years. He would arrive home on Friday evening and prepare the sermon for Sunday services. He studied on Sunday afternoons and left for Fremont again on Sunday nights. The children attended a one-room school in District No. 28. They rode their bikes the two miles to school. In the spring of 1961, Henry was ordained at Central Synod of the Lutheran Church of America in Oklahoma City, Oklahoma. All the family who had traveled by car were in attendance. He was officially Reverend Henry Yurk.

On his return to Nebraska, he started a dual charge—two churches—with a church in Madison in addition to the church in Platte Center. In the fall of 1963, he moved the family to another dual charge at Peace Lutheran in Lewiston and St. John's Lutheran in Sterling, Nebraska. His son Klaus said, "We were poor, but as children we didn't realize it. My dad always said it was against the law in Nebraska to not be a Cornhuskers fan." Baby number six, Arnold, was born that year in Sterling.

In 1967, the family moved to Gurley, about twenty miles north of Sidney, in far western Nebraska. With each move, there was a small increase in salary for a preacher. Klaus added, "We were too dumb to know we were poor. Mother was a wonder. She was a great cook, nurse, housekeeper, psychologist, housewife, helpmate in every sense of the word. Even though the outside world spat on her and her children, she always made us feel valuable and loved."

The family moved a final time in Henry and Hildegard's ministry career to Cordova, Nebraska, population 165. The parsonage was brand new. Henry converted the "mud hole" around the house into the loveliest yard in town. His green thumb and botanical skills were the envy of all.

Epilogue

Henry finally got in touch with his mother through his mother's sister, who was living in Sheboygan, Wisconsin. He found that his mother was still alive. Even though she was in her eighties, she was still being punished by the Soviets for writing to a traitor. He sent her a message and told her a bit of his good life and family in the United States. She wrote two letters, but they were heavily censored. Everything was blackened out but the prepositions by the authorities. There were even burned spots on the paper.

In the spring of 1982, Henry was diagnosed with gallstones. During surgery, cancer was found which had "eaten" his bladder and spread through his organs. He was sent home to die with Hildegard as his caregiver. Klaus said:

> Dad was in terrible pain. He told me, "Even Jesus Christ had been asked to suffer horribly. So why not a simple sinner, Henry Yurk. I have been a lucky man. God had saved me. If it was now my time to go, then so be it. It could have happened years ago in the snows of Russia."

God had given Henry forty more years. His six children were all grown. Most had gone to college. Whether rich or poor, they were good people.

His last words when he aroused on his death bed while holding Klaus's hand were, "Die Russen kommen!" which translates to, "The Russians are coming!" He fell back to sleep and died. The war was always with him. Henry died on June 23, 1982, at 0618 hours. His son Klaus reflected, "I held his hand and felt his last heartbeat. His long journey from Central Russia was over. He had left home along that great moving Volga River to the 'Flat River,' as the Indians called the Platte River of Nebraska."

Ikrom Artiko

A farm boy from Uzbekistan persevered to get into an American foreign exchange education program.

"Back home, we say that Uzbeks are like walnuts—hard on the outside but soft on the inside when you get to know us. In the US, it is the other way; it took time before the folks would let you into their world and you needed to earn their trust." —Ikrom

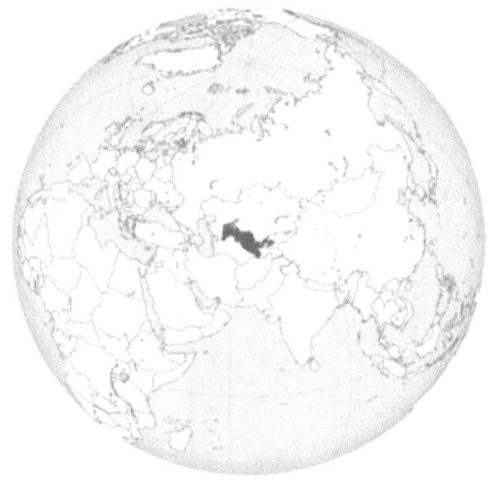

Ikrom

Uzbekistan is one of only two countries in the world that is double landlocked (the other is Liechtenstein). This means that it is separated from the ocean by two countries on all its borders. On the northwest, Uzbekistan is bordered by the Mangystau region of Kazakhstan, the country which continues to border to the northeast. Its southern and eastern borders are shared with Afghanistan, Tajikistan, and Kyrgyzstan. This large area is geographically considered Central Asia. It was gradually incorporated into the Russian Empire during the nineteenth century. The 1924 national delimitation of Central Asia created the Uzbek Soviet Socialist Republic as an independent republic within the Soviet Union.

The suffix –stan comes from a family of Indo-Iranian languages which means "place of." Uzbekistan has a population of 35 million. It is 173,350 sq. mi., or the combined size of Colorado and Nebraska in the United States. It has ample supplies of gas and oil and has a gigantic power generating capacity. It is a major producer of cotton. It has a colorful history of being ruled in the third century BC by the Macedonian ruler Alexander the Great, who conquered the lands ranging from the Balkans through the Middle East, Central Asia, and parts of southern Russia.

Eastern Iranian nomads known as Scythians and a series of kingdoms occupied the area for nearly 1400 years from the eighth century BC through the sixth century AD. This was followed by the Muslim conquest of Persia in the seventh century, which placed much of Central Asia under the rule of the Arab Caliphate. There were nomadic tribes that lived throughout this area. One of the tribes was the Shaybanid Uzbeks, which became a settled tribe that gave a foundation to several ancient cities in the Central Asian valley through which the Silk Road laid its path. This area (now occupied by modern Uzbekistan) became the center of the Islamic Golden Age, until the thirteenth-century Mongol invasion led by Genghis Khan destroyed the key towns of this settlement.

When Uzbekistan became part of the Soviet Union (USSR), the Soviets pushed for greater cotton production. The Soviets were making the different Soviet states intentionally dependent on each other. Cotton was sent to Ukraine to be used in the textile business, as that republic specialized in textile business. Cotton plants required copious amounts of water, which required irrigation. Over seventy years of heavy irrigation took a toll on the ecosystem of Uzbekistan. The Aral Sea, which was once the fourth largest freshwater lake in the world, was drained and is now a desert. Overuse of water has caused high salinity and contamination of the farming soil with heavy metals.

In addition to cotton, Uzbekistan produces more than ninety tons of gold annually, making it the tenth leading producer in the world. It is eighteenth in the world in natural gas and twentieth in copper production.

In 1985, *perestroika,* a movement concerned with political and economic reform, opened the closed borders of Uzbekistan to the rest of the world. With the Soviet Union breaking up, the country sought educational opportunities for its students to travel abroad. A goal and purpose were to bring back knowledge in the sciences and engineering to Uzbekistan. Uzbekistan declared independence on August 31, 1991.

Ikrom Artiko was born April 27, 1975, in Samarkand, Uzbekistan. His father, Sanakul, was a professor of physics at Samarkand University. His mother, Noila, taught at the medical college. Both of his grandfathers served in the Soviet Army in World War II. Approximately 1.5 million Uzbeks served with the Soviet Army in the war, and nearly a third of those were either killed or injured.

Ikrom was sixteen years old when Uzbekistan became independent in 1991. Ikrom shared:

> Samarkand is a multinational and diverse city. It is home of
> Iranians who had migrated centuries ago; Tajiks, Uzbeks,
> Koreans, and Crimean Tartars [resettled by Stalin after
> World War II]. Growing up with all these different groups, I
> learned to live in peace and harmony. During my

education, in addition to the native Uzbek language, I learned Russian, Tajik, Korean, and Iranian. In middle school and high school, we were required to learn at least one other foreign language such as German, French, or English. These were requirements grandfathered from the Soviet system, where it was mandatory to learn at least one foreign language starting in the fifth grade. I chose English.

Ikrom learned about a program in the United States called the American Collegiate Consortium (ACC). The program offered an academic scholarship for exchange students with all expenses covered at one of the state universities in the United States. He was a student at that time in college at the Samarkand Institute of Agriculture studying food science. He explained:

It was somewhat of a family tradition, as most of my close family were in either the restaurant business, culinary chefs, or food technologists at food preservation or production plants. When I applied to the Consortium, I was overwhelmed. I interviewed in person. My English was so poor that I only kept nodding my head as I understood barely anything as my interviewer kept asking me questions. I was so embarrassed for wasting her time and being so ignorant. She was extremely nice and gracious about it. I made a promise to do everything in my power to prepare better for the next time. I applied a second time. I failed to be accepted, but the interview went better. Upon the third application, I finally passed. At the interview, the folks that interviewed me the previous times admitted with a smile, "I remember you," and giving each other a look and saying, "that's the guy." In hindsight, I think they probably noticed my tenacity to accomplish my goal to speak English as best as I possibly could and come to America.

Ikrom flew to America in 1996 and entered Louisiana State University (LSU) in Baton Rouge as an undergraduate in food science.

> I thought my English had improved until I met Louisiana. I could barely understand the southern accent. I remember trying to order pizza and drinks at one of the Pizza Hut joints, and when it came to drinks, I recall a cashier saying, "if I wanted root beer." I only understood the beer part and thinking it was beer I said "yes." To my amusement it was a soft drink. For some reason, the smell and taste reminded me of the Soviet hospitals. Naturally, I was appalled and did not finish my drink. As years passed, I am still not fond of root beer or Dr. Pepper. However, I got to learn Cajun culture and all the people were so friendly, smiled, and hugged if they were given a chance. I still recall my college advisor that hugged me at every opportunity and would say she was proud of my accomplishments. For my US experience there was pizza, McDonald's, and so many choices. The people were so friendly. Back home, we say that Uzbeks are like walnuts—hard on the outside but soft on the inside when you get to know us. In the US, it is the other way; it took time before the folks would let you into their world and you needed to earn their trust.

Upon completion of the one-year program at LSU, Ikrom returned to Samarkand in 1997. "It is a city as old as Rome. It has four seasons, much like Colorado. Oh, what a change from my year at LSU and the south," he smiled. Upon his return home, he worked with a couple of joint ventures that included Case International. He completed his bachelor's degree in food science with flying colors at the same time.

In 1998, Ikrom applied to the University of Nebraska-Lincoln (UNL) to enroll in graduate school. Some of the documentation had been mistranslated, so he ended up in the Department of Agriculture rather than pursuing a graduate degree in food science. He only found out differently as he landed, they could not locate any records of him in the food science department. He was told, "The good news is you are in the right University; the bad news, you are in the wrong department." It was decided and "stamped" that Ikrom would pursue his degree in the agricultural science area of soils study. "I had to learn and change on the fly," he said. Two years later, he received a master's degree in soil science.

He returned to Uzbekistan in 2000, where he thought he would be more valuable working for the government. He worked for the Samarkand Region in the Governor's Office as a deputy in the Information Analysis office. "A fun fact," said Ikrom, "the current president of Uzbekistan was the governor at the time, and I had the privilege to administer some of his meetings." Ikrom was responsible for providing analytics around the socio-economic status of the region along with writing decrees, clauses, and statutes based on federal documents of similar nature.

"My interests were not in production, but in agriculture business," Ikrom shared. He returned to Nebraska to pursue a second degree in agriculture business. He met Stacy, and they dated for two years until they married. They were married in a beautiful wedding venue in a farm setting. Nebraska is known for its rapid weather changes. The days leading up to the wedding were warm in April 2005. On the day of the wedding, the temperatures dropped below freezing and the wedding couple and guests were bracing for the outdoor ceremony. However, everyone was shivering and rushed into the big spacious barn, scrapping the plans to celebrate outdoors. The couple exchanged their vows in full Uzbek formal wear with a turban and traditional coats, called *chapans*.

"It was a whirlwind week as I was married to a wonderful girl from Kearney, Nebraska. That same week I received a call from Pioneer Hi-Bred International in Des Moines, Iowa, offering me a job in market research. It was the best present I could ever imagine for a poor college student," Ikrom said with a smile.

Epilogue

Today in 2023, Ikrom works at Wells Fargo in Banking. His wife, Stacy, works at Principal Insurance as a project manager. Together they have two sons, sixteen and thirteen years old. The oldest son is a computer and history "nerd," and the youngest is a youth club swimmer and member of the school orchestra. Ikrom smiled as he said, "They say we are very restaurant friendly. That is because our family sits four at a table."

Ikrom shared his philosophy:

> I look back on my home country of Uzbekistan. In the 1930s through the 1970s, the USSR's ideals of equality for all of its people seemed to benefit even all of us in the separate Soviet republics. However, it was not sustainable. Human nature is such that one needs to cultivate kindness and honesty. As years went by, the system became flawed—it didn't provide incentives to those that pursued these ideals, and to the contrary, rather favored those that found loopholes.

Though raised a world away in Samarkand of Central Asia, this man now works using his mathematics abilities in the finance industry in America.

Fun fact: the same city was the home of another great name, Al Khorezm (Algorithm). This famous seventeenth century mathematician's name is the foundation of the current word "algorithm" which is used every day in problem solving and computer calculations.

Isabel Posso Diedrichs

A woman from Ecuador fell in love with
language education and a military man, which
took her all over America and the world.

*"Our school was implementing the Audio, Lingual, and Methods of
Teaching curriculum. We went crazy with this program. The student first
listened, then spoke, then read, and finally wrote the language. They were
learning practical language and speaking skills."* —Isabel

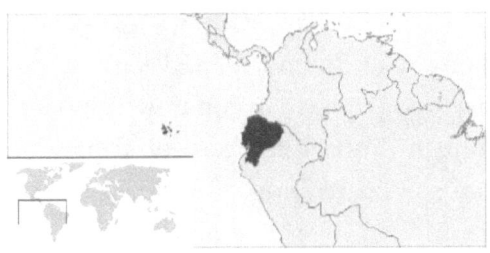

Isabel

The Inca Empire expanded north through modern-day Peru during the fifteenth century AD. During this time, Ecuador was incorporated into the empire, and was home to a variety of Indigenous groups. In 1531, the Spanish, led by Francisco Pizarro, landed in South America, leading to the end of the Inca Empire by 1533. Between 1544 and 1563, Ecuador was part of the Spanish Empire's colonies in the New World.

The Spanish brought new diseases such as smallpox, which were endemic among Europeans and caused high fatalities among the Amerindian populations. Ecuador's independence from Spain came in 1822. It was the first country of people in Latin America to obtain their independence. The nineteenth century was marked by instability for Ecuador with a rapid succession of rulers. Slavery was abolished in 1851.

The legacy of both the Inca and Spanish Empires is reflected in Ecuador's diverse population. Today, most of its 18 million people are Mestizos, followed by large minorities of European, Native American, African, and Asian descendants. Spanish is the official language. Ecuador means "equator" in Spanish. Quito is the capital. It is located twenty-five miles (forty kilometers) or one fourth of a degree south of the equator. Its population is eighty-five percent Christian, of which sixty-nine percent are Roman Catholic and seventeen percent Protestant. Quito's population is 2.7 million, and Guayaquil, the industrial city in the northwest, also has a population of 2.7 million.

Ecuador has 283,561 sq. mi. (283,561 sq. km.) which is approximately the size of the state of Nevada (USA). Ecuador borders with Colombia on the north, and Peru to the east and south. There are four geographic regions which feature volcanoes, snowcapped mountains, Amazonian jungles, fishing, and farming.

Ecuador's constitution requires all children to attend school until they receive a "basic level of education." In the rural areas, less than 10.5% go to high school. The mean numbers of school years attended in rural areas is 7.38 years, compared to 10.86 years in urban areas.

The Trans-Ecuadorian Pipeline System was completed in 1972, which brought oil from east of the Andes to the coast, making Ecuador the second largest exporter of oil. Ecuador joined the Organization of the Petroleum Exporting Countries (OPEC) in 1973. In 1978, the city of Quito and the Galapagos Islands were inscribed by UNESCO as World Heritage Sites, making them the first two landmarks in the world to become heritage listed sites.

Ecuador is the world's largest exporter of bananas. Exports, in order of their value, are listed: oil, bananas, crustaceans, processed fish, cut flowers, and cocoa beans. It produces forty percent of the world's output of platinum. The US dollar has been the national currency since 2000. There have been wars and conflicts with Colombia and Peru over water rights of the various rivers emptying into the Amazon and territories of the Amazon basin.

Isabel Posso Diedrichs was born on June 5, 1939, in Quito, Ecuador. Her parents were Roberto and Laura Posso. This date is a holiday in Ecuador, celebrating the day of founding of the Liberty Party, a fact that her father would often remind his daughter.

Isabel attended and graduated from the American School of Quito. The school was founded by Galo Plaza, the Ecuadorian president, and later Secretary General of the Organization of American States. It was a total immersion English and Spanish school. Many of the graduates applied to colleges in the United States.

Isabel had a summer job with the American company, Utah Construction and Mining Company, in Quito. The company was building a hydroelectric dam in Ecuador. She met the head of the company, William Palin, who had noticed her proficiency in English and her management skills. She shared with him that she wished to travel to the United States to attend college. William and his wife, Aleta, offered to sponsor Isabel should she apply to colleges in the United States. They suggested the Pacific Northwest, as Isabel wanted to go to an area where very little Spanish was spoken. When she received a scholarship to the University of Montana at Missoula, the Palin's were excited because William's sister Louise also lived in

Missoula. "Louise Jette became like a mother to me for the next five years in Montana," Isabel remembered fondly.

At nineteen years old, Isabel boarded a plane for the four thousand-mile flight to Montana. She had been informed that the area was known as the Big Sky Country, but she was not informed that it was also noted for its big snow winters. Isabel lived for the next four years at the Kappa Alpha Theta sorority house. Her counselor noticed her gift for language and suggested that she take French to supplement her education. What great advice this was, as it later opened opportunities in three continents!

Isabel graduated from UM in four years with a degree in business administration and education. She accepted a job in Arvada, Colorado, in the Jefferson County School District, where she taught Spanish and French. She said of her first teaching years in Colorado:

> The old method of teaching languages was by giving the students lists and having them memorize the nouns, verbs, and phrases. They were just like parrots; they spoke the words but did not know what they were saying. Our school was implementing the Audio, Lingual, and Methods of Teaching curriculum. We went crazy with this program. The student first listened, then spoke, then read, and finally wrote the language. They were learning practical language and speaking skills. We "play-acted" conversational skills and lessons such as restaurant. One student would act as the waitress, wait on the table, and present the menu. The other students would order, and then the roles would be reversed. I had the students to my home, where they conversed with my mother in Spanish. Their comprehension of the language became much improved over the former method of memorization of lists.

A summer school program for language teachers was offered by the National Defense Education Act (NDEA) at the Institute of

Higher Learning in Washington DC. Isabel was chosen from her school to attend for two summers. She shared the importance of this experience for teaching in the schools:

> My school sent me to this summer program. The first year I was in New York City where I met the Ambassador from France. The next year, the teachers went to Arcachon, France, which is in the western France area cf Cote d' Argent. The trip truly was educational.
>
> I first went to Mont-Saint-Michel. At the restaurant at the top, I ordered *Mouton pré-salé* (salty mutton). The location of Mont-Saint-Michel is noted for its high tides. When the tide is out animals come to the beaches to eat the herbs and vegetation. Sheep thrive on these greens and thus their meat has some of the salty flavor from their diets.
>
> The second stop was across the Loire River where it empties into the Atlantic. The castle there is Chateau de la Loire. I learned from the literature and got to know some of the attractions in the castles. We were exposed to literary authors and music from periods such as King Louis XV and the soc ety of the times. I can still hear the clanging of the champaign glasses as we teachers were welcomed—*Santé.* Finally, I reached the little town of Arcachon. It is across from the University of Bordeaux. Parisian, French, and Arcachon dialects are d fferent. For the next three weeks, we studied and learned the language in speaking and grammar. We met with the professor at the University who helped correct our pronunciation. This exposure in French provided by the NDEA so benef ted my teaching and further in-depth background in the language.

Isabel was conscious that her visa to the States for education required that she return to Ecuador for at least two years to fulfill the scholarship guidelines. She remembered, "I was making money, and I loved this America. I had even done tax preparations for the head of the language department in Montana. I was contacted by Immigration Services that I was to return to Ecuador for the two-year commitment. You don't play games with Immigration Services in the United States."

While in Washington for the summer at the Institute for Higher Learning, Isabel visited the Ecuadorian Embassy. She met with the Ecuadorian ambassador Manuel Calisto who she had known back in Ecuador. She told him that she wanted to stay in the United States. She was informed that if she was to stay in the States she could not teach. Manuel had connections and told her she was to apply for a job as a secretary. Since she was now trilingual, she applied at the International Monetary Fund and the Organization of American States (OAS). This became the ticket to stay in the States. She was accepted and approved by the offices. She was required to turn over her passport and was to be sent to Africa on a two-month mission mainly as an interpreter. The problem came when Immigration looked at Isabel's passport. Immigration said no. It was congratulations on your new job, but she was not allowed a visa to go to Africa.

Isabel returned to Ecuador, this time as a thirty-year-old looking for a job. Isabel recalled:

> I wanted to teach but could not find a job to support myself. I visited the American Embassy and inquired about employment. I was told that they needed someone in the Peace Corps. I was directed to see Eric Hoffman, who was of German origin and worked in a big building in the presidential area. I interviewed with Mr. Hoffman, and he said, "Can you stay today?" I started the next Monday and oversaw radio communications for the Peace Corps.

While working at the Peace Corps office, Isabel met Daryl Diedrichs. He had just received his draft notice for the Armed

Services and was being sent to Lincoln, Nebraska, for his physical. Back in Nebraska, Daryl's state of residence, he failed his army physical. He was not able to return to Ecuador, so he took a job with the Red Cross. This two-continent relationship with Isabel became more serious, and Daryl proposed to Isabel in a letter.

When the two-year obligation in Ecuador was completed, Isabel came back to Denver, Colorado, to visit her family. Two months later, at the age of thirty-one, she became officially engaged to marry Daryl. A minor problem existed and that was religion. Since Isabel was Catholic, her mother wanted the wedding to be in the Catholic Church in Colorado. On the other hand, Daryl was Lutheran. Isabel laughed and reflected:

> Daryl was related to about half of the state of Nebraska. My mother asked to see the book of marriage in the Lutheran church. Upon reviewing it she said, "They are Christian, and we are Christian, so I approve of your marrying him in the Nebraska Lutheran church in Nebraska."

The newlyweds moved to Fort Hood, a military base in Texas. The year was 1970 and Daryl spent the next twelve months in Vietnam with the Red Cross. The first six months were in the south at Phan Rang. The next six months were at Phu Bai along the Demilitarized Zone (DMZ) in the north. "I was in Denver with my mother while he was in Vietnam. I listened to the news intently. It was horrible having my husband with the Red Cross in the middle of the fighting. He was given a rest and recovery (R&R) for a few weeks in Hawaii where I joined him, and it was lovely."

From this hazardous duty assignment in Vietnam, Daryl's next assignment with the Red Cross was in Hawaii which seemed like a paradise. For the next three years, the couple shared the beauty of the islands. Isabel easily found a teaching job in languages. Their baby, Danilo, was born in the Kapiʻolani Hospital in 1973. "All of my students came to see the baby. They all loved seeing their teacher and the newborn," Isabel remembered.

Following this three-year, holiday-like assignment in Oʻahu, the Red Cross had Daryl on the move again and he was sent to Detroit, Michigan, for eight months. His next move was to Washington DC at the American Red Cross National Headquarters. He was a desk officer as the person for international disasters for the next five years. He traveled to these disasters and helped the on-ground administration for the Red Cross.

Isabel and Daryl lived in Maryland within commuting distance to Washington DC. Isabel became a United States citizen at the courthouse in Baltimore. She took classes at night at the University of Maryland in College Park for a master's degree. She worked from home as a translator for the Red Cross. Baby Maria Isabel was born in Washington DC on April 20, 1977.

Daryl was promoted to the International Committee of the Red Cross (ICRC) in Geneva, Switzerland, in 1979. Isabel was back in the classroom teaching at a private school, Collège du Léman. For the next eighteen years, she taught all levels from grades one through thirteen at the school. She taught both Spanish and French. Her own children became proficient in German, French, Italian, and Romansh (an official language of Switzerland). During these eighteen years in Switzerland, the couple was not allowed by the government to buy a house since they were not Swiss citizens.

The Diedrichses retired in 2002 and moved back to Lincoln, Nebraska. Daryl thought the small farm home of his family would be a nice place to live in retirement. Isabel, on the other hand, had a slightly different mind when seeing the farm home. They purchased a one-level home in Lincoln which had been built by Russell Stover for his two single daughters. (That's right, Russell Stover of chocolate fame). The house had been on the market for some time because it was just one level on a slab foundation. It was decorated exquisitely with a lanai and formal garden.

By coincidence, a professor at Nebraska Wesleyan University in Lincoln was going on a one-year sabbatical. Isabel took her position and taught Spanish and French for that year. While getting her master's, she worked at the University of Nebraska and taught beginner's Spanish. She was also refreshing her French, when she was asked to substitute in a French 200-level course.

Epilogue

This attractive lady continued teaching at the university level well into her seventies. She retired in 2013 to care for her sister who had cancer in Colorado. Isabel had come full circle with her return to Colorado, where she had taught school forty-five years earlier. She was able to see her daughter Maria and her grandson who live in Longmont.

Maria started college at the University of Geneva and finished at Nebraska Wesleyan University. She is a professional musician. Her talents in voice and piano are well-known in Denver's musical circles. She has performed a sixtieth anniversary tribute of Edith Piaf in Geneva, Switzerland, and sang at the Brown Palace Hotel in Denver. She teaches French and Spanish at schools in Denver. She is a member of Alliance Française and translates for the organization.

Isabel's son Danilo earned an engineering degree from École Polytechnique Fédérale in Lausanne, Switzerland. He has a PhD in math and computational sciences and teaches at Wheaton College in Illinois.

Once a child in Ecuador yearning to come to America, Isabel did indeed become an American citizen. She has taught on three continents, and fortunately took the advice of a counselor, which led her to many educational opportunities and brought new languages to thousands of students.

Paco Rosic, *The Sistine Chapel in Spray Paint*, 2006, at the Rosic family restaurant, Galleria de Paco in Waterloo, IA.

Jacky Rosic

A Bosnian man used his trade skills to survive war-torn
Bosnia before he escaped with his family to Waterloo, Iowa.

"Talk with everyone, eyes to eyes. Always be positive, energetic, and do it with your hands and that special hardware computer in your head. If you listen, you are special. We must understand each other. Believe in man, God, and nature." —Jacky

Jacky

Bosnia and Herzegovina has been a country since 1995, following the Dayton Peace Accords signed by Croatia, Serbia, and Bosnia-Herzegovina. Though only twenty-nine years old (as of 2024) as a country, its history on the Balkan Peninsula has been a center of many Empires for the last 2,200 years: the Roman Empire, the Ottoman Empire, the Austro-Hungarian Empire, Nazi Germany (1941-1943), and Yugoslavia from 1920 to 1992.

Bosnia-Herzegovina borders Serbia and Montenegro to the east, and Croatia to the north and west. It has a narrow twelve-mile (twenty km.) shoreline on the southwest into the Adriatic Sea. The country is mostly mountainous with half of the land forested. Rich fertile farmlands are located along the Sava River and surrounding areas in the north.

Sarajevo is the capital. It has been the center of some of the most tragic events of the twentieth century. The assassination of Archduke Franz Ferdinand on June 28, 1914, by a Bosnian revolutionary was the event that triggered World War I. At the outbreak of that war, the people of the region were 50% Muslim, 25% Christian, 15% Orthodox Christian, and 10% Jewish. Nearly 10% of the Bosnian Army was killed in the war, but none of the fighting was done on Bosnian soil.

At the outbreak of World War II and the German invasion, most of the Jewish people of Bosnia were exterminated. Hundreds of thousands of Serbs died in either extermination camps or mass killings. The Serbs took up arms to form Chetniks, who were responsible for widespread persecution of the non-Serbs and Communists. Sandžak of Yugoslavia was their primary target, where 80 to 100 thousand Muslims were killed in their villages, or about eight percent of the Muslim population.

Following World War II, the Federal Republic of Yugoslavia officially made Bosnia and Herzegovina one of the six constituent republics of Yugoslavia. The six were Croatia, Slovenia, Serbia,

Montenegro, Macedonia, and Bosnia-Herzegovina. They were all ruled by the Communist leader Josip Broz "Tito."

Sarajevo showed the world its beauty in the 1984 Winter Olympics. It was the first winter games in a communist country. The events were held in the Dinaric Alps and the surrounding sporting centers.

When Slovenia and Croatia declared their independence in 1990, it placed Bosnia-Herzegovina in an awkward position with its three-constituent people: Croats, Serbs, and Bosnians. A public referendum, boycotted by the Serbs, ruled in favor of independence on March 1, 1992. Serbian offenses began shortly after the referendum, officially beginning the Bosnian War. The first casualty of a war is usually known. However, in this case it was an unknown Bosnian woman killed by a sniper as she was protesting a barricade in Sarajevo. Deaths in the war totaled more than one hundred thousand, of which 1,500 were children. At the Srebrenica massacre, eight thousand Bosnian Muslim men were murdered. Over two million refugees fled the war-ravaged countries.

At the outbreak of this three-year war, the populations of Sarajevo and surrounding villages were nearly 500 thousand; among them 49% Bosnian, 30% Serb, 10.7% Yugoslav, 6.6% Croat, 3.6% Jewish and Romas. Twenty years later the population was 80% Bosnian, 3.78% Serbian, .94% Croatian, and 10.54% other.

Jacky Rosic was born in Breza, twenty miles from the city of Sarajevo, Yugoslavia, on July 18, 1955. Being the first born in a Muslim family, he was given the name Muhamed Dzerad Dzeki. Jacky's father, Ibrahim, worked as a city clerk. His mother, Melva, was a housewife and cared for their three children.

Jacky started school at the age of seven. After eighth grade, the students are directed to a vocational training curriculum or to a gymnasium, which is the program for those who are directed to go to university. His father died when Jacky was fifteen. He suffered from a horrific automobile accident which fractured his skull. "My life was upside down. My uncle in west Bosnia encouraged me to come live with him and that he would get me education and I could work for him as a butcher."

Upon moving to live with his uncle in Pećigrad, Jacky found the promise of more education did not happen. He did learn the trade of being a butcher. This training and knowledge of meat would help him for the rest of his life. He also worked there in a restaurant and bar.

Jacky loved music and was a singer and performer at an early age. He was in a five-piece band with four other boys, and they performed at bars, restaurants, school gatherings, and social functions. Rolling Stones music was his favorite. He "became" Mick Jagger on stage with a microphone in his hands. "I knew all the words in English but had no idea what the words meant. I also sang Phil Collins and all the popular music from England and the United States."

When Jacky was eighteen, he received papers from the army. He had no money and no schooling. His uncle loaned him money for the bus ticket back to Sarajevo to see his mother. "I was never going back to my uncle. On induction into the army, I started training to be a paratrooper. One problem was that I was claustrophobic. Another problem was that I was scared to jump out of a platform or plane. I was then designated to be a cook. I was promoted and earned two stripes while learning to cook for the next fifteen months," shared Jacky.

While in the army, Jacky met a gentleman at Sarajevo airport and was asked to be in his band, which played at army facilities. People flocked to their disco music. "I was a crazy singer—Mick Jagger—and people loved it," Jacky remembered. On the dance floor one night while playing at the gymnasium, a girl appeared who would change Jacky's life. "I was singing and saw her as she came in. I was at the best song and stopped instantly!

"The organist yelled 'what's happening?'

"I was in a trance and said, 'I quit.'

"'What? You can't quit now.'

"'You heard right. I quit, and maybe I'll be back. I have to see someone.'"

Jacky jumped off the stage and rushed to see the black-haired beauty. Jacky remembered:

When I spotted her, she was so awesome. My heart was beating. My hair was even so large. When I reached her, I pulled her to me to dance. I squeezed her. I didn't even know her name . . . I made it back to the stage to finish the set. We went into a fifteen-minute break. I looked for her, but the lady was gone. Was it a dream? Is it true? I was sick. When I got back to the band after the break, they said, "What is going on? This is your job. Don't make any mistakes. We are going to finish."

For the next two months, Jacky looked for this unknown lady. One night in his basement apartment, he met a girl who was going to the gymnasium. He asked her if she knew the person he was trying to find. "She looked at me and I said, 'Hold everything. Do you know who she is?' 'Yes,' she replied. I begged her to tell me more about the girl. She told me her name but that she feared me for coming on her so fast at the dance," he detailed.

"She is scared of you because you held her so tight. She hates you!" the gymnasium girl yelled.

This was the opening for the love story that would last for the next fifty years. Jacky finally located Gordana Bosnjak (Anna) that April. For the next month, he started sending Anna sandwiches and food packages with candy and fruit using a delivery boy to the gymnasium. Classmates were asking, "Who is sending you this wonderful food basket?" Slowly over time, Anna found out it was Jacky. "I met her. I told her, 'I love you.' And she became to love me, too. I told her you will marry me, and you are going to have a super life with me," Jacky relived the moment they met.

Just a month later in May 1976, Anna and Jacky were married. There were a few minor complications. One issue was religion. Anna was half Croatian Catholic and half Serbian Orthodox, and Jacky was Muslim. This was considered a mixed marriage in Yugoslavia. The couple went back to west Bosnia, where Jacky's uncle recommended him for a construction job. They were living in an apartment where the new bride was not happy with the surrounding neighbors in the complex. A knock at the door was from two policemen who told the couple they were to come to the police station. At the police station were Anna's parents, requesting a conference. They were unaware that Anna was now married and demanded that Anna return with them to Sarajevo. Jacky remembered the scene. "Anna's father was a very successful big restaurateur, I mean 'over the mountain' big. Being that we were married, he wished us well. It would be many years later in America that I wept when they lowered his body into the grave. In many respects, my father-in-law saved my life."

Anna was soon pregnant. The couple moved back to Sarajevo where their son, Alan, was born in 1977. A second son, Evelin (Paco), was born in 1979. Jacky worked for the next ten years as a butcher. Jacky's days in the band had to come to an end with his growing family. They celebrated all the holidays of their families' faiths, including Ramadan, Christmas, the Serbian Orthodox Easter, Pentecost, and Ascension. With his knowledge of meat, Jacky was recruited to work for a veterinarian as his assistant technician, inspecting meat products at food facilities. The pay was three times what he was making as a butcher. He had to go to a university in Zagreb, Croatia, to get more training.

In 1990, the breakup of Yugoslavia created religious conflicts throughout Croatia, Serbia, and Bosnia. The vote for independence for Bosnia in March 1992 was the lightning rod to set off the powder keg for the three-year war of genocide and ethnic cleansing. Jacky reflected:

> Terrorists from other countries around the world were
> selling weapons and bombs that infiltrated and broke our
> country. There were Serbs and Croats shooting each other.
> The civilians were all caught in the middle. The snipers
> were in all the corners, and all had AK-47s. We had lost our
> freedom. Our life was so upside down. It is so hard to
> explain the horror and the killing. Our money, the dinar,

became worthless. It couldn't even buy a toothpick . . . We chewed grass and ate leaves. We chewed on wood and pieces of old leather. It was just survival. Of course, we knew nothing of what was in store for our country in the next three years. Why were people so manipulated, and Serbs are people too. Your emotions, your soul, your life. Where were the politicians to see these emotions?

With his family's lives in question, Jacky found a driver who would help them go to Germany in May 1992. They could not leave without a military signoff. His cousin in Breza did sign and gave them permission to leave. They also were required to get a Catholic and Serbian Orthodox signoff but chose to ignore that requirement. Traveling north, it took four days to reach Germany. The family was taken to a Catholic organization called Caritas Internationalis, which helped the wounded and amputees from the war. Jacky could speak many languages including Serbian, Russian, Bosnian, Croatian, and some German. Through a translator, he was able to find a job as a butcher for the next five years.

In 1997, a letter from the United States Embassy in Frankfurt was delivered to Jacky, summoning him to the embassy to discuss the family's request to come to America. At the embassy, interviewed by an immigration agent, Jacky was informed that his request to come to America had been accepted. The special status was because Jacky was a refugee from the Bosnian War and was in a mixed-religion marriage. The agent suggested that they may want to come to Dallas, Texas, his home state. Jacky asked, "What about Waterloo, Iowa?" The agent said, "Yes, that is America, too." Jacky smiled as he remembered in school in Yugoslavia learning about Texas, "I had been educated that Texas maybe wanted to be its own country, and I just wanted to make sure I would be in America for good."

The agent gave Jacky and Anna two envelopes and told them not to open them until they got back to their house in Germany. On their way home, the temptation was too great, and they opened the envelopes to find four airplane tickets to Waterloo, Iowa, for Jacky,

Anna, Alan, and Paco. In two weeks, they arrived at JFK Airport in New York City. They were given green cards. They arrived in Waterloo on September 24, 1997, and lived with Jacky's sister for twenty days. Within ten days, Anna and both boys had jobs at the Hy-Vee grocery store.

Through a friend and translator, Jacky was able to find an apartment where his family could live together, so they moved out of his sister's place. Jacky started taking English classes at Hawkeye Community College. There were more than three thousand Bosnians living in Waterloo at this time. The classes were fully enrolled, and learning the new language together was very important.

On a November morning during a heavy snowstorm, Jacky went to the Hy-Vee store where he found the sidewalks were covered with the new snow. He saw a snow shovel and started clearing the sidewalks. An assistant manager coming to work saw him and told him he did not need to do this. Jacky did not understand the English, and another manager came out who could speak Bosnian. She was immediately touched by Jacky's spirit, personality, work ethic, and previous knowledge as a butcher. She asked him to come in and introduced him to the meat department. There were no openings in the meat department, but she offered him a job in the produce department. "I did not understand the word produce and thought it must mean something to do with meat. I told others about my new job, and I had no idea that produce meant the fruit and vegetable area," Jacky laughed these twenty-five years later. Within a few years, he became an assistant manager at the Hy-Vee store.

Jacky became a United State citizen in 1999. A man in the meat department helped him in some of the areas he needed to study for the citizenship test. All the other workers had no knowledge of the history and constitution of the United States. He shared:

> I passed the test in flying colors. There is no place in the
> world that has the freedom that we have here in America.
> All the rest of the world's population wants to come here.

> This is such a unique place, and I do worry that our
> politicians are trying to take some of those freedoms away.

Jacky wanted a more permanent house of his own, but was told that he needed to establish credit before he could be considered for a loan. He had an account at a credit union. He sent money to the government to repay the four tickets that were given to him to bring the family to America. By repaying this debt, he was given the credit rating that he needed. He and Anna bought a house in 1998.

After ten years and saving for his own business, Jacky purchased a storefront in downtown Waterloo. His son, Paco, used his phenomenal artistic talents and, using spray paint, he painted the vaulted ceiling in what is called the Sistine Chapel of America. Its meaning and how much power and kindness that went into the project was to be shared with the public. Their restaurant, Galleria de Paco, opened for fine dining in 2006. Its reputation and unique art and fine cuisine was requested by bus tours and visitors from all over the world. It has received national and international acclaim and front-page news stories in many Untied States newspapers. "I believe my son is a genius, too. There is no need to go outside the United States to see this art. This is the meaning of immigration," bragged Jacky.

Epilogue

The Rosic family continues to live in freedom in their new country. They love their children and grandchildren. Jacky philosophizes:

> Many Americans cannot believe the beauty and
> uniqueness of this country. Many have no clue what it
> means to be free. Talk with everyone, eyes to eyes. Always
> be positive, energetic, and do it with your hands and that
> special hardware computer in your head. If you listen, you
> are special. We must understand each other. Believe in
> man, God, and nature.

This country should not have hate. No north, no south. No
Red or Blue states. We are all the same, black, white,
brown, Asian, Jewish, Orthodox, Catholic, and Muslim.
Freedom is not going around the world killing people.

Their son Alan and his wife Dina have two children: Isabella, age
thirteen, and Dominique, age five. Their son Paco continues his artist's
studio and markets art throughout the world online.

Jacky's final words of advice are, "It is a privilege to be aged. You
are not old until you are dead!"

Kutlu "Jon" Isin

A Turkish exchange student became a
teacher and counselor in Kansas.

*"I learned that the hard red winter wheat had come to Kansas with the
Mennonite immigrants from Russia in the 1870s. I witnessed with amazement where field after field of this golden wheat was harvested . . ."*
                                                                    —Jon

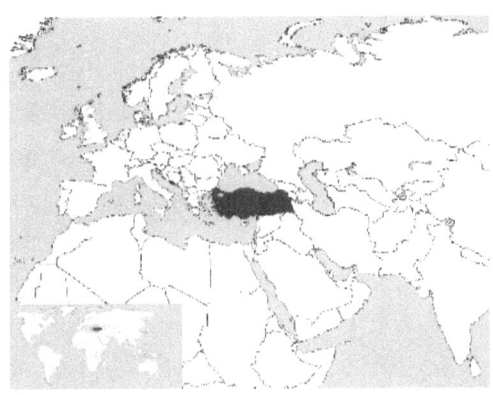

Jon

Türkiye has a remarkable history. The apostle Saint Paul was an Anatolian and born in the then Roman city of Tarsus along the eastern Mediterranean coast of what is now Türkiye. He traveled through Asia Minor (a.k.a. Anatolia), speaking of Jesus. His first journey from 47-49 AD was from east to west along the Mediterranean coast and stopped in Antioch (now Antakya), Seleucia (Silifke), Selimiye (Side), and Attalia (Antalya). His letter to the people of Galatia became the ninth book of the New Testament Bible. The seven churches of Revelation were in Asia Minor: Ephesus, Smyrna, Pergamum, Sardis, Philadelphia, Laodicea, and Thyatira. Saint Paul's fourth and final trip was from 59-60 AD.

Turkey was created from the fall of the Ottoman Empire. The Ottoman Empire ruled the region from 1453, when Sultan Mehmed II captured Constantinople, ending the Byzantine Empire. It retained its power until the end of WWI, when new international borders were established throughout eastern Europe.

Modern Turkey was established in 1923 when the Grand National Assembly declared Turkey as a republic with Mustafa Kemal Atatürk (Father of the Turks) as the president. Among the great changes implemented by Atatürk were the abolishment of the Ottoman Fez, giving women full rights, creating a new writing system based on the Latin alphabet, and moving the capital from Istanbul to Ankara, in the interior of the country.

The Republic of Türkiye is the only country in the world that spans two continents, Europe and Asia. It is larger than either France, Germany, or Texas. It is twice the size of California in the United States. Its land mass is 302,455 sq. mi. (743,356 sq. km.). The past one hundred years since the new republic was established has brought many changes for Türkiye. Military coups, Kurdish wars, rise in political Islam, Istanbul attacks, secularist protests, and Islamic party victories have continued to change the political landscape in this country of eighty-five million people (2020). The official language is

Turkish. The population is approximately 70-75% Turks, 19% Kurds, and 6-11% other minorities.

In 2022, or one hundred years after the new republic was formed, the country's name was changed to the spelling Türkiye. It is sandwiched between the Black Sea and the Mediterranean Sea, and shares borders with the countries of Georgia, Armenia, Azerbaijan, Iraq, and Syria to the east, as well as Bulgaria and Greece to the west. Türkiye's major exports are electronics, food products, textiles, plastic, transportation equipment, machinery, metal manufactured products, and apparel.

Kutlu "Jon" Isin was born on December 3, 1937, in Mersin, Turkey, located near Tarsus—the birthplace of Paul the Apostle. His parents were Ziga and Necmiye Isin. Birth certificates were issued late in those times because there was such a high infant mortality rate. The records and certificates of birth were usually issued after the child was several years old. Jon's birth certificate reads the date of birth as January 1, 1938. His father, Ziga, was an agriculture agent for the government. Ziga was drafted three times into the Turkish Army. Necmiye did household work and took care of the children. Jon was the oldest of five children.

The family had three homes. The main home was in the city of Mersin, along the coast of the Mediterranean, which became very hot in the summer season. The second home was about twenty-two miles into the mountains. The mountain home was much cooler and could only be reached by horses. The third home was located alongside the family's orchard. The orchard grew lemons, grapefruits, and oranges. All these fruits had to be picked by hand. The family did not do much farm work, as it all was done by hired workers.

Since Jon's birth certificate had been forward-dated, he was able to start school at the age of seven and a half, instead of the normal eight years standard at that time. He graduated from high school in 1956. He went directly into the Turkish Army for eighteen months of service. Since he was a high school graduate, Jon became a second lieutenant and a transportation officer. Jon's father encouraged him to go to college and study agriculture.

At the age of twenty, Jon enrolled at the University of Ankara. The university was very crowded and very competitive. Jon had to take tests. The class sizes were sometimes three to four hundred students. The few textbooks were either in German or French. Jon recalled:

> I had to get summaries of the courses written by other students. In microbiology we had three microscopes. We were allowed two minutes to look at a slide and then go to the board and draw the organism we had seen. I could not get a handle on everything. After one year, I quit the university. I applied for several other schools, but they had no programs in horticulture or agriculture. I had wanted to learn about our citrus crops and orchard programs. My father was disappointed but suggested that I find a school in America that could lead me into this agriculture education.

Jon had heard of a program called International Farm Youth Exchange (IFYE). He applied to IFYE and was accepted to come to the United States for the summer. IFYE was part of the 4-H program in which the students went abroad and lived with farm families and learned about the culture and farming experiences. The Turkish government had no funding for this type of program. Jon's father paid his way to come to the States in the summer of 1960. Jon arrived in Washington DC on May 10, 1960. Following an orientation with other incoming IFYE students from all over the world, Jon boarded a bus for a two-day trip to Santa Clara, California. He spent three weeks with a family and saw the great citrus orchards in the San Joaquin Valley. He then bused to Kansas to stay with four new families. It was wheat harvest time in the breadbasket of the country. Jon saw the enormous combines and the golden grain being moved into storage and markets at the mammoth concrete silos on the flatlands of Kansas. Jon shared:

I learned that the hard red winter wheat had come to
Kansas with the Mennonite immigrants from Russia in the
1870s. I witnessed with amazement where field after field
of this golden wheat was harvested. There were no weeds
in the wheat fields and the precision of the combines, the
trucks, and the elevators for storage was unlike anything I
had ever seen in my home country.

Jon's English was limited. He studied all the time and used his dictionary. He had basic grammar in high school in Turkey. He watched television shows and listened to the radio. Before the summer was over, he was able to communicate in this new country by speaking English. A family in Sawyer, Kansas, suggested that Jon should stay and go to college here in the States. There had been a revolution in Turkey on May 27, 1960, just three weeks after he had arrived in the States. There was uncertainty about returning home with no prospects for schooling and the possibility of more military time. He applied to the nearby Pratt Junior College and was accepted to start school in September 1960. He was able to obtain a student visa. Jon received his two-year degree from Pratt and then enrolled at Pittsburg State University. He studied auto mechanics and metals. He graduated with a teaching degree in the spring of 1964. His first job for one year was at Anthony High School in Anthony, Kansas. He then taught at Junction City High School for the next four years. The opportunity to teach in Saint John, Kansas, provided him with a new district in the same area of the state that he had come to as an IFYE participant.

As a teacher Jon reached all levels of students. He proudly shared:

I had always observed that some students even with a
156 IQ literally could not change a spark plug even with a
demonstration and training. And yet, others who could
not read and write to pass a test could learn skills in
mechanics. I approached the principal at the high school,
and we came up with a program that tested students in
their verbal skills. We applied to the State of Kansas

> Department of Education for a grant to develop a
> program called "High Performance." We were astonished
> to receive $150,000 to develop and implement the High-
> Performance program. All kindergarten children from St.
> John, Stafford, and Macksville were tested from 1972
> through 1983. Those that tested ten points or higher in
> "performance skills" were introduced to a program.

Jon became the elementary guidance counselor in addition to teaching auto mechanics and metals courses at the high school. One summer he received a letter from the Kansas Board of Education telling him that his qualifications to be a counselor were insufficient. He enrolled at nearby Emporia State University, and over several summers, received a master's degree in counseling. The State acknowledged that since he was working toward the counseling degree, he could continue counseling at the high school level, but not at the elementary level school until his degree was completed.

Jon became a United States citizen at the courthouse in Junction City, Kansas, in 1971. He married Shirley Pihl, a kindergarten teacher, in St. John in 1973.

In 1983, Jon, Shirley, and their daughter moved to Salina, Kansas. Jon became an elementary guidance counselor for the Salina School District for the next eighteen years before retiring in 2012.

Epilogue

Approaching eighty-five years old in 2023, Jon takes care of his wife of fifty years, whose health is declining. He volunteers on Tuesdays for Care Givers. He is the only man of this group, alongside fifteen women, who help families with Alzheimer's patients. He has hobbies in photography and reads nearly everything he can find. His favorite thing to read is historical fiction. He has a love of geography. He has not returned to Türkiye to visit family since the Covid pandemic. He takes pride in his yard and mows it meticulously.

People don't know freedom and that they have responsibility to help others along the way. In 1923, when Turkey became a republic under Atatürk, it freed itself from British and French control. He gave the country six months to get rid of the Arabic system. They were only to write in Roman. The language was very phonetic. There were no spelling tests, because if there were, everyone would get a 100% because of the phonetics.

Jon reflected on his life as an American:

My city in Turkey was forty thousand [people] when I came to America in 1960. Today it is one million. There are many Syrians, Russians, and Afghanis living there with the native Turks. When I came to America, I had the opportunity to travel with a friend to Mississippi. I could not understand why the black-skinned people would not look or talk to me. My friend said, "Don't worry about it." I tried to understand it because I had no prejudice. It was back in Kansas just a few years ago, when I pulled into a car wash. There was a black man who came into the same car wash area. I was astonished that he did not get out of his car because I was a white person in the car wash bay. We continue to learn, and hopefully in this country of the free that there is no place for ignorance and prejudice. I suggest a great read titled, *The Book of General Ignorance,* by John Lloyd.

Jon Isin: a teacher, innovator, counselor, and cultured man who has given many students and families his service and shares his graceful life in his new country.

Karoline Shaele Win

A girl and her family fled Myanmar (Burma) and spent nine years in a refugee camp in Thailand, before coming to the US for work and educational opportunities.

"One night when we were coming home from church, we could see the light of the bullets being fired in the woods. We were so frightened, and we ran as fast as we could . . ." —Karoline

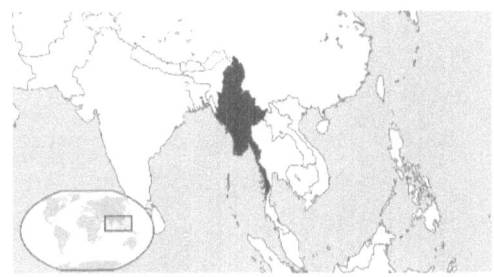

Karoline

Burma, renamed Myanmar in 1989, has over thirteen thousand years of history. It had a Buddhist culture when it was overrun by the Mongols in 1287. In the 1800s, Burma bordered with China to the northeast, Siam (Thailand) to the southeast, and British India to the west. King Bodawpaya turned westward for expansion to the ill-defined border with British India. The British instigated a rebellion in Manipur in 1819 and Assam in 1821. Raids across the border led to the First Anglo-Burmese War from 1824-26. Burma unilaterally ceded all of Bodawpaypa's western acquisitions (Arakan, Manipur, and Assam). The Second Anglo-Burmese War in 1852 was brought on by the British who were alarmed by the consolidations in French Indochina. The Third Anglo-Burmese War in 1885 had the British annexing the remainder of the country, sending the Burmese king into exile in India.

The Burmese language and culture dominated the entire Irrawaddy River Valley, eclipsing the Mon language and ethnicity by 1830. Growth of Burmese literature and theatre continued with an extremely high literacy rate for that era.

After the Suez Canal opened in 1869, rice became the principal export. Vast amounts of land were opened for cultivation. The Burmese economy grew but the power and wealth remained with British firms, a few Anglo-Burmese people, and migrants from India. Britain made Burma a province of India in 1886, with Rangoon as the capital.

A nationalist movement in 1900 founded the Young Men's Buddhist Association (YMBA), leading to freedom of religion and more autonomy for Burma within the administration of India.

Britain separated Burma from India in 1937 with a constitution calling for a fully elected assembly. Ba Maw became the first prime minister in 1937. He was followed by U Saw, who was arrested by the British for communicating with the Japanese. Aung San co-founded the Communist Party of Burma. Aung San tried to unite with the Chinese Communist Party, but the Japanese offered him support by forming a secret intelligence unit with the purpose of closing the

Burma Road (a road connecting Burma to southwest China) and supporting the nationalist uprising. Japan declared Burma independent in 1943.

Upwards of 250 thousand civilians died during the Japanese occupation of Burma during World War II. With British negotiation, the Aung San-Atlee Agreement was signed on January 27, 1947. However, the communists and some conservatives went underground. Many leaders, including General Aung San, joined to form the Union of Burma. U Saw, a conservative pre-war prime minister had Aung San assassinated, along with his eldest brother, Ba Win. Rebellion broke out and July 19 became known as Martyr's Day. The Burma Independence Act in 1947 was passed by a new cabinet.

Beginning in 1947, Burma had a relatively peaceful fourteen years. From 1962 to 1988, coup d'états and bloodless coups became a common state of unrest. Burma became a socialist state and was isolated from the rest of the world. The military government in 1989 changed the name of the country to Myanmar.

This background is provided to show the endless civil strife endured by the Burmese people for the last two hundred years. Civil war has been nearly constant, with the warring sides very ill-defined.

Karoline Win was born on March 5, 1990, in the village of Moso, located in the state of Karenni, which is near the middle of the country of Myanmar. Her father was a teacher and pastor. Her mother, Rosar, was a farmer. Karoline was baptized by a priest from Italy who was in her village. Her uncle was a Catholic bishop and called her a special girl.

Rosar farmed land away from the village. She often left the children alone and spent the night in a tent next to their farmland. She raised peanuts and alternated them with rice every other year. Corn was raised next to the family's bamboo home in the village.

Karoline remembered:

> One night when we were coming home from church, we
> could see the light of the bullets being fired in the woods.
> We were so frightened, and we ran as fast as we could.

Since our home was just bamboo, which offered no
protection, we ran for cover to the church and to the
priest's home, which were made of concrete.

It is from this strife-torn country that Rosar, Karoline, and her
brother Angelo fled. They went to Thailand, into a refugee camp, in
the year 2000. A sister, Jo Paule, was left behind and stayed in a
boarding school. Karoline's father, Grato D Phoe Ei (pronounced Dee
-Poh-Ee) had fled in 1993, when the rebels were coming into the
villages to find men to supposedly volunteer for their cause. Rosar and
D Phoe Ei had written letters to communicate for these seven years
which they were apart. The safety of his family and their future led
them to Thailand. They were afraid of both sides in the conflict
between the army and the rebels.

Rosar was not a timid lady and stood her ground better than some
of the village women. "When the army men would come through the
villages, they took our food and even our chickens. Mother yelled at
them, 'You are not taking my chickens!' And they knew she meant it,"
Karoline remembered proudly. She had been only seven years old at
the time.

Rosar led the children, and they walked for three weeks to reach
the Salween River separating Burma and Thailand. They boarded a
ferry boat to cross into Thailand. They stopped at a refugee camp run
by the United Nations High Commissioner for Refugees (UNHCR),
where they met up with D Phoe Ei. Their tent was on a lot which was
twenty-five square feet. Karoline laughed, "When one would cough in
the next tent, we could hear everything."

After two years in the camp, the family had to move, as two camps
were made into one. It was two years in one camp and then seven
more years in the second camp. Karoline was able to go to a school at
the refugee camp. At the age of seventeen, she had to drop out of
school and was hospitalized for depression. She was not able to finish
high school due to her illness.

Karoline explained:

Many countries choose students who are smart. I loved math and always dreamed of becoming a nurse. In 2009, the United States chose my family to start a new life. My father had one question for any country that was seeking immigrants. That was, "We want to feel human rights!" He applied and there were two types of interviews. The United States chose us, and we were very happy. There were about two hundred from our camp that came to America. We were sad for those left behind. We did not know where we were to go, but everybody was in the same unknown.

They had moved from Burma to Thailand, and then to the United States, with each step being to find a better future. Karoline recalled:

We left the camp in a car, and then were transported by bus to Bangkok. I had never seen a hotel before, where we stayed for just two hours. Sheets on the beds, towels in the bathroom, and a faucet with running water. My brother and I did not know how to touch the hot water. The hotel was amazing.

All two hundred immigrants were bused to the busy Bangkok airport for a flight to Japan and then on to Chicago in the States. Karoline recalled:

The authorities tried to explain that we would be flying. I had no concept of how long it would take and what to expect, being in an airplane for such a long time. It took us nearly twenty-four hours. When we arrived in Chicago, all the news was that Michael Jackson had just died. I thought he looked like a girl.

The family was met at O'Hare International Airport by a case worker. Everyone was very happy and energized. Karoline told:

> Many people had taken medicine for motion sickness, but
> not me. We were taken to an apartment in uptown
> Chicago where we lived for a year. *Ahh*, but everything was
> so expensive. My father, at the age of fifty-seven, had a
> couple of jobs, but his health suffered and he had nose
> bleeds.

Karoline found a job at O'Hare, where she worked as a cleaner on airplanes. She took three buses and two trains to get to her job. She left the apartment at 8:00 PM to arrive at work at 10:00 PM. She took a break for lunch at 3:00 AM, and then left work at 8:00 AM to return to the apartment. She then went to class where she was working to become a Certified Nursing Assistant (CNA). English was the hardest language for her, even though she had some teachings at school in Burma and Thailand.

A lady from Moline, Illinois, was recruiting immigrants to work at Tyson, a meat packing company in Waterloo, Iowa. The potential worker did not have to speak much English.

Karoline shared, with tears in her eyes:

> My father came first to Waterloo. I visited him two times
> by bus transportation. My brother Angelo had just finished
> tenth grade. I prayed I would not have to work at the
> "meat factory." My father persuaded me to come here. In
> my heart, I wanted to do anything to stay together with my
> family. Everyone always said I was Daddy's girl.

D Phoe Ei had Karoline help fill out applications for other Burmese immigrants in Chicago to also come to Waterloo, Iowa. In 2012, the family was reunited and moved into a house on Locust Street.

Karoline shared with a smile:

> I met my husband, Han Win, when he was working at
> Tyson. It was such a wonderful happenstance because we

had gone to [the same] school in Thailand at the refugee
camp from the third grade through the tenth grade. Our
families had communicated, as his family had come to the
state of Washington. We had encouraged them to come to
Waterloo to work and make a life here. After three weeks
of their reuniting, Han Win and I were married with our
parents' approval.

The newlyweds first lived with Karoline's parents. They then lived in several rental houses. Her brother, Angelo, bought a house with money given to him by his mother. "Mother then pooled her money and gave it to my husband and me to help with a down payment for our house. We applied for a loan and now have our own home near my parents," Karoline said with a grin.

Han and Karoline have three children, ages nine, six, and five months old. They attend school at St. Edward school in Waterloo. Han still works at Tyson and has had many promotions. Karoline's parents live about two blocks away. Grandmother Rosar helps with the children.

Karoline continued:

The happiest day of my life was the first day of getting
accepted into school to get my GED. I had to take a test to
get into the program. So far, I have only one more exam to
pass and that is reading. I have already passed the math,
science, social studies, and writing portions. The process
has been interrupted somewhat while having babies at
home. My father said that I should stay home with the
children. I love garage sales, but my husband will not allow
me to bring any more into our home.

In 2016, Karoline took the test to become a United States citizen. "My husband is making a nice living for us. So, I want my children when they grow up, to go to the University of Dubuque," she said.

With a twinkle in her eyes and an ever-present smile, Karoline shared:

> My two children in school are so good at English. There are times where they make me pronounce the words that they do not understand what I am saying. They are so smart and are certainly great English-speaking Americans.
>
> My father encouraged me to learn to drive and get a driver's license. He said to live in America you need to learn to drive. His favorite saying is, "In America, the car is your shoes," and, "No car, no go!" The English-speaking people taking the test have it easy. All they must do is chose the correct answer, "yes" or "no." With the test in the Burmese language, we had four choices that we had to know.

Epilogue

Hopes, dreams, and extremely hard work brought Karoline and her family to America. The fear of war and refugee camps are part of the past. She and her family have assimilated into this new land, and the rest of Americans who were also once immigrants welcome them with open arms.

Their children will have dreams, and hopefully will someday attend college and even go to the University of Dubuque. And yes, this young mother with her childhood love of math, will someday fulfill her dreams, too, and become a nurse.

"Since I am American, there is a lot of responsibility on me," said this beautiful lady who wore a t-shirt that says, *Christ, Coffee, Cardio.*

In parting, Karoline added, "Thank you to the UNHCR, thank you to Thailand, and thank you to the United State of America. Every day I am blessed! And I pray that someday, through some humanitarian group, that we will find a way to bring my sister and her two children from Myanmar to America, too."

Kofi Opoku

A man followed his ambitions from Ghana to the US,
where he found work to make a living and support his family.

"When I was six years old, I had a dream to go to America. All the Americans I had met were so nice . . ." —Kofi

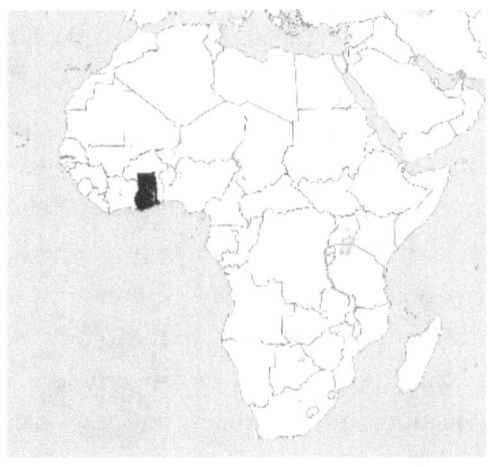

Kofi

The Republic of Ghana is located in West Africa, to the north of the Gulf of Guinea. It borders Togo to the east, Burkina Faso to the north, and Côte d'Ivoire (Ivory Coast) to the west, with a land mass approximately the same size as the state of Oregon.

Ghana's population is thirty-three million, which is more than the population of Texas, on land which is one-third the size of Texas. The capital is Accra, and the official language is English. There are eighty different ethnic dialects in Ghana, with the most prominent language being Twi. Ghana's history can be archeologically dated back to 2000 BC, near the Bronze Age.

European colonization started in the fifteenth century when the region was called the Gold Coast. The word "gold" was more than symbolic. By 1471, the Portuguese arrived and traded for gold, ivory, and pepper. The Dutch built two forts in 1598, and in 1637 they captured the Portuguese forts and castles. The Danes, Swedes, and British all built forts along the coastline. Because of the European influences, the area accumulated the highest concentration of military architecture outside of Europe. The Gold Coast went from being an exporter of gold to an importer of slaves, as well as an exporter of slaves to the Americas. Initially, they relied on other African areas to send captured natives to the Gold Coast to be shipped across the Atlantic as enslaved people. In later years of its history, their own people were captured and sold into slavery. By the last quarter of the nineteenth century, the Gold Coast was under British control. The Danes departed in 1874. Protestant missionaries were very active in the country during the nineteenth century. They believed it was their mission to civilize what they saw as slaves, sinners, and savages.

Three main areas make up modern Ghana: the Ashanti Colony, Northern Territories, and the Gold Coast Colony. The British were able to unite these three regions, and the poverty level dropped as they brought communications and railroads into the country. A leading crop, cocoa, was introduced when the cacao tree was brought to the country in 1879. It adapted very well in eastern Ghana. Exports were very profitable in gold, cacao, and timber. Financial education advanced to be the best in West Africa. Independence from Britain came on March 6, 1957. A constitutional monarchy existed until 1960, when a referendum passed declaring Ghana a republic. By 1964, under President Kwame Nkrumah, Ghana had become a one-party state. He sought to form a United States of Africa. The Soviets and Chinese trained revolutionaries that were sent into neighboring Mali and Congo.

A military coup in 1966 governed for three years until 1969 when the first free elections were held since independence. The government was declared the Second Republic of Ghana. Prime Minister Kofi Busia expelled noncitizens to relieve the country's unemployment. A companion measure was established to limit foreign involvement in small business so that the Lebanese, Nigerians, and Asians were not able to monopolize trade.

Into these times, Kofi Opoku was born on May 30, 1968. His parents were Kojo Baah and Mary Opoku. His father had a store and had five wives. He was old when Kofi was born. His mother was a farmer. Kofi shared:

> Mother raised potatoes, onions, plantains, corn, and cabbage. She went to bigger towns to buy goods and came back to our village to sell these goods. The family had to walk a mile and a half to get water for their dwelling. We had no electricity. Being very close to the equator, our days and nights were almost exactly twelve hours each. When night came, it turned dark almost immediately, and there was no dusk. It just turns from light to dark. We had candles or a lantern after dark. Mother had a vision to send all six of us kids to school. Our dwelling was a mile and a half from the source of clean water. We walked this each day to bring back water for cooking, cleaning, and bathing.
>
> When I was six years old, I had a dream to go to America. All the Americans I had met were so nice. I was living with my

stepmother when I came of age to go to school and start kindergarten. My parents were a poverty family and not rich by any means.

Kofi went to school for eleven years, all in the same one-story building. He remembered, "English was started in kindergarten. I studied by candlelight or by the lantern. Since we all had to use this lantern, I often got it after all were asleep and studied my schoolwork after midnight. Our language was Twi, which is the most spoken language in Ghana among our eighty other dialects."

After high school, Kofi went to Accra to live and work with his uncle, who made shirts at his own screen-printing business. After a year with his uncle, Kofi had saved enough money to rent a bedroom in a compound house. He explained:

> This compound house was in a ghetto area and the rooms were separated by sheets. Other families and people rented other rooms. We all shared a bathroom. Since I was not there much because of my work, the one-bathroom situation did not bother me. It was the first time I had ever had an indoor bathroom with running water.

Kofi wanted his own business. He went to the market and met a man who offered him an opportunity. He started selling music cassette tapes through this contact. He traveled by car across the border into Togo, where he bought the cassette tapes. He brought them back to Ghana and resold them. Kofi continued to work on his English because it was the language for the best communications.

After two years of selling and working for someone else, Kofi started his own business. Compact discs (CDs), music, and movies were now becoming popular. Using his experience, he started driving to Nigeria to buy CDs and bringing them back to Ghana to resell. "I found the Nigerians very smart and intelligent. They were honest and I was so impressed with their business abilities," said Kofi.

In 2003, after selling CDs for three years, Kofi wanted to fulfill his dream of going to America. He was married and had two children. His sister had been in America since the 1970s, living in Massachusetts. He had saved enough money and applied for a visa at the British Embassy in Accra. He was turned down and then subsequently turned down twice at the German Embassy. In 2004, Kofi walked to the United States Embassy and got a visa on the first visit. His sister in Massachusetts purchased an airline ticket for him. He flew KLM out of Ghana, then to the Netherlands, and finally to JFK in New York. From there, he bused to Milton, Massachusetts. "I was not frightened by the travel. My English got me by fairly well," remembered Kofi. Within a week of his arrival in the USA, he had a job in Boston at a 7-Eleven convenience store.

Through a friend's recommendation, Kofi moved to Virginia and worked in a warehouse for five years. He continued to save money. Through another friend, he was told that he could make more money in Iowa. He moved to Waterloo, Iowa, in 2009 and started working at Tyson (a meat packing plant) as a meat cutter. His night job was with a janitorial service, ABM. He was contracted by the business doing janitorial work. One of his jobs where he was contracted to clean was at the office of Tom Strub, a dentist, who shared, "Kofi did the best job in cleaning our office that I ever had. He was so honest, conscientious, and trustworthy. A truly remarkable person."

Kofi applied for citizenship in 2019. This started a very complicated series of events. He received a letter from Immigration Services saying that there were questions of irregularities about his applying for a green card years before. He was turned down for citizenship.

Epilogue

In 2015, Kofi sent money for his two children to come join him in America. Frank, then seventeen, and Sandra, age fourteen, moved to Cedar Falls, Iowa. Kofi's wife remains in Ghana and will not be eligible to get a visa until Kofi becomes a citizen. Frank started high school in Cedar Falls. He showed interest in music and wanted to join the band. His counselor directed him to Mr. Ramsey, the band instructor. He asked what instrument Frank played. Frank smiled as he shared his reply:

> The drums. Mr. Ramsey handed me a sheet of music and asked me to play the notes. I told him I had never seen sheet music in my life. He then said, "Okay, just play me something that you do know." I had three great years in the band. I even learned to play the notes. He gave me special solos in the pep band, jazz band, and concert band. It opened me to a group of friends through music. And of course, I was pretty good and popular on the soccer field, too.

Frank recently graduated from Wartburg College in Waverly, Iowa, with a degree in computer information systems. Sandra is now in nurse's training and working to become a registered nurse. Kofi is awaiting a court appearance in Omaha, Nebraska, 250 miles away, to get a ruling on becoming a citizen in the United States of America. And then he hopes to bring his wife to America.

Lidija, Olga, Karl, Kristaps, Martha, and William in Camp Wentsdorf, Germany, July 1949

Kristaps and Olga, wed Aug. 11, 1935

Kristaps and Olga Undsenaite Volskis

A family escaped from Latvia during WWII before being sponsored to Nebraska in the US.

"My parents were able to somehow get us moved from different DP camps, having heard that some camps had a greater chance of getting to immigrate . . . Father used his shoemaking skills, and stayed busy making and repairing shoes. I do not know if he received any pay, but he may have been able to save some money for our eventual immigration." —Kristaps

Kristaps and Olga

Latvia is a rather flat country with alternating rolling hills. It borders the Baltic Sea and the Gulf of Riga,. It also borders Estonia on the north, Russia to the east, Belarus to the southeast, and Lithuania to the south. Latvia is somewhat smaller than South Carolina in the United States, with a population of 1.9 million, or about the same population as West Virginia.

Latvia is one of the three Baltic states of northern Europe which has been ruled and occupied for much of the past eight centuries by foreign countries. It is a prominent division of ancient groups of people known as Balts. It was known for its amber trade with the Mediterranean world and with the Roman Empire.

In the tenth and eleventh centuries, it was subject to double pressure from the Slavs to the East and the Swedes to the West. During the Crusades, the Germans and Saxons were seeking overseas expansion and reached the eastern Baltic shores. Because people occupying the shores were the Livs, the German invaders called the country Livland, or Livonia.

In 1561, Latvian territory was partitioned along the Western Dvina River. North of the river was Livonia, which was incorporated into Lithuania. The area south of the Western Dvina River was Courland, which became semi-independent under the Lithuanian sovereign. In 1581, Riga was incorporated into what became the Polish-Lithuanian Commonwealth. This was short-lived, as the Swedes took over sixty years later in 1621.

Russia's Peter the Great broke through the Baltic to Sweden in 1710 and took Riga from Sweden. By the end of the eighteenth century, all of the Latvian nation was subject to Russian rule. There was unrest in Latvia until the emancipation of the serfs throughout the Russian Empire in 1861. This allowed the people the right to purchase land from the landlords, who were mostly German.

The last twenty-five years of the nineteenth century (1875-1900) saw a national revival throughout the Latvian territory. Universities and cultural institutions were established.

With the Russian Revolution in 1917, a complete political autonomy was considered at the Latvian National Political Conference in Riga. However, on September 3, 1917, during WWI, the German Army took Riga. By December 1919, the Red Army, with the aid of Latvian units, had pushed the German troops out of this territory. In August 1920, the Latvian-Soviet peace treaty was signed in Riga by the Republic of Latvia and Soviet Russia. Latvia experienced nearly two decades of economic growth. Over 145 thousand peasants were granted land.

The "secret protocol" of the German-Soviet Nonaggression Pact of August 1939 decided the fate of Latvia. WWII started in September 1939 with the German invasion of Poland, and by October 1939, Latvia had to sign a dictated treaty of mutual assistance in which the USSR obtained military, naval, and air bases in the Latvian territory. The Red Army invaded and occupied Latvia in June 1940. A "year of terror" ensued in which thirty-five thousand Latvians, especially the intelligentsia, were deported to the eastern portion of the USSR. Many were sent to prison camps in Siberia.

With the German invasions of the USSR, from July 1941 through October 1944, Latvia was a province of the larger Ostland, which also included Estonia, Lithuania, and Belorussia (Belarus). By the fall of 1944, two-thirds of the country was occupied by the Soviet Red Army. More than one hundred thousand Latvians fled to Sweden and Germany before the arrival of the Russians. Included in the exodus was the Volskis family.

Kristaps Volskis was born on December 6, 1901, to Fredrich and Anna Volskis in Volhynia, Russia. His mother, Anna, twenty-five years younger than his father, was Fredrich's third wife. His first two wives had died in childbirth. Kristaps's parents worked the land for a rich land baron. In 1909, when Kristaps was eight years old, the family left Russia and moved to Latvia near the town of Kirshenhof.

In his teen years, Kristaps worked as a hired man, milking and herding cows. His formal schooling began at the age of fifteen and only lasted two winters. When he turned eighteen in 1920, he served in the Latvian Army. He trained in the 4th artillery battery and learned to play the baritone and violin, as well. When Kristaps became ill with swollen feet, he spent some time in a Riga, Latvia, hospital, unable to walk for a month. He was treated with seawater and mud packs.

From 1920 through 1935, Kristaps had various jobs. He packed apples for a gardener and dug ditches and wells for a land baron who owned a castle. When the castle became a trade school, it was Kristaps's job to deliver heating fuel to the school. He also worked as a shoe repairman and later used these skills as a shoemaker in the Displaced Persons (DP) camps following the war in Germany. He worked on his brother Wilhelm's farm while Wilhelm pastored a church. Kristaps was very active in his church; he played in the church band and sang in the choir.

Olga was born on March 22, 1912, in Lithuania to Martinas and Anna Undsenaite. Her father was a merchant marine and made at least two trips after 1915 to New York and Boston in the United States, where he earned money to buy property in Lithuania. Olga's mother was a seamstress. Martinas would be gone for long periods of time, leaving Olga's mother to support and care for the family. There was not much to eat, and the family survived by eating raw potatoes. Her mother and four-year-old brother, Kastas, fell ill with dysentery and died within hours of each other. Six-year-old Olga and her eight-year-old sister Elsa were left alone in the home all day before the neighbors found them. They then stayed with the neighbors for several days before their father returned.

Martinas soon remarried. Life with the new stepmother was not easy for Olga. At times she was beaten with a switch and made to kneel in a ditch for hours until her father came home. Her father felt bad about the abuse, but the stepmother, being of stronger will, usually won the arguments. Her father started drinking heavily and spent his time in town drinking away their money. One cold night after Martinas had been drinking, he passed out in the back of his horse-drawn wagon. The next morning in front of his home, he was found frozen to death. He was forty-five years old. When Olga was thirteen years old, she left home and found a job as a house girl. In 1929, at the age of seventeen, Olga moved to Tilsit, Lithuania, where she worked as a cook in a boarding house.

Olga met Kristaps in Riga, Latvia. Kristaps had spoken to the minister of his church about wanting to marry a nice woman. The minister arranged a meeting between Kristaps and Olga. Two weeks later, they were married on August 11, 1935. Kristaps was thirty-four, and Olga was twenty-three years old. Kristaps later commented, "It was important that we married quickly because my knees were giving out from pedaling my bicycle twenty-six miles each way to court Olga." After the marriage, the couple moved in with his family in Jēkabpils, Latvia, to help them farm.

Communications between the newlyweds and Kristaps's family were challenging. Olga spoke only Lithuanian. Kristaps spoke Latvian, German, and Russian. Olga learned to speak Latvian and German. She and Kristaps could communicate slightly in Latvian, but she had to learn German to converse with his parents. On June 15, 1936, their daughter Lidija was born, and on March 27, 1938, a son Karlis was born. When immigrating to America fifteen years later, Olga mastered English.

Following the Russian invasion of Latvia in June 1940, collectivization of agriculture was started by the Communists. Kristaps worked for a widowed landowner. When Hitler overran the country the next year, the farms were divided, and Kristaps was given ten acres to farm.

In 1944, with the advancing Russian Army, the Communists would come by night and load families in trucks to take them away. Kristaps and Olga feared for their safety because they were aware that families were often separated.

They joined the long lines with thousands from Latvia, Estonia, and Lithuania traveling hundreds of miles south and west into Germany. They were heading to Kristaps's sister's place near Heiderode, Germany. The family needed papers to get into Germany, so Kristaps and Olga rode ahead on bikes to get the necessary paperwork while leaving the rest of the family to wait in a barn for their return. They were picked up by German soldiers who offered to give them a ride back to where their family was in the barn. Miraculously, they met Elsa and the rest of the family headed in the opposite direction. They had hitched the horse and left their hiding place in the barn as the fighting was coming near. Food was becoming scarce. One lucky day, a German Army supply wagon traveling in front of them hit a bump and a loaf of bread and marmalade fell out. Young Karl jumped out of the wagon and picked it up. It seemed like another miracle.

Their horse died from lack of feed. They continued by train and crowded into a cattle car. Making it into eastern Germany, Kristaps was taken from the train to dig ditches for the German Army. The rest of the family continued to his sister Flora's house, believing they may never see him again. When they finally reached Flora's, they all had lice from the extremely close quarters on the train. They had been traveling for three months and fourteen days.

Kristaps was taken to a work camp where he remained for two months. He and several men escaped one night and hid in a rye field. He took off his German-issued jacket to sleep on it. The next morning, he forgot and left the jacket in the field. The other men had left their jackets on, and when they reached a train station, they were recaptured by the SS because they recognized their jackets. Kristaps boarded the train unnoticed. Two months later, he made his way to Flora's house. He was a physical mess when he arrived. He was covered with lice, and Olga had to boil his clothes to get them clean.

The Russians were getting closer to Heiderode, so the family was on the move again, headed to Elsdorf, Germany. They arrived by train on January 28, 1945. Kristaps and Olga worked on a farm with the Grube family in the Badenhorst community.

After the war, all displaced persons were required to go to one of three hundred displaced persons camps. The camps were under the care of the United Nations Relief and Rehabilitation Administration. Olga, Kristaps, and family entered Camp Seedorf on June 28, 1946. Life in the camp was good; there were many other Latvians. The

Latvian population was able to organize an educational, cultural, social, and religious infrastructure. Lidija and Karl attended school.

Kristaps and Olga started filling out papers to immigrate to the United States. They moved to the Rotenburg camp for three years. Refugee packages came from the United States with coffee, sugar, flour, dried milk, and Hershey candy bars.

They were settled in this displaced persons camp. Kristaps attempted to find his brother, Wilhelm, back in Latvia. Wilhelm and his family had not fled Latvia and remained there under the Russian occupation. Kristaps placed an ad in a Latvian newspaper flyer in the camp. Miraculously, Wilhelm saw the clipping and responded that he was indeed still alive.

At eighty-five years old in 2023, Lidija shared:

> The DP camps allowed us to live in a house beside a
> German farmer where father worked as a farmhand.
> When my sister Martha was born, I remember having to
> go out to the adjoining barn while mother gave birth in
> the house. My parents were able to somehow get us
> moved from different DP camps, having heard that some
> camps had a greater chance of getting to immigrate.
> These particular DP camps were mostly of refugees from
> Latvia. Father used his shoemaking skills, and stayed busy
> making and repairing shoes. I do not know if he received
> any pay, but he may have been able to save some money
> for our eventual immigration.

Interviewed and quoted forty-six years later in 1990 for the Minden, Nebraska, newspaper, Lidija told the story of the 1944 escape:

> We hurriedly packed up in a small, covered wagon, taking
> whatever we could get in the cart. We put a cow behind
> the wagon for a milk source and took some dried bread.
> Besides the necessities of blankets and clothing, a few
> photographs and handiwork items were also packed.

Father was a shoemaker, so he took his shoe molds with him. His trade kept him busy later in the German refugee DP camps for the next five years.

Our family joined a line of people traveling east in search for shelter with relatives or friends. Sometimes only a few would be in a group and at other times it was like a "big wagon train."

It wasn't until 1949 after living in several DP camps in Germany that we were allowed to immigrate to the United States. Two more babies were born in the DP camps: Martha in 1946 and Willis in 1948.

Lidija continued with the newspaper interview in 1990:

A letter from Margaret Grummert from Nelson, Nebraska, reached Kristaps in February 1949. The letter was dated February 19, 1949. It was addressed to Kristaps Volskis. It started:

Dear Mr. Volskis,
You may have learned through Rev. Adolfs Majorins that my son and I have provided assurances of home, employment, transportation, and such as our law requires for your coming to the United States. They have been sent to the Church World Service in New York . . .

My parents, our grandmother, and two aunts and the five children came on a ship from Germany to America. I was the only one that did not get seasick. Then we were put on a train west across America which seemed like three days.

It was late on a stormy night when the family finally arrived at the Hastings [Nebraska] train depot. When we arrived, it was so stormy that no one from Nelson was there to meet us until the next day. We had to spend the night in a nearby hotel.

We moved into the old Nuckolls County farm dwelling for more than a year while father worked for the Grummert's. It was a huge house. We all had a room for ourselves. The neighbors had given us a we come shower to fill the house with household goods and groceries.

I credit my country schoolteacher for helping catch me up with the other children my age. She took a lot of time with me and within one year, I was caught up. My former classmates still tease me about how agreeable I was when I first came to Nelson. All I knew to say was "yeah," and smile.

The Volskis family moved to Minden, Nebraska, in 1950. Kristaps worked there for another farmer and later as a construction carpenter. Olga did house cleaning. The Volskises bought a house at 642 E. 8th Street in Minden in 1955. They took great pride in their home, yard, and flower gardens. The home was a showpiece in the community. Olga raised beautiful varieties of peonies and sold them for Memorial Days.

Epilogue

Kristaps and Olga raised their four children in Minden, Nebraska. All four graduated from high school at Minden High School. Karl went into the Navy. Lidija married and became a farm housewife and telephone company employee. Martha became a college graduate and teacher. Will graduated with a degree in chemistry from Metropolitan State University of Denver.

Louis (Rovnaer) Ruffner

A Jewish peddler from Kiev, Russia, became a beloved
citizen and businessman in West Virginia, USA.

*"Honest, upright, industrious citizen, a kind and devoted husband and
father, a true friend to all . . ."*   —Louis Ruffner's obituary, April 1922

Louis

Ukraine is the second largest country in Europe, after European Russia. Its area is 233,000 sq. mi. (603,000 sq. km.), which is slightly smaller than the state of Texas. The Russian invasion of 2022 and war ravaging this beautiful country is just one more chapter in Ukraine's struggle for autonomy. Its archeological history dates back thirty-two thousand years.

During the Middle Ages in the ninth century AD, it was the region of early Slavic people or the East Slavic Culture. The Mongols invaded in the thirteenth century. For the next six hundred years, this area was under the rule of many empires, beginning with the Polish-Lithuanian Commonwealth, followed by the Austrian Empire, the Ottoman Empire, the Tsardom of Russia, Cossack Hetmanate (which was partitioned between Poland and Russia), and ultimately the Russian Empire.

The Russian Revolution of 1917 resulted in a short-lived Ukrainian People's Republic. The Bolsheviks consolidated it into the Ukrainian Soviet Socialist Republic (Ukrainian SSR) in 1922. When the Germans invaded in 1941, most of the Ukrainian Jews were killed or sent to extermination and work camps.

The Ukrainian Jews had lived under the tyranny of Catherine the Great from 1761 to 1796. She had been a German princess who deposed her husband, Czar Peter III, to become the Czarina of Russia. She restricted Jews to the Pale of Settlement within Russia in 1791. "The Pale of Settlement was a western region of the Russian Empire with varying borders that existed from 1791-1917," per Wikipedia. Within the borders of the Pale, Jews were allowed permanent residency. Outside the Pale, Jewish residency, permanent or temporary, was mostly forbidden. "The archaic English term *pale* is derived from the Latin word *palus,* a stake, extended to mean the area enclosed by a fence or boundary. The Pale of Settlement included all of modern-day Belarus and Moldavia, much of Lithuania, Ukraine, east-central Poland, relatively small parts of Latvia, and what is now the Northwestern Federal District of Russia."[1]

In 1861, serfdom in Russia was abolished. The Jews continued to suffer under Alexander III, who escalated anti-Jewish polices. Pogroms were targeted, violent mob attacks on the Jewish population.[2] From 1881-84, two hundred anti-Jewish Pogroms were conducted in Kiev, Warsaw, and Odessa.[3] The Jews were being blamed for the assassination of Alexander II. When economic conditions worsened, the blame was focused on the Jewish money lenders. In the 1890s, anti-Jewish Pogroms escalated across the empire. More than two million Jews fled between 1880 and 1920.[4]

In this country in the city of Kiev, Louis Rovnaer was born on October 22, 1865. His parents were Hyman and Ester Rovnaer. His father was a peddler. At the age of fifteen, Louis immigrated to Baltimore, Maryland, USA, and lived with a relative. The Baltimore city directory in 1884 shows Louis Ruffner living at 247 Orleans.

It is believed that because of his strong, Russian, guttural pronunciation of the word Rovnaer, the officials recorded the name as Ruffner.

Louis (Rovnaer) Ruffner moved to Cincinnati, Ohio. The Cincinnati city directory in 1891 records: Louis Rovnaer, peddler, living at 380 Kenyon. Just one year later in 1892, the Cincinnati city directory shows a different spelling and address for Louis Rovner (sic.), peddler, living at 210 Kenyon Av.

The account by a judge in Hamilton County Ohio records Louis's marriage:

> Louis Rovnaer and Minnie Sibverstein (sic) were married in Cincinnati, Hamilton Co., Ohio. THE STATE OF OHIO, Hamilton Co: Personally appeared before me, the undersigned Judge of the Probate Court within and for the county of Hamilton, Louis Rovnaer, who being duly sworn, deposeth and saith he is more than twenty-one years of age, and has no lawful wife living, and that MINNIE SILBERSTEIN (sic) is more than eighteen years of age, and has no lawful husbanc living; that she is a resident of the county of Hamilton aforesaid: and the said LOUIS

ROVNAER further says that said MINNIE SILBERSTEN (sic) and affiant are not of nearer relation to each other than a second cousin, and that he knows no legal objections and the marriage contemplated between them and further this deponent saith not, sworn unto subscribed before me LOUIS ROVNAER, this 30th day of July 1890. Hermab Goebel, Probate Judge . . . Married on the 3rd day of August 1890, LOUIS Rovaener and Minnie Bell Silberstein (sic) by me, a minister of the Jewish Gospel; (Reverend Simon Levy).

Authors note: It is quite amazing how official recording can attempt to spell names. For the purpose of this story, Louis Ruffner and Minnie Bell Silverstein (sic) were the ones married in Cincinnati, Ohio, on August 3, 1890. Their names will continue with this spelling.

Louis and Minnie traveled on the Ohio River. Their daughter was Goldie Ruffner. She shared with her son, Charlie Kirkwood, as she remembered years later that her father traveled from Cincinnati on a flatboat put together with logs, sitting on a barrel of his belongings. They landed at Charleston, West Virginia. Minnie's parents were Abraham (AP) and Rebecca Kahn Silverstein, but they may have already been in Charleston at the time when Louis and Minnie arrived by boat. AP Silverstein wrote in 1893 that Louis Ruffner was one of the four founders of the B'nai Jacob Congregation in Charleston, West Virginia. They met in the upstairs room over a business in town. The first service was held at the Court Street home of Mr. and Mrs. Julius Nearman. Pack peddlers came in from the hills on Friday to observe the sabbath.

The B'nai Jacob Synagogue became the first Orthodox Jewish Synagogue in the area. In 1906, it took ownership of a $16,000 building which had previously been built in 1873.

Louis was a peddler of dry goods. He and the family moved from Charleston nearly twenty miles south along the Kanawha River to Montgomery, West Virginia, in 1900. The Kanawha and Michigan

Railroad crossed the river and connected with the Virginian Railway at nearby Deepwater. In the early 1910s, Montgomery was the shipping point for twenty-six different coal operations. It was to these coal company villages that Louis traveled to peddle his dry goods. There are different accounts of how he carried his goods. In 2023, his grandson, Charles Ruffner, recounted:

> I was told that Louis carried a knapsack and boarded the train to destinations along the line. He would disembark and find a location to open his knapsack and spread out his wares. He would then give a boy a penny to go and tell all the surrounding residents that he was in the area, and they could come and order from his displayed selections. He then went back to his warehouse in Montgomery, filled the order, and brought back the goods which had been ordered. Though my grandfather had died before I was born, I remember visiting my grandmother's place and seeing the big warehouse out back. My grandmother's house was elevated up onto blocks, and chickens shaded themselves and made nests under the house. There was a big vegetable garden outback. An iceman would carry a big block of ice and put it in their wooden ice box.

Louis Ruffner was a faithful member of the Knights of Pythias Lodge. He proudly wore his Knights uniform and displayed his sword in pictures. At the time of his death in 1922, he was remembered in a Lodge document from his family's collection:

> *The great order of knights of Pythias in West Virginia loses one of its most faithful members, and a local lodge Fayette. No K of P will never see his place filled in that lodge . . . He was kindly and liberal to a fault, and his benevolences and kindly ministrations to the needs of his fellowmen were not limited to his hometown, but wherever he went in his daily*

travels, to help others seemed to give him greater
happiness than anything else . . .

Epilogue

Louis Ruffner died of pneumonia. His obituary in the local newspaper:

DEATH REMOVES SPLENDID CITIZEN- Shortly before 10 pm,
Wednesday April 5, 1922, he ceased conversation with the
family to cough. He remarked that he believed he was
dying, and in a minute the second hemorrhage occurred
and in a short time he breathed his last.

The passing from this life of Mr. Ruffner removes a figure
familiar to men, women, and children in both the New
River and Kanawha Valleys . . . for he spent more than a
score of years in these valleys merchandizing business and
at his death had a large clientele . . . Honest, upright,
industrious citizen, a kind and devoted husband and father,
a true friend to all . . . a good citizen, a strong believer in his
home town and lost no opportunity to boost it, and
welcomed and assisted in any movement that had for its
purpose the advancement of Montgomery and the
surrounding territory morally or otherwise. . . born in Kiev,
Russia in 1866 (56 YOA).

Louis Ruffner is buried in the B'nai Jacob Cemetery in Charleston, West Virginia. His wife Minnie B. joined him there in 1940.

From a boy born in Kiev, the same year as the end of America's Civil War, he immigrated to America. His family's Jewish faith had been despised in Ukraine and the greater Russian Empire. In America, he was a simple peddler, but he provided a life for his wife and eleven children. He was cherished by his clientele in the backwoods coal mining hamlets, as well as the townspeople. From the very year that he arrived in West Virginia, he was one of four who organized the Jewish

Synagogue in Charleston. From a revered family man, to businessman and lodge member, Louis left an honorable footprint in his new country in his short fifty-six years of life.

WORKS CITED

1. "Pale of Settlement," Wikipedia, The Free Encyclopedia. Wikimedia Foundation, 18 Dec, 2024, https://en.wikipedia.org/wiki/Pale_of_Settlement.

2. "Pale of Settlement," Jewish Virtual Library, www.jewishvirtuallibrary.org

3. Jewish Chronicle, May 6, 1881 cited in Benjamin Blech, Eyewitness to Jewish History.

4. Sankt-Peterburgskie Vedomosti newspaper No. 65, March 8 (20), 1881.

The artist

Sisters: Marie,
Natile, and Luby

Luby Grinkiv Miller

A Ukrainian woman won a green card to immigrate to Illinois,
and went on to build a life for herself as an artist in Iowa.

"I took a written test and was sworn in with a group of other people taking the oath of allegiance to my new country. It was a very troubled time for me. I had loved my Ukraine life and now it was becoming my former country." —Luby

Luby

Ukraine is the breadbasket of Europe. Centuries of conflict and wars have been imprinted on these eastern European people. The Greeks, Lithuanians, Polish, Habsburgs, and Russians have overrun and ruled this nation. It shares its borders with no less than seven countries: Russia, Belarus, Poland, Slovakia, Hungary, Moldova, and Romania. Its southern exposure to the Black Sea gives it export access to the rest of the world. Ukraine's population is forty-four million, and it has a land size of 235,384 sq. mi.: slightly larger than Nebraska and the Dakotas in the United States.

When the Habsburg Empire collapsed following WWI, Ukraine became one of thirteen Soviet Republics in the Soviet Union (USSR). In WWII, this land was being overrun by the Germans attacking the Russians to the east. Then, in 1944, the Russians pushed the Germans back to Berlin. In 1947, Ukraine, under the title of the Ukrainian SSR, became a member of the United Nations—one of three Soviet Republics to do so.

With the breakup of the Soviet Union in 1991, Ukraine became a self-governing country, though many communists remained in government positions. Numerous Ukrainians fled or immigrated to North America.

In 2014, the Russians took over Crimea in southwestern Ukraine, where they then built a twelve-mile causeway connecting Crimea to the Russian mainland. The Russians claimed they were attempting to liberate Ukraine on the grounds of freeing the people from a "Nazi" government. The eastern provinces of Donbas and Slobozhanshchyna are militarily controlled by the Russians. In 2022, the Russians invaded Ukraine. To date, tens of thousands of Russian and Ukrainian soldiers have died in the bloody and devastating war. And no less than four million refugees have fled to Poland alone.

Lyubov Grinkiv Yaroslavna, born April 29, 1979, was the middle daughter of Yaroslav and Olga Grinkiv. The name Lyubov means "love" in Ukrainian and is shortened to "Luby." Luby's mother, Olga, was born in 1960 in Odessa, a key port city on the Black Sea. Olga's father was imprisoned after WWII by the Russians for ten years because of his military involvement in fighting against the Russians. After his release from prison, his health declined. He received frequent visits from the KGB to make sure that he would never rise against the Russian government again. Olga's family had some Jewish descendants. She spoke a combination Ukrainian and Russian dialect and had a very distinct accent. She was blonde with blue eyes.

Luby's father, Yaroslav, had six siblings in his family and was brunet with very bright blue eyes. Yaroslav was a carpenter, and the family lived on a one-acre plot. He had horses to cultivate the land for a large garden. With the Russian revolution in 1917 and the Communist takeover of Ukraine, the government confiscated his land. With the breakup of the Soviet Union in 1991, some of the family's original land holdings were restored, but it was scattered in many directions. Yaroslav also served in WWII, after which, he had bullets stuck in his leg for decades from the fighting. Early in Luby's life, he was forced to have his legs amputated.

Luby attended school through the equivalent of eighth grade. Since her family could not afford art school to further her education, she attended a local trade school. Her dad's cousin was a deacon at the college and helped with her tuition. She took woodworking and a high-class carpentry course She was enamored by art, which was supported by the few classes at her trade school.

When a third child was born to Yaroslav and Olga, they qualified for a larger lot of land because of their family's size. The couple built a house themselves on the lot from scratch. In 1996, a gas line passed by their home, and the family was connected to natural gas. At the time in 1998, when Luby came to America, there was still no indoor plumbing. Their television had three black and white channels, and they used pliers on the controls to find them.

Luby married at the age of eighteen, and soon after, she received a packet in the mail indicating that she had won a green card. This allowed her to come to Chicago with her new husband. Luby shared her first impression, "Chicago was a culture shock for me. I had never seen so many cultures together like this in my life." They moved into a small house, living with her husband's father and brother in Bensenville, Illinois. The living conditions were squalid. Her husband's father and brother were both in the United States illegally. There were eight people living under this one roof, with two more coming in later. For six months, these conditions escalated. Luby's husband returned to Ukraine to see an old girlfriend, and their relationship deteriorated.

Luby moved out of this home. She found a job with a family with five children, who she nannied for the next five years. Luby told:

> I learned what English I could from the children, but it was only "children English." I lived on my own and afforded my own apartment. I sent money back home to my family in Ukraine by Western Union to my mother. It was convenient and fortunate that my husband had filed for divorce in Ukraine.

> I had grown up when Ukraine was still under communism. When it broke up, it was like living in a cage and all the little mice running in a circle. Someone feeds them and cares for them. When it [communism] broke up, they opened the cage door, and everyone started stealing and running. There was no discipline. No one knew how to run the country. No one knew how to run a business. Yet, the Russians still kept their people in the government to control it. There were no jobs and people started fleeing the country.

> By 2003, I visited a friend in Arizona. He had been a police officer in Chicago and helped protect me from a very jealous ex-husband who was threating me. It was December in Arizona, and I was shocked by how green and warm it was.

> In Chicago, I wanted to learn better English. I received a certificate in computer applications from Truman College. I

wanted to improve my English, because I only knew "children's English."

I met a person from the Chicago Art Institute and was mind-blown away with the art.

On her birthday, April 29, 2004, Luby loaded a four-by-eight U-Haul, hooked it up to her Acura, and headed for Arizona. She traveled for three days and two nights with only a map for guidance. There was no such thing as GPS or smartphone to travel the 1,750 miles from Chicago to Phoenix. She shared:

I pulled this huge, big thing behind me. I had a calling card to call back home to my parents . . . My parents had no phone [in Ukraine], so I had to call my uncle who was their neighbor, or another who was a police officer neighbor. They would then go get my mother to come to their home so we could visit over the phone.

In Arizona, Luby had a difficult time finding a job. Even though she had a certificate in computer operations, her skills were compromised because she had difficulty in spelling and sentence structure. She got a job at Aunt Chilada's, a restaurant in Phoenix. It was a family business owned by Ken and Candace Nagel, and Luby did everything. She went from waitressing, to bartending, to maintenance, painting, and cleaning. She also had a part-time job at a hotel, and later got hired as the general manager for Samurai Sam's restaurant.

Luby became a United States citizen in 2005. She shared, with tears welling up in her eyes:

I took a written test and was sworn in with a group of other people taking the oath of allegiance to my new country. It was a very troubled time for me. I had loved my Ukraine life and now it was becoming my former country. My great friends at the restaurant had organized a party for me that

night. I was so emotionally distraught that I did not attend
my own celebration party.

Luby met a friend, Susan Sombrovich, who inspired her to
concentrate on her passion for art. They went to many art events,
studios, and anything you can imagine. She was able to paint and sell
her art again, which made her very happy. She said "I love knowing
that someone will enjoy my art."

Luby married a second time and a son, William Dimitry
Thompson, was born in 2008. She reflected "In just my five years in
Arizona, I made a lot of money. I bought a $210,000 condo and a new
car. Then the market crashed in 2008."

With her new husband, they drove three different summers to
Buffalo Center, Iowa, to visit a friend of her husband's and escape the
brutal Arizona temperatures. The topography in Iowa was more like
Ukraine. Luby was enthralled by the green and calmer temperatures,
which reminded her of her home country. She remembered:

> In Arizona, God had a different plan for me. I was a
> bartender and had a lot of cash. When I became pregnant,
> it was going to cost $23,000 just to have a child, and that
> was only if there were no complications.
>
> I couldn't believe how some people were using the system.
> They were coming across the border to have a baby in the
> US, all at no charge, covered by the government. For the
> one and only time, I was forced to use this system to cover
> my delivery, which cost me about three thousand dollars.

During the third visit to Iowa, Luby and her husband bought a
house in Buffalo Center. The entire city block was owned by the
Catholic church. The house they purchased had been the Catholic
parsonage and had been built on July 7, 1913. Ironically, they
purchased the house one hundred years later on July 17, 2013.

Luby painted houses in Buffalo Center, both inside and outside. Her skills and word of mouth kept her more than busy. Her work ethic, honesty, beautiful blonde hair, green eyes, and sweet personality became known to many.

Luby's second marriage started to fail and literally went south. Her husband found Iowa a shock to his urban upbringing. He moved back to Arizona, and Luby was once again single—but this time with a son of school age.

Her painting skills were noted by a friend who directed her to Creative Spirits in Forest City, Iowa. It was a business that teaches people to paint. "It was a good experience in my life, as it taught me that everybody has art in them, and I was able to help show them their creative bubbles, and that it was a huge world out there to express themselves," Luby said. When Creative Spirits was disbanding, Luby was still painting houses. She met Dawn and Royce Janssen in Lakota, Iowa, where she painted the walls and floors of a unique condo complex in the refurbished, closed Lakota High School. The walls and hallways of the former high school were painted in a hometown main street pattern, and Luby's creative genius is every bit as great as that which is found in a Grant Wood painting or a Thomas Hart Benton mural. She opened a restaurant within the former high school cafeteria. Luby ran the restaurant for the next four and half years and recounted:

> I did everything. From the cooking, preparation, cleaning, waiting tables, and running the cash register. As a child at home, when I wanted to play with friends, my mother would tell me you have to go weed the garden first. I milked the cow by hand, fed the pigs and chickens, and had a work ethic instilled in me.

While working at Creative Spirits five years earlier, she met Jeremy Miller. She continued:

I had never intended or thought I ever needed to marry again. I dreamed of having a café and having a romance like in the Hallmark movies. I think God put me in this place at this little café. God let me have it and put me in the perspective to rely on him and not just my wants and dreams. Jeremy was more Christian. We were married on October 10, 2020. Back home in Ukraine, we were Catholic. The people could party and pick and choose what suited them. Here I can read the Bible and learn my religion in a much more meaningful way.

In the summer of 2022, Luby's mother arrived from Poland to visit Buffalo Center, Iowa, for her first time in America. She had fled the Russian invasion and war in Ukraine and made it to Poland. She was granted a refugee visa to come to America. She found her now-American daughter in the middle of a construction job, as the walls of the house were stripped down to the studs. Art comes in many forms. This woodworking project and carpentry project is just another of these "do-it-yourself" things that this artist can do. One of her large paintings hangs at the end of the expansive dining table. This display showed Luby's mother the talents and expressions of her American daughter.

Epilogue

It has been more than two years since Russia invaded Ukraine, and the war continues. Luby's mother is still living in Iowa with Luby. The refugee visa was initially for two years. There is uncertainty about any return to Ukraine in the near future.

Luby's perseverance and determination to work and provide for her family has not changed. She paints and does construction projects. Artists have a way of describing life with a brush.

She continues to be loved by her customers from the restaurant, and their friendships have made this lady very happy in her new country of America.

Maria, Marijke, Leendert, and Hendrik

Marijke Vermeulen Klahn

A Dutch girl moved from Jakarta to the US with
her family at the age of five, where they worked to
both assimilate and find pieces of home.

*"I may not have known what the words meant, but boy could I spell and
pronounce them. I believe the immersion and assimilation was the ideal
time to learn the English language. I later became a teacher and learned
from the experience to use as a Title I teacher."* —Marijke

Marijke

Marijke was born on September 9, 1948, to parents Maria and Leendert Vermeulen at a hospital in Batavia, Dutch East Indies. She was named after the Netherlands' Queen Juliana's youngest daughter, Marijke.

Her parents were engaged and pledged to each other when Leendert, an architect, was conscripted into the army in March of 1942. He was sent to the Dutch East Indies (now Indonesia) as reinforcement to protect and defend this archipelago of 17,500 islands, which were rich in rubber and oil. The Indies had been a Dutch colony since 1800, when the Netherlands took over administrative control.

When the world was thrown into turmoil with the Second World War, the Netherlands were defeated after an eighty-eight-hour battle against the German invaders on May 15, 1940. On December 8, 1941 (one day after the attack on Pearl Harbor), the Dutch government in exile (in London), known as the Dutch London Cabinet, declared war on Japan. The Japanese invaded and overran Java and Sumatra and occupied the Dutch East Indies for its rich oil fields to support their war machine. Leendert Vermeulen, along with 100 thousand Dutch, British, Australian, and American troops, was taken prisoner for the next three and a half years. They were used as forced labor. The death rates reached nearly thirty percent. At the time of the Japanese surrender in August 1945, the rebels seeking independence for Indonesia were emboldened to push the Dutch out of the Indies. Leendert was soon traded to be imprisoned by the Indonesian rebels. He said the next three months were the hardest and the worst of all his captivity. Leendert suffered from malnutrition and physical torture at the hands of the rebels. Upon his release, this 6'2", thirty-year-old skeleton of a man weighed eighty pounds. He was sent to Ceylon by ship, where he was hospitalized for the next eight months and recovered from his nearly four years in captivity. He was returned to the Netherlands by ship, arriving in late November 1946. He was reunited with Maria. She had waited these long seven years and had been faithful to her engagement. The Dutch Protestant tradition of placing the engagement ring on the right, fourth finger was emblematic of her love for him.

In December the couple received their "Under Marriage" receipt from the Dutch government, and Maria and Leendert were married on January 29, 1947. The wedding ring was then placed on the right, fourth finger, per the Dutch tradition.

Post-war jobs in the Netherlands were scarce after the trying five years of occupation and brutal rounding up of the Jews by the Germans. Anne Frank had journaled this occupation while hiding in Amsterdam. This diary was later printed posthumously as *Anne Frank: The Diary of a Young Girl.* The government was employing workers to go back to the Dutch Indies to help in its reconstruction. Just one year after their marriage in 1947, Maria and Leendert were on their way back by ship to the same land as his five-year captivity.

For the next six years in Jakarta, the Vermeulen's lived in a modest home of a former diplomat. They had seven domestic helpers. Indonesia gained its independence in 1949 following the guerrilla war with the Dutch. In 1954 Leendert and his family left by ship with only a few crates of their possessions to go back to the Netherlands. The domestic workers pleaded to go with them, but unfortunately the Vermeulen's were unable to make adequate provisions for them.

Jobs and opportunities back in the Netherlands were still very limited. Housing was at a premium, if not nearly impossible to obtain. The Vermeulen family was able to find rentals along the coast and moved from house to house, room to room. Leendert found a job with a concrete company in Amsterdam but had to commute daily. A "white lie" with the government housing authority finally secured a house for the family in Amsterdam. Leendert had stretched the truth and implied the family was living with an aunt and uncle and their family, and the occupancy of so many people in one house was against regulations.

Marijke started school in Amsterdam and had the same wonderful teacher from second through sixth grade. She learned French and some German. Her brother, Hendrik, was two years younger and attended the same school.

With so few prospects in the economy at the time, the government was encouraging those who could find a sponsor to immigrate, especially to Australia, Canada, or America. On January 9, 1960, the Vermeulen family, with only a four-by-four wooden crate, embarked on the USS Ryndam for America. With the high seas in the North Atlantic, it took two extra days to reach America ten days later. The family, and most aboard, were seasick. "Pappa always said he had lost everything he had three times in his life, and he arrived in New York harbor with just the clothes on his back," Marijke remembered. After a long wait to go through customs, they reached the front of the line. The family before them had to unload everything from their wooden crate for customs inspection. Leendert was relieved when their crate was hardly looked at, and the Vermeulen's were officially in America.

From New York the family traveled by train for three days to Council Bluffs, Iowa. On Friday January 22, 1960, they were met by their sponsor, William Mott. He loaded them into his rather old station wagon. Marijke remembered:

> We went directly to a cafeteria where he fed the family. I had never seen so much food and the selections were unbelievable. I had not seen corn on the cob before, but Mr. Mott assured me I would like it. We had not eaten much for nearly three days, and I heaped my tray with about everything. Of course, whether my eyes were bigger than my stomach, or maybe it had shrunk from not eating, I was not able to eat everything I had taken. I was very embarrassed when I told him I could not eat any more. Mr. Mott then took us to his home for the first few nights. I was shocked to find that a privy in the backyard was the only toilet for his family and guests.

Being somewhat familiar with church, and having occasionally attended the Dutch Reformed Church back home, the family was introduced the next morning on January 24, 1960, at the chapel in the YMCA of Omaha. Marijke explained:

> I was informed this was the Friends Church. I knew that
> church always had a pastor or at least a pulpit for a
> speaker. When no one appeared for the longest time, the
> congregation sat so quietly, it startled me when someone
> behind us stood and gave a short sermonette or testimony.
> I remained in fear that our family would have to do the
> same, but we were spared this time.

The sponsor family, Mr. and Mrs. William Mott, and other church families had provided the Vermeulen's with a small furnished home in Council Bluffs, Iowa. The next day, Monday, January 25, Leendert traveled by bus across the Missouri River to Omaha to seek employment. He could speak some English and returned the same day with a job at an architectural firm. He was able to do all the work as an architect, however, since he was not licensed in America, he was not compensated nearly as well. "That first Easter with his second paycheck, Pappa bought me an Easter dress and a toy, and also a bicycle for my brother Hendrik," Marijke lovingly remembered.

Her mother, Maria, first found a job at Swanson's chicken processing plant. She and Leendert commuted by bus to Omaha. She could not speak English and the heat and working conditions were exhausting.

Marijke and Hendrik were soon sent to elementary school. Though they were the ages of sixth and fourth graders, the principal wanted to start them in the first grade. Their mother protested and had none of this. She insisted the children be placed with their peers in sixth and fourth grades, respectively. The children spoke no English. Marijke started school in January of 1960. She learned English one word at a time. After three weeks, she was receiving perfect scores on her twenty spelling words. Marijke remembered:

I may not have known what the words meant, but boy could I spell and pronounce them. I believe the immersion and assimilation was the ideal time to learn the English language. I later became a teacher and learned from the experience to use as a Title I teacher. I soon had no accent. Being a new student from another country, I was taken in as a special person and became friends with many.

Marijke and the family moved to Grand Island, Nebraska, and she started eighth grade at Barr Junior High School. Leendert started a new job at George Clayton Architectural Firm. Maria was employed at Handlers News Agency. This agency distributed all the magazines such as *Time, Ladies Home Journal,* and *Newsweek* to stores and news outlets. Maria then returned and removed the unsold magazines and replaced them with new editions the next week. The covers of the unsold magazines were torn off and returned for credit to the publishers for accounting purposes. "Momma brought home some of the rest of the magazines for us to read. I loved the news and fashions and explored the pages in my new homeland," said Marijke.

High school in Grand Island was a joy for this skinny, 5'10", blonde and blue-eyed girl who resembled her parents. The family joined the Presbyterian church, which they thought was the most like their Dutch Reformed Church background. Marijke sang in the choir and was the president of the youth group. She played volleyball and was active in the Girls Athletic Association (GAA). She joined the German American club which prided itself in service and giving back to others. She was a friend to all. Her gregarious spirit was infectious, and she was loved by many. How often do people in their seventies still Zoom with their beloved high school friends? That would be Marijke.

Freshman year at the University of Nebraska found Marijke overwhelmed. Being very social, and carrying eighteen hours with Advanced German, Botany, English, and electives, she returned home at semester break with grades unbecoming. She confessed:

I was so embarrassed to go home at Christmas with my
marks. My parents had worked so hard to have the money
to send me to college and I had let them down. Being
eighteen years old in 1966, the majors for girls seemed
limited to only a few opportunities such as nursing,
teaching, and even a flight attendant. I transferred to
Kearney State, a teacher's college in central Nebraska, to
bring up my grades and concentrate on my studies. My
dad came often to visit and check up on me. He always
gave me a ten-dollar bill. I went home almost every
weekend to work, and I learned discipline and how to
study.

Her friends called her Lucky Lady 13. It seemed she truly was
lucky. Just nine days after breaking up with her boyfriend, she met her
husband-to-be, Bernie Klahn, on a blind date on the thirteenth of July
1968. They were engaged on Friday the thirteenth in February 1970.
She later won a car on Friday, May 13, 2005.

Marijke and Bernie were married on August 22, 1970. Bernie had
three choices during this Vietnam era. One was to be drafted, another
to flunk the physical, and the other to join ROTC and go into service
as an officer. With a biology major and an ROTC commission, Bernie
was trained in the Army Chemical Corps. He was stationed in
Alabama and Texas. In the summer of 1975, after attending the
Defense Equal Opportunity Management Institute at Patrick Air
Force Base in Cocoa Beach, Florida, he was sent to Germany with the
2nd Armored Brigade. Marijke remained in Killeen, Texas to fulfill her
second grade teaching contract. The couple was reunited and found an
apartment in Grafenwoehr, Germany, for the next three and a half
years. This time going back to Europe was by airline and not ship. The
countries had rebuilt significantly since she had left the Netherlands
twenty-four years earlier.

Annelies Marie (after Anne Frank) and Erik were both delivered at
the US Army Hospital in Nuremberg, Germany. They have desig-

nations on their passports stating, "United States citizen—born abroad."

Marijke's life has been blessed with happiness at many stops. From Germany, Bernie was reassigned to a Chemical Corps position at Aberdeen Proving Ground, Maryland. Civilian life brought them back to the middle of America. Bernie became an administrator and teacher at Kansas Wesleyan University in Salina, Kansas. After eight years, he earned his doctorate at Kansas State University. Marijke taught Title I reading and math for eighteen years at Bartlett and Whittier Elementaries in Salina, Kansas.

Epilogue

One of life's interesting twists and ironies found Bernie's next higher education opportunity in Wichita, Kansas, at Friends University. Yes, the same denomination which had welcomed the Vermeulen's to America thirty-three years earlier became Bernie's employer. Marijke taught fifth grade at the Independent K-12 school, retiring at sixty-four years old in 2012.

Marijke's beautiful smile, love of life, and magnetic personality still bloom for all she meets. *Yes Dorothy, it is Kansas,* where this little Dutch girl born in Batavia, now called Jakarta, Indonesia, continues to inspire and lead others.

Marion Rosemeck nee von Wetter

An Estonian-born woman, after escaping the grasp of WWII in Europe, moved across North America while raising a family, establishing her autonomy, and answering her calling as a weaver.

"All the strangers were holding onto each other. We were all so frightened . . . We could see the Russian tanks on the ridge above us shooting. We could see flames. It was very, very hectic." —Marion

Marion

The Baltic Sea to the north separates Estonia and Finland by only a few miles. The northeastern corner of Estonia borders Russia, and the southern interior borders Belarus. The three Baltic States of Lithuania, Latvia, and Estonia are referred to as Baltic Germany, as opposed to the Slavic countries of Russia and Belarus.

Marion was born July 5, 1924, to Otto Friedrich Hermann von Wetter and Inga Helene von Taube near Tallinn, Estonia. Her great-great-grandfather's brother, Gustav Heinrich von Wetter-Rosenthal, came to America and fought in the American Revolution under the name Major John Rose. John Rose was the only Russian national to fight with the Continental Army in the War of Independence in America. He was adjutant to Generals William Irvine and J. Jackson. He later returned to Estonia.

Marion's families were members of the Baltic German communities who established large estates in Estonia as far back as the 1600s. They became the von Wetter-Rosenthal's in 1652 when the Swedes controlled the region (1629-1710).

Marion's father, Otto von Wetter-Rosenthal, was a landowner. He studied at Dorpat, a university in Estonia. When Estonia was under Russian occupation, he joined the Czar's Hussars at the Court of the Czar in Saint Petersburg. Estonia had been pulled back and forth between occupations of Sweden, Denmark, Russia, and Germany. During the Russian Revolution of 1917 and the abdication of Czar Nicholas II, Otto fled back to Estonia. Though Estonia was independent, all the land and estates were divided and given to the native peasants. Since the Russian Hussars had such fantastic and decorative uniforms with white, very fine leather pants, he had to find someone he trusted to give him clothes. This was a challenge, as Estonia was filled with communists.

The ancestors of Marion's mother, Inga Helena Baroness von Taube, came from Sweden, and those ancestors can be traced back to the twelfth century.

Otto and Inga lived with an uncle in Valka, Estonia, where Marion was born in 1924. Her brother, John, was born in 1929. In 1930, Otto became the manager of a large estate in Finn, a community that had not been divided up during nor after the revolution. It belonged to a finishing school. Since it was tax exempt, it was also exempt from the division of land. It had horses, cattle, pigs, over one hundred milking cows, and produced wheat in the fields. Forty to fifty young women were taught manners, as well as how to cook, sew, garden, make cheese, and set a table. The main objective was to train them for marriage and raising children.

At the finishing school there was a huge loom for weaving. Marion became fascinated watching the feet move back and forth. This would begin her weaving life thirty years later.

In 1937, Otto moved the family to Reval (now Tallinn), Estonia, and into a modern rented apartment on the second floor. Running water and electricity were a novelty to them. There was continual worry about the Russians, and in 1938, this fear accelerated. The Russians were checking the borders and rattling their sabers. In August of 1939, Stalin and Hitler signed the Molotov-Ribbentrop Pact, assuring Hitler that Russia would not attack. Hitler had to give away the Baltic States of Estonia, Latvia, and Lithuania. He had absolutely no authority in the Baltic States, but that was the deal. The agreement was that all people of German descent who wanted to go back to Germany would be allowed to leave the Baltic States providing they were not Jewish. The adults were very upset and sad because they were leaving the land where their forefathers had lived for centuries. Inga, the children, and several relatives boarded a large ship at Reval in November 1939 for Stettin (now Szczecin), Poland.

In April 1940, Otto fled Estonia. The Russians had taken over housing and more of the land. It was too dangerous for the Baltic men left behind. He came to Stettin in western Poland and met the family. Germany now occupied Poland, and the Polish war was over. Otto was given several huge Polish estates to manage. The food raised went directly to Germany. Marion went to a boarding school for girls who were from Estonia and Latvia, created for the Baltic people. The teachers were from Latvia and Estonia and were not influenced by Hitler. She attended this school for the next three years and graduated high school.

Marion was drafted for six months into the *arbeitsdienst* (labor service) for the country. She was shipped to one of these camps and donned a blue dress, neckerchief, and work boots. Field work. Housework. Dirty little kids. Primitive conditions. Her father tried to get her to the farm that he managed, but since he had not joined the Nazi party that he despised, he had alienated himself with the occupational German troops and Marion was not allowed to go home.

Marion was supposed to go to the Ruhr in Western Germany which had a huge complex of factories that the British were bombing continually. With help from Otto, she stayed in the labor camp and got further training in home economics to become a teacher. She learned sewing, dress making, housekeeping, and gardening. In the camp, no one could be trusted. Should they have different ideas than the Nazis, or if someone denounced them, they were sacrificed.

From the tape recorded by Marion Rosemeck in 2007:

> One never knew much about the war, who was winning or losing. When the war with Russia started, it was just propaganda that we heard. By the fall of '44, my father began to prepare for a flight out of Poland because he could see the Russians coming.

> I spent Christmas and New Year's with my parents. My father had given me the name of his sister in Berlin and instructed me to remember the address. If anything happened, I was to go there. I was barely back in the labor camp when the war started to go drastically wrong. We heard that during this very severe winter in January 1945, the Germans were retreating from Russia into Poland. The trucks promised to evacuate the labor camp never came. The Russian tanks could be seen on the ridge and were

rolling along the horizon. The town deserted. Everyone was fleeing. We put on our warmest clothing, buried our treasures in the woods, and started walking west. We marched through the snow and ice and the bitter cold. The roads were just chockablock full. Horses, people, drawn carriages, drawn sleds with oxen, cows, and frozen people lying dead in the ditches.

The first night, we had nowhere to sleep. I remember standing between two horses to keep warm and holding onto their necks. No shelter. Snowing. In a deserted village, a bakery was found with a dairy next door. And I filled up. I was carrying a small little satchel. I had a change of underwear and socks. I wore a heavy coat, pants, gloves, and a knitted cap.

I managed to squeeze onto a train and stood. The train ride was slow—a narrow gauge track, and they were small, and it was full. You couldn't fall because you were standing so close. Right in front of me sat a little old lady all bundled up and she had a basket of eggs in her lap. She was trying to keep those eggs from breaking. It is odd to remember after all of these years, but I can still see that little old lady hunched over her eggs so afraid somebody would fall and break all of her eggs.

The train ride was terrifying. It was trying to beat the Russians from cutting it off and was going at such a speed it was swaying. All the strangers were holding onto each other. We were all so frightened. It was mostly old people. At Gladex, we stumbled out. We could see the Russian tanks on the ridge above us shooting. We could see flames. It was very, very hectic. Since we were still in uniforms, we were put to work to evacuate the train of senior citizens. They were bedded down and told they would spend the night and the next morning. They would be taken the next morning back to the train and taken on. Well, that never happened. We were done taking care of them and all of a sudden we were told, "If you want to get out of town you better go to the railroad station and hop that last train." They [Russians] were about to destroy the bridges [over the Oder River]. We got to the train, and it again was full. And it was terrifying because that train rattled along much faster than most German trains ever traveled.

That train took us to Berlin, and we went to a Red Cross camp for displaced people and were fed. My aunt had fled Berlin. I left notes with the Red Cross and filled out cards in case relatives were looking for us. This was in February 1945, and I stayed there until March. It was a most hopeless feeling because there were these sad people trekking and dragging themselves to safety. Berlin was surely not safety.

I went every day to the card files and read notes. I came across an awful lot of cards saying about my parents were last seen and not being able to cross the Odor because the bridges were destroyed and hadn't made it across. They were assumed dead. My father was not going to be caught by the Russians. He had a revolver and was going to shoot himself and my mother and brother because he would not want the Russians to catch them.

After going to the Red Cross every day, I finally found a card from my father instructing me to go immediately to their friends near the city of Magdeburg (fifty miles south). Berlin was being destroyed. The first sight of my father was him plowing a field with two very stubborn oxen. We stayed there in one of the outbuildings until the Russians pressed further forward.

When the war ended, the family moved to Wardenburg in the north, near the North Sea, where Marion found work in nearby Oldenburg. She met Max Holz who later became her husband. Since she was a high school graduate and her English was reasonable, she was placed in a German bakery that had been taken over by the allies. The troops there were British, using the German bakers to do the actual work, but wanting to use their English recipes. Sixty years later, Marion recorded:

> So, every morning I had to come to work early to get all the recipes for the next day's orders translated into German measurements and language. And that happened every day and I had to figure out the quantities.

> There were many allied troops in Oldenburg and several commissaries that needed the baked goods. There were restaurants that served only the troops, and they also needed baked goods.

In 1949, Otto and brother John had gotten permission to immigrate to Canada. Otto was to chaperone about fifteen young men who were seventeen to twenty-two years old on the trip, all being sponsored by the Lutheran church. The church had arranged jobs for all of them. Some were going all the way across Canada to British Columbia.

> Some stayed in Ontario. My father was given a job on a farm. The farmer received money, but they had to work for a year. There was an agreement with the church that they had to work for a year. They had to be paid a certain amount of money so they could pay back the costs for the trip across the ocean.

After a year, Otto and John had earned and saved enough money to bring his wife Inga to Canada. Since Marion was pregnant, she,

Max, and little Inez had to wait to immigrate to Canada until the next year in 1950.

> We stayed in a camp at Bremen to get our medical examinations. Our trip was very rough . . . we were taken across the ocean in a freighter named Beaver Bray—that is imprinted in my brain forever. It was a very steady ship when loaded with wheat. But, loaded with people and luggage, it was very unsteady. A lot of the people aboard were Germans from the southern part of Russia. They were of German origin plus Arabian . . . people who had never seen water, had never been near water, and were seasick while we were still docked.

Arriving after a ten-day voyage through the North Sea and Atlantic Ocean in cold November, Marion and family stayed first with her parents, Otto and Inga. Just a month later, during the Christmas season, Marion had taken a short-term job at a florist shop. She became friends with a lady who worked in the office of the shop. The lady was Jewish and invited the family to their house for a Christmas dinner.

> You must remember that Jews do not celebrate Christmas the way we do. They were practicing Jews. They couldn't eat with us, and they couldn't eat off the plates after we had eaten on them. All the dishes had to be borrowed from somebody who was non-Jewish, and yet, these people did that for us out of the goodness of their heart. And we had a lovely Christmas celebration with a Christmas tree, with gifts under the tree and a special dinner. They didn't eat with us, they didn't partake in the exchanging of gifts, the children and adults were just there to make it for us. It was really very, very special.

Max found a job at a Wonder Bread bakery. He then sold insurance. Another son, John, was born while the family lived in London, Ontario, for the next nine years. They saved and bought two houses and rented the second one out. Max developed cancer on his vocal cords and required surgery. He did recover following a heavy dose of radiation, but the doctor suggested the harsh Canadian climate was not good for Max. Through some of his business contacts, he was able to find a sponsor in San Diego, California, who worked at a Volkswagen dealership. Max and Marion's marriage was not very happy. He really did not want his family to follow him to the States, so he left for San Diego by himself. Marion stayed behind and tried to make enough to support herself and the two children. After a year, she gave in and decided to move to San Diego with the children to be with Max in 1960.

Max had a job and was doing well. They bought a house, the children started school, and things became more normal. Marion started and stopped the tape several times and then said:

> As a European woman or wife, I was used to being under the thumb of my husband, whether I liked it or not—that was the way it was in Europe. In Canada, we were so poor there was no choice for me but to do what I was told. But after living for a while in the US, I found a job in a car dealership and was working and made fairly good wages. We had a house and the kids settled . . . I, all of a sudden, saw how American women lived, or how American families lived, and how much power American women had within the home. Not so much in the workplace, but within the home. And uhm, I rebelled, because I did not want to be held down anymore. I wanted some freedom. I wanted my paycheck. I did not want to turn it over, all of it, and then ask for whatever money I needed for necessities, personal things for myself. So, life became a struggle, a power struggle between Max and me. When Max decided to take our son John to visit Dorcian Venacamp . . . that was the

year I decided to leave Max and make a clean break and struggle on my own with the kids. It was very, very scary, because I still didn't earn much and I didn't know how we would have survived . . . but for a while I became a dressmaker, and I took in sewing. I did alterations. I did drapes, I did slipcovers. I did all kinds of things . . . that was one thing I had learned in Canada. I had worked for a lady from Scotland in Canada . . . But in the evenings, she and I went to a local sewing class at a high school. And I learned a lot. I learned sewing and what I hadn't known before, I perfected. And so, my sewing could earn a living with it.

Marion moved to Coronado, California, where she did a lot of sailing. She met Theodore Harmon and crewed with him on his sailboats. Coronado was a small town, and she made many friends. There were many Navy people there, and she never had any trouble finding enough sewing to do without having to advertise—it was just by word of mouth. Ted had been raised in New York City. His parents had immigrated from Hungary. Through the Depression and World War II, he had many jobs—from a taxi driver to a mechanic for the taxis. He worked for the government at different naval stations as a mechanic, from Quantico to Norfolk, both in Virginia. When Marion met Ted in 1961, he was a twice-divorced bachelor living at Coronado. They married. Ted had raised three children, and Marion had partially raised two.

We had never expected to have a child, but we were very lucky, as on May 17, 1963, our son Mark Frederick was born. Ted never had time to be a father to his kids because he had two jobs, and life was very difficult during the depression years. It was a beautiful experience after all these years having another child for him.

Marion became a United States citizen in 1965. Her life seemed to have become, at last, nearly perfect. Unfortunately, that was not to be.

Ted only enjoyed his son for the first four years of Mark's life. He had an aneurysm, and after many operations, survived, but was not the same Ted.

> He was just a man, an unknown man who sometimes did
> not recognize either of us. He lived in a rehabilitation
> home for four more years and died on Christmas Day 1971.

Marion and young Mark were fortunate that Ted had a good government pension, and with her skill as a seamstress, they survived. Ted had bought a new home when Mark was born, and they were a very happy family for those four years. Marion lamented on the tape recording.

> But it was good, it was a good four years, and I will never
> regret having been married to him and raising a child later
> all by myself. I am proud of myself.

Marion moved to Port Angeles, Washington, in 1981. The area reminded her of her homeland in Estonia. Here she took her talents to another level. She had taken weaving lessons in California. And after taking another course in weaving, she acquired a loom. She joined two weaving guilds and attended many workshops in Port Angeles. Her memories from back in 1939 at the school in Estonia had come full circle. She became a master weaver and instructed over one hundred students along the West Coast to also become weavers. She developed her own patterns and wove a wide range of materials. Her favorite approach was shadow weaving. Her linens and pieces of her handiwork are spread across the country. She was the president of the Olympia Weavers in 1992.

Marion married Frank Rosemeck. Following his death, Marion moved to Colorado, and then to Vermont to be next to her youngest son, Mark, and his family. She volunteered at the hospital and was both a master weaver and master gardener.

Epilogue

Marion died on February 9, 2017, at the age of ninety-two, having spent her tragic young life in Estonia through the six years of WWII, then having shared her adult life, from Canada to America, with three marriages and three children. She lived in four of the most beautiful areas of the country, from Coronado, California; Port Angeles, Washington; the foothills of Colorado; to her final resting place in the Green Mountain State of Vermont.

Marion was an enthusiastic volunteer at the Rutland, Vermont Regional Medical Center for many years. She is survived by two sons, Mark Harmon of Londonderry, Vermont, and Ingo John Holz of San Diego, California; a daughter, Inez Holz of San Diego; a brother, John, in Hamilton, Ontario; one nephew, four grandchildren, and one great grandchild.

Norma Margrit Jutta Jahn
and John Paul Leone

A couple shared their respective experiences as children
during and after WWII: their families' survival stories, their
lives in America, and how they eventually found each other.

"I really didn't like to dance much, but if I didn't try, the other guys would
cut in. In Germany, it seemed that we danced every night."'   —JP

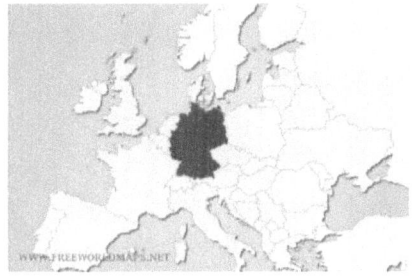

Norma's Story:

Norma was born in Holland in 1942. Her parents were Alfred and Ilse Jahn, who were German. Norma's father, Alfred, was from Bremen in northern Germany. Alfred had been in the German Army since 1939. Her mother, Ilse, had asthma since childhood and a doctor had suggested that regular swimming in the Rhine River might help strengthen her breathing and health in general. She became so adept at swimming that in 1933 she was awarded the German swimming championship and was handed an autographed picture of Adolf Hitler. Although she surely would have made the German swimming team for what was to become the infamous 1936 Berlin Olympics, her father forbade her to live there for the year it would have taken to prepare for the Olympics.

Grandfather Jacob Bollinger worked as a contractor for the Didier Company, which included natural gas furnace factories. In 1905, he married Elizabeth Premm and the Bollinger's lived in Paris, although Jacob went on all his business trips alone. They moved to the Spanish island of Mallorca for ten years (during the First World War) while Jacob's sales business took him to Spain, Paris, Rome, and Poland. The Bollinger's came back to Koblenz, Germany, in 1923 and continued in the furnace business. They built a home there. In 1933, a business opportunity was presented to Jacob, which required relocation to Holland. The Bollinger's were willing to do so, with the stipulation that he would no longer need to travel. Norma's mother, Ilse, and her two sons moved to Holland to live with her parents.

Alfred and Ilse married in 1942 in Holland, and that fall, baby Norma was born. The bombing in Holland brought most Germans back to their homeland by order of Hitler's government. Norma, her mother Ilse, and Grandmother Elizabeth came first to the Ruhr region in Northern Germany where Elizabeth's sister lived.

Norma remembered:

> We were made to go to air raid shelters. Mother was
> allowed to have a bed in the shelter because I was just a

baby. There was no room even to stand in the shelter. Everyone had rosaries and they were praying out loud. Mother got bed bugs from the mattress and itched all over her body. When we came out of the shelters, the terrible smell of sulfur was in the air. My mother decided to take us to the farming country n southern Germany by the Black Forest. We traveled on the train south. She kept me under her coat as much as possible to keep me warm. Mother had terrible sores on her arms and face (from the bed bugs). She told the other passengers that they were from flea bites, which she thought sounded better than bed bugs from the bomb shelters. We saw bombing along the way south and had to get off the train three times to hide for fear of the train being bombed. We came to Trossingen, which I consider my hometown. Only three bombs were ever dropped here; one of them hit a cigarette factory.

Norma, Grandmother Elizabeth, and Uncle Kurt lived in a bowling alley in Trossingen. Norma shared, "I remember there were so many mice that Uncle hit the side of his bed just to quiet them at night. One morning, Mother opened a cabinet, and a mouse jumped and landed down her blouse and stuck in her cleavage."

On January 29, 1945, the beautiful Bollinger home in Koblenz was bombed. "So, we had absolutely nowhere to go back to," Norma recalled, "I was just two and a half years old at the time."

Norma's father Alfred and his family had a different journey. Having lived in Bremen, Germany, Alfred's brothers and sisters had immigrated to the United States in 1926, while Alfred remained in Germany. One brother stayed in New York, and one went to Detroit, Michigan. His sisters moved to Pittsburgh, Pennsylvania. In 1938, Alfred came to America to visit his family. He went back to Germany and witnessed the Kristallnacht on November 9, 1938, when the Jewish shops were burned. Alfred was conscripted into the German Army for the next six years. He fought in Poland, France, and

Moscow. He was in Paris when the Germans marched under the Arc de Triomphe on June 14, 1940. Norma "My father always said the Polish people were the politest," Norma shared.

At the end of the war, Alfred was a prisoner of war at Nuremberg where he became a cook in the POW camp. Trossingen was just a half hour from Switzerland and the Black Forest area in southern Germany near Bodensee Lake. Here he learned that his wife and now three-year-old, Norma, had fled Holland and were subsisting nearby, and he was able to send food packages to them. Norma remembered:

> We had no heat, and each morning my mother had to break the ice on the bucket of water in the kitchen. We had so much less food to eat than during the war. Mother put one of the other children in a pram and went to the countryside to beg for food. Grandmother would not allow her to use me in the pram while Mother went to the farms.

When Alfred was released from the Nuremberg POW camp, he came to Trossingen to find his family. He wanted to go back to his hometown at Bremen in northern Germany. Ilse worked there at a bakery and was able to borrow some flour for the family.

Norma and the other children in the town played in bombed-out buildings. They played on the horse tie rails, doing flips. They had bike races, swam in the river, and did headstands. "I remember sneaking into horse races under the wooden fence," Norma smiled at the memory.

Norma attended school in Bremen and Trossingen depending on whether she lived with her parents in Bremen or with her grandmother in Trossingen. Norma and her grandmother traveled back and forth from Trossingen and Bremen. In the north they spoke Low German, and the dialect in the south was High German. Norma explained, "The language was completely different, so I guess I became bilingual at the age of five. In Trossingen, the boys wore lederhosen. The headmaster often spanked them. I was so afraid I was going to be spanked, too."

Alfred, Ilse, Norma, and little brother Frank came to America and landed in New Jersey on July 31, 1951. Norma reminisced:

I remember all of us had been seasick as hell on that boat. Alfred was interrogated at least three more times about his German Army past and whether he was a Nazi. We all were on pins and needles worrying about him. When he finally was cleared, we were met by my Aunt [*Tante*] Selma and Uncle [*Onkel*] Kurt from Pittsburgh [who had paid for their passage across the ocean]. That was 360 miles away by car. I had never ridden in a car before and would you believe it, I got sick as hell all over again.

We stopped at another Onkel Robert's farm at Shohola, Pennsylvania, on the border of New York in the Poconos. Robert lived in Manhattan and had bought the Shohola farm as a getaway from the city. We all stayed there on the farm a few days and then came on to Pittsburgh. Mother had told me as much as she knew about the city and America. When we first arrived, I asked her, "But where are the golden streets?" I was very worried about coming to America, and often asked Mother, "Are there any Catholics in America?" Mother had always reassured me, "Yes, America is full of them," which I later learned she was only guessing. Well, she was right on this one because there were Catholics everywhere in our neighborhood in Pittsburgh. Mother was Catholic, and my father, Alfred, was a Lutheran.

None of us knew any English. Father got a job as a butler and Mother became a cleaning lady. I (now nine years old) took care of my little brother, Frank, who was four and a half years old. I entered school at Saints Peter and Paul Catholic School in Pittsburgh, which was taught by nuns. At first, I was put in the fourth grade, where my age of kids

were placed. Because of my lack of English, I was put back
in the third grade and I remember being so bored. The
spelling was so remedial because we were forced to write a
word fifty times and then, on Friday, have a spelling test on
ten words. German schools were so much more advanced
because we would read a story and then spell the words. In
German kindergarten it was all about social interaction and
playing. In America, they tried to teach numbers, letters,
and spelling. In Germany, I loved school and always cried
when it was out in May.

Alfred's next job was as a sheet metal worker. He had taken
English lessons to get the job. He then sold windows and doors. He
bought a truck to pick up the windows and take the old ones to the
dump on his days off and after work. In 1977, at the age of fifty-eight,
twenty-six years after coming to America, he opened a window
factory. The business did well and employed more than forty people.

Grandmother Elizabeth Bollinger flew to America at the age of
eighty-seven to visit. She had come three times before by ship and
stayed about a year each time. She had loved our President Kennedy
and was inspired by him. She sent money to many of the Catholic
charities. Norma described her grandmother:

It is incredible to me that she flew for the first time and
came all that way to visit us. She was such a dynamic
woman. Her travels and bravery from Germany, to Holland,
and back to Germany were a testament to her strength
and survivability. She loved American Western movies: *The
Lone Ranger, Maverick*, and anything with John Wayne.

In May 1961, Norma graduated from the Divine Providence Girls'
High School in Pittsburgh, with thirty-seven in her class. She worked
at Hartford Insurance. In 1964, she made her first return trip to
Germany by ship. She later made thirteen more trips back to
Germany. She felt such an immediate love for her former country and

the beauty of the Alps, Munich, and Vienna. It was the same year that the movie *The Sound of Music* with Julie Andrews was released. To Norma, "the hills were truly alive with the sound of music!" She thought, "Hey. Why are we in Pittsburgh?" This twenty-two-year-old *fräulein* got a job at Stuttgart working for the Americans as a secretary at the army post. The Germans paid her salary as part of the war reparations agreement made at the end of World War II. She lived in the barracks in Ludwigsburg, north of Stuttgart.

Who knew, on that first trip back to Germany, that she would meet the love of her life? On the ship crossing the Atlantic, Norma had met an American girl. They became fast friends. Her boyfriend, Jerry, introduced Norma to an American GI, John Paul Leone (JP), at a dance in Stuttgart. Dancing was not JP's thing. But he was instantly attracted to this pretty little outgoing *fräulein* from the States. He, too, was a child of World War II, born in Italy in 1945, the year the war ended.

Norma and JP's first date was to dinner at Wienerwald (a chicken restaurant). Norma had a salad and JP had half of a chicken. "We ate out as long as the money held up, because the food back at the barracks was not the greatest," JP remembered. Before long they were constant companions and dance partners. JP said, "I really didn't like to dance much, but if I didn't try, the other guys would cut in. In Germany, it seemed that we danced every night."

John Paul's story:

How JP came to be an American is yet another story. JP's father, Gaetano Leone, was born in 1916 in New York City. His family moved back to Sicily, which was their native home. When World War II broke out, Gaetano was conscripted into the Italian Army for the next ten years. He met Conforte Bidini in Italy. She was much younger, having been born on June 23, 1923. They married in 1942. Like many Italian soldiers, he first fought against the Americans; then after Benito Mussolini's death and the German and Italian surrender in North Africa, the Italians switched sides and fought with the Americans against the Germans. It was this action that Gaetano always worried about regarding his American citizenship. Since he had been born in the States, and thus, was legally a naturalized citizen, he may have been in trouble with the United States government. He worried, since he had fought along with the Italians and Germans from 1941-1943 against the Americans, that he would be forever expelled from the United States.

The first male born in an Italian family is named after the father's father. The second male born is named after the mother's father. John Paul, or his Italian name, Giani Paolo, was born February 4, 1945, in Caprese Michelangelo (Michelangelo's hometown). Since his father was away at war, JP's mother named him as she wanted. After the war was over for Italy in May of 1945, Gaetano was reunited with his wife and babies, Giani Paolo and Tony, and moved them back to live with his family in Sicily.

In 1947, Gaetano moved back to Brooklyn and lived with his brother, Gaspare. Gaetano borrowed $1,000 to get a ticket for his family to also come to America. He had asked his father for the loan and thought he was good for the money. His father talked it over with an acquaintance who said that one should never loan money to a family member. Thus, the loan for $1,000 had to be secured from others.

On November 14, 1948, the SS *Saturnia* sailed from Genoa to Brooklyn. On board, ship passenger logs show three Leone's:

> *Leone Bidini Comforte (Sic.)—Italian 25 years*
> *Leone Giani Polo (JP) (Sic.)—Italian year 3*
> *Leone Antanio (Sic.)—Italian year 5*

In New York, the family moved in with Uncle Gaspare, Aunt Sadie, and their two children to a three-room apartment in Brooklyn. That made eight people together in this small apartment.

JP started preschool in 1952 at a Catholic grammar school. He then attended St. Barbara's and St. Joseph's schools. In 1963, he graduated from Bushwick High School in Brooklyn. During his senior year, another baby boy, Frank, was born to the Leone family. "Here I was, eighteen years old, and Mama has another baby. Frank turned out to be a brain. Tony and me always asked our dad why he kept all the brains back for our little brother," laughed JP. The family moved to a three-story building in Glendale, Queens, where a store was on the first floor, the Leones on the second floor, and the third floor was rented out. This later became the family's third deli.

In 1954, Gaetano bought a deli in Brooklyn. JP, at the age of nine years, helped at the deli. He barely managed to lift the heavy crates of cold cuts. The fifty-five-gallon barrels full of olives were his daily chores. JP remembered:

> My job was to smash the olives to get the olive oil for the deli sandwiches. I used the bottom of a Pepsi bottle to roll and crush the olives. It seemed like a bottomless barrel or pit. I also candled eggs purchased from Long Island farms. I looked for double yolks, blood spots, and occasionally a half-grown chick. After an hour of intensely staring or candling at these eggs, I felt like I was cross-eyed and could barely focus.

JP enlisted in the American Army in his new country and was sent to Germany in 1964 on a ship. He recalled, "It was a two-week journey. I was sick as hell the whole time. Guess it's good I was not meant for the Navy!" The ship landed at Bremerhaven, and he was sent directly to Würzburg where he was in the infantry. The following year he was sent to Stuttgart to an armor company and worked in supply and mail. That assignment led him to an occupation for his career.

When JP's army tour was up, he left Germany on a military flight on November 22, 1967. This was quite an upgrade from the ship ride three years earlier. He went to Queens, where his parents were living. Then he boarded a bus to Pittsburgh to meet Norma and her parents. They visited with a priest on December 11. He had to report to Fort Bragg in December, and the commander questioned him thoroughly, asking, "Are you sure that you want to get married?" JP was given a weekend pass, and Norma and JP were married back in Pittsburgh on January 12, 1968, at the Blessed Sacrament Church in Eastwood. The new couple traveled by car to the Fort Bragg assignment the next day.

Following JP's army discharge on August 18, 1968, the newlyweds lived for two months with Norma's parents in Pittsburgh and then into a three-room apartment. With JP's four years of army experience and being a veteran, he was able to secure a job as a mail carrier. The next year in 1969, JP's father, Gaetano, asked him to come back to New York to join him in the family business. One week later, JP called him to tell him, "what a son always dreads telling their loving father," that his job at the post office was a good one and he had to decline the offer. JP was very successful with the new job; he retired thirty-two years later as the postal supervisor in Verona, Pennsylvania.

Epilogue

Norma and JP Leone had two sons, born in 1970 and 1972. Brandon also worked for the post office and owns a pizza business. Gregory graduated from Indiana University of Pennsylvania and earned a master's degree from Carnegie Mellon. JP's little brother, Frank, went to Princeton and became a medical doctor (pulmonary specialist), and speaks all over the world at medical societies and universities. He practices in Philadelphia at the University of Pennsylvania.

The Leone's retired to Florida to garden, dance with the best, cruise every chance they can, and even drop a few shekels at the casinos for fun.

A little German girl born in war-torn Germany and a boy with Sicilian and Italian parents each immigrated to America and have contributed to their communities. Their patio in Florida is usually filled with visitors, friends, and a five o'clock crowd.

Nouran Othman

After being forced out of her home by the Syrian Civil War, a young woman followed educational opportunities to the United States.

"When I left to come to America, she held me in her arms and said, 'You will always be a piece of my heart, but I will never stand in your way to better yourself.'" —Nouran

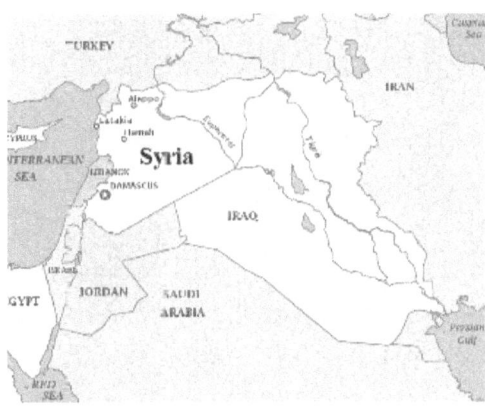

Nouran

Ancient Syria was part of the Roman Empire. Its domination by foreign interventions has more than three thousand years of history. In the four-hundred-year period from 1518 to 1918 (the end of WWI), Syria was part of the Ottoman Empire. Greater Syria, in the final years of Ottoman rule, included present-day Jordan, Israel/Palestine, Lebanon, and parts of Turkey and Iraq.

This Arab country has a majority Sunni Muslim population. The last one hundred years, since the end of WWI, has been a continual turnover of leadership, from military leaders to kings, and for the last forty years until they were overthrown on December 8, 2024, the Assad family. Following the Suez Canal Crisis and the Israeli invasion of the Sinai Peninsula in 1956, Egypt and Syria agreed to unite and became the United Arab Republic, or the UAR. The UAR lasted for only three years.

Internal struggles and conflicts between more conservative groups in the country led to sectarian violence. Numerous wars with Israel, the Syrian occupation of Lebanon, and the Soviet Communist influence fostered further division in the country's leadership. The Arab Spring in 2011 marked the beginning of the Syrian civil war. As of 2024, Syria was being led by a transitional government with more than fourteen million displaced persons. Refugees have been spread across Europe and surrounding Arab countries in the Near and Middle East.

Nouran Othman was born in Damascus, Syria, in 1992. She had two brothers and a sister in her family. Her mother was born in Palestine and had eleven brothers and sisters. She shared, "I had over sixty cousins and our family gatherings were so special. We had wonderful family values and loved each other." Her great-great-grandfather was a general in the Ottoman Army in the 1800s.

Fearing for their safety because of the Syrian civil war, Nouran and her family fled Damascus for Amman, Jordan, in September 2012. They traveled the four-and-a-half-hours trip by car to visit and stay with her mother's sisters who lived there and had married Jordanians.

Since they were living with relatives, they were not considered refugees. Nouran's father did not allow them to return to Syria because ISIS (Islamic State of Iraq and Syria) was coming to Syria and kidnapping girls. She remembered, "It was hard to see my country being destroyed. Our beautiful neighborhood in Damascus was rubble, and chaos existed every day for those left behind."

Nouran's mother had a sixth-grade education. Nouran graduated high school from a Shiite school in Damascus, though she was Sunni. She spoke both Arabic and English. As a twenty-year-old in Jordan, she was able to find a job as a secretary for a family doctor who took care of foreign workers. She met Amy West from Cedar Falls, Iowa, who lived near her aunt. This lady was a United Nations worker and had Nouran act as an interpreter because of her English and Arabic language skills. She helped at a refugee camp, and they became friends. "She knew of my desire for education and to improve myself," said Nouran. The camp was sponsored by Mercy Corps, and she helped start a Girl Scout group at the camp. She was discriminated against in pay because she was Syrian and not Jordanian.

Amy West told Nouran about a program at the University of Northern Iowa called the Culture and Intensive English Program (CIEP). Another friend from Washington DC helped Nouran fill out the forms to get into the program. It was April 2014, and she had missed the deadline for applying by one day. After two years in Jordan, she was finally accepted but had to wait until the spring semester of 2015 to start at the university.

Nouran went to the United States Embassy in Amman and in ten days had a visa to travel and a ticket to fly to New York. She was met at JFK Airport by two friends. One had just graduated from Princeton and the other from Georgetown. She laughed and shared:

> Neither of them knew where Iowa was and said they
> would have to "Google it." After five days with them, I
> boarded a bus for a fourteen-hour trip to Michigan to visit
> my uncle. It was then another fourteen-hour bus trip to
> the Waterloo, Iowa, bus station. I had two suitcases. It was

January, and the blizzard there had shut down the city and the schools were all closed. I was informed that Waterloo had not had taxis for over fifteen years. I did not know how to get to the family that I was to stay with in Cedar Falls, which was about ten miles away. Fortunately, the bus station lady must have taken pity on this stranded and frightened girl and found me a private driver to take me through the nearly isolated streets. I had seen snow in Syria only a few times, and it was always melted in a few hours. This was really a "white out," as I would later hear the term. I arrived at Andrea and Bill Vanderhaar's . . . which was to be my home for the next five months.

The spring semester at the University of Northern Iowa (UNI) started the next week after her arrival in the blizzard storm. Since Nouran had no phone, the Vanderhaar's planned their week together on what time and place they would drop her off and pick her up after class. She had taken English since kindergarten but did not learn to speak the language until coming to America. Her first course of study was with a cultural English program which included reading, writing, and listening for eight weeks. This course was followed with another eight-week semester. Nouran received a scholarship to finish the summer of 2015. She recalled:

I so wanted to go back to Jordan, as I longed for home. I then got the news that Jordan would not let me back. I could have gone to Turkey, but making the arrangements back to Amman seemed impossible. I applied for a work permit job with Rob Green [the mayor of Cedar Falls in 2023]. I found a job that summer doing web design at the UNI Library and Museum. I moved to live with Paul and Kathryn Koople that summer.

In the fall of 2015, Nouran tried to get paperwork to get protected status in the United States. She moved in with the Krukow family and stayed in their living room because they had another student who had the extra bedroom. She then moved into the Alicia and Eric Duncan home for the next eight months where she babysat to help pay the rent.

Nouran waited for a work permit from the US Citizenship and Immigrations Services. She started working for the next two years at Side Car Coffee near the campus as a barista. She was saving her money and babysitting to help pay her rent. She started a third job as a housekeeper at Bickford Cottage, which was an assisted living facility. She was not able to apply for a scholarship because she was not a citizen.

From Nouran's income, she started paying taxes in 2015. She had to pay every year to continue with the Temporary Protected Status (TPS). She did paperwork for the next eight and a half years to maintain her status. She had to drive 120 miles to Des Moines each year and have annual fingerprints taken. She proudly said, "I did this without the help of a lawyer. Over that time, I paid close to $3,000 to continue getting the TPS."

By January 2017, Nouran had saved enough money to go to Hawkeye Community College in nearby Waterloo, Iowa. She became a bank teller that March at Veridian Credit Union. She later would move up to a loan advisor position.

Having applied for asylum in 2015, she had not heard anything about her status for five years. Though she was living in Iowa, she was assigned to the Vermont office with her asylum request. She married another student, William Boelts, in 2019. Together they bought a "fixer-upper" two-story house. As it is the custom in her eastern tradition, Nouran kept her last name. Now, since she had married an American citizen, it was not difficult to get a green card.

After one and a half years at Hawkeye Community College and two full years at the University of Northern Iowa, Nouran graduated with a degree in management information systems, and a second degree in supply chain management.

Nouran applied for fifty-seven jobs. One of those was with RSM McGladrey, a tax auditing company. They had eight different job sites and one of them was in Denver, Colorado. She accepted the Denver job in Data and Digital Application and Consumer Service, where she helped them with coding. The Denver location allowed her husband to continue his graduate studies.

Nouran was the first of her family to leave home. Her mother had married at sixteen years of age. She was divorced when Nouran was sixteen years old. "When I left to come to America, she held me in her arms and said, 'You will always be a piece of my heart, but I will never stand in your way to better yourself,'" Nouran tearfully remembered.

Nouran's brothers were able to flee Jordan by paying fifteen thousand dollars to be accepted as refugees into Canada. They are now Canadian citizens. They were able to get their mother and little sister out of Jordan as well, and they are waiting for Canadian citizenship in Alberta, Canada.

Nouran was able to fly to Canada in the summer of 2022 to reunite with her family for the wedding of her brother. That little piece of her heart was reunited with a special mother who had so willingly and bravely encouraged her daughter to come to America and fulfill her educational dreams.

Epilogue

Nouran Othman became a United States citizen at 8:00 AM, on June 22, 2023, at the Centennial, Colorado, United States Federal Building. She had studied for the test with her husband for two weeks before the interview. There were one hundred questions for the test, and with her husband she was able to answer one hundred out of one hundred correctly. She was disappointed at the interview when they only asked her six questions. The test included an interview and reading and writing sections. She raised her hand and took the oath with thirty-two others from twenty-seven countries. The friend from Jordan, Amy West, who had sponsored Nouran to come to America, was visiting her in Denver and was able to attend the ceremony.

Penelope Gonzalez Quevedo

A young woman from Cuba persevered through political, economic, and personal hardship to pursue her love of working with animals and being a business owner.

"It was crazy how I had started and sold the other two business salons just up the street. And now on Miami Shores, I have a unique Penelopets."

—Penelope

Penelope

Penelope Gonzalez Quevedo was born on August 25, 1977, in Havana, Cuba. Her father went to law school with Fidel Castro. He worked in the Cuban government and was sent abroad to bring business to Cuba. Her mother was in elementary school when the Cuban Revolution broke out. She was able to bypass all the other grades and go directly to university as a result of all people being equal, in alignment with the Soviet regime.

Cuba is the largest country in the West Indies at 777 miles long, 119 miles at its widest, and 19 miles at its narrowest. It is nearly three fourths the size of Florida. Cuba is 90 miles from the Key West shores of Florida, just south of the Tropic of Cancer. Cuba's contemporary history dates to the Spanish landing of Christopher Columbus in 1492. The Indigenous population was estimated at 130 thousand at that time. Much of this Native population was devastated by the white man's diseases and armed conflict. Cuba was the most important source of raw sugar for the Spanish in the eighteenth century.

Spain fought several campaigns to maintain its control over Cuba. They were defeated in 1898 in the Spanish-American War, which was triggered by the sinking of the battleship, USS *Maine*, in Havana Harbor. The war is renowned for the bravado of the Rough Riders, led by Theodore Roosevelt in the Charge of San Juan Hill. Cuba became a United States possession with the Treaty of Paris, signed on December 10, 1898. Although Cuba was soon given its independence, it was still under the shadow of the United States.

The Cuban Revolution began in 1953. The leadership of Cuba under Fulgencio Batista was challenged by a charismatic guerrilla, Fidel Castro, who was fighting from mountain hideaways. On January 1, 1959, Castro proclaimed his leadership in Cuba. In less than two years, Cuba became aligned with the Marxist-Leninist nature of the revolution with close links to the Union of Soviet Socialist Republics (USSR). This isolated Cuba from the rest of the neighboring countries, particularly the United States. Consequently, the US placed an embargo on Cuba that still exists in 2024.

In the 1950s, two thirds of the island country's foreign trade was done with the US. By 1961, only four percent was with the United States. With the fall of the Berlin Wall and the collapse of the USSR, Cuba became even more isolated, causing wide shortages of goods. At the time of the collapse, three fourths of its foreign trade was with the USSR. By the twenty-first century, some of Cuba's restrictive economic and social policies were relaxed.

At the time of the Revolution in the 1950s, the population was five million. Almost seventy years later, it has nearly doubled. During the 1980 Mariel boatlift, over 125 thousand Cubans escaped primarily to the United States, Venezuela, and Haiti. In the 1990s, over 200 thousand became legal US immigrants. Money from these Cubans living in the US was allowed to flow back to Cuban relatives and friends in 1993. Yet another exodus occurred in 1994, when nearly thirty thousand Cubans escaped in another flotilla to the United States.

As a young girl in Cuba during the late 1980s, Penelope was a dancer and took ballet for six years. In a 2023 interview she remembered, "When I was eleven years old, I told my parents that I wanted to leave Cuba as soon as possible. I [wanted] to be free and go to a country with justice." That chance of leaving arrived with an immigration crisis and uprising in Cuba in 1994, when she was sixteen years old. Her choices were to leave or stay and go to college. If she stayed for a college education, she was told she would have to stay until the age of twenty-five. The only others that had a chance to leave were those affiliated with sports if they were under the age of twenty-one.

During the Cuban Raft Exodus in 1994, Penelope's parents knew she was having a long-distance affair with a boy named Gerardo from Mexico. They were soon married, which allowed her to leave and fly to Mexico City with her husband. She was just sixteen years old and moved into Gerardo's parents' family home. Her mother went to a hotel to make an international call to see how Penelope was doing. She believed she was being treated very poorly. After twenty days, she was back on a plane to Havana. Back home in Havana, her mother told her that times in Cuba were not safe, and, worried about a civil war, her mother told Penelope she needed to get out of Cuba. From her mother's balcony, Penelope saw masses of people carrying makeshift boats and rafts on their heads. There were people selling them compasses, water, and life vests.

While making the call from the hotel phonebooth, trying to communicate with Penelope, her mother had met a couple from Mexico who had found her in the lobby crying and tried to console her. They encouraged her to let Penelope fly back with them to Mexico.

Upon arrival again in Mexico City, Penelope stayed with this couple. The woman had a menagerie of animals living in the house. There were monkeys, cats, dogs, rabbits, and snakes. Penelope's first job was as a waitress in a restaurant. She soon had a second job as a nightclub dancer. Since she was not paying for her room, she started to save money. This was short-lived, as the couple divorced. The woman told Penelope she would have to start paying rent. When Penelope retuned from work one night, she found that the woman had broken into her bedroom and taken all her money. Penelope called the ex-husband, who told her to pack up her things and that he would come by after midnight to pick her up. He put her into a hotel at his expense. She had thought the woman was crazy to have all the animals, but while living there she had also purchased a snake for herself. When Penelope packed to leave, of course the snake also came with her.

Penelope continued with her jobs. One night upon returning from work, she found the snake was missing. The snake was found in an adjoining room by the manager. Penelope was evicted. The next morning, she showed up at work with all her belongings in bags. Her coworkers asked, "What are you doing with all of your things?" Luckily, she found a room across from the restaurant where she worked. One problem: it did not have electricity. This did not deter Penelope for long. She found wires and cords hanging down in the hallway corridor. She hooked up the electricity with cords into her room. "Coming from Cuba, I was very raw and had no manners," admitted Penelope.

She was shocked six months later when her mother came to visit from Cuba. She informed Penelope that she had thyroid cancer which had been surgically removed in Cuba. They found another apartment and a friend rented the place next door for her mother. Her mother got a job as a mathematician at Mexico City University.

Penelope shared openly in 2023, "Mexicans are very macho. Being a female from Cuba, I was hit on." She became friends with a man who had horses. She fell in love with his horses. In a riding accident, she broke her arm, but this did not stop her from riding nearly every day. There were many equestrian clubs around Mexico City. She bought a horse for $1,000. Her boyfriend helped her pay for the horse, but not its daily expenses. She named this eighteen-year-old horse Old Habana. She started competing in jumping equestrian events with this horse. "I became part of this family and started teaching kids how to ride. Many of these horses were broken down thoroughbreds from the track, which could be retrained to be jumpers," Penelope explained. She bought a second horse named Tropicana for $500. After training this mare, Penelope sold her for $5,000. Things were going well, and Penelope quit her other jobs.

She became friends with the owner's son. Penelope reminisced:

> I lived nearby and could ride my horse home to eat, and tied her up in front of my place. I felt very lucky, and I am blessed. It was a perfect life. I did this for eight years. I moved to an even more sophisticated club which was more into English pleasure horses. I soon decided I needed to do more with my life. I made the biggest mistake of my life when I met a man, Cesar, who would become the father of my child. We were living together but were not married. One day the call came that Old Habana had died. I needed to move on. Cesar was a model and was making good money. He convinced me that I could also model. We were very well paid. Mexico was like a trampoline—I did not want to live there forever.

On August 13, 2004, when she was eight months pregnant, she and Cesar drove their car more than six hundred miles north from Mexico City to Brownsville, Texas. The law at the time was that the border was open. Cesar was in a detention center in Brownsville for about a week. Penelope was housed in a hotel. The only English she knew was from schooling in Cuba. She had purchased records as a young girl that had an insert with English lyrics to the songs. This taught her a few more English words. Penelope continued with tears in her eyes:

> I had gone to the US Embassy in Mexico City to seek a visa. I was denied a visa but was told I could just cross the border, since I was Cuban citizen. I had known that if a baby was born in the United States, it would automatically become a US citizen. My father, who had previously fled to Florida, had told us to come to Miami to live and come to his home. It was the summer of 2004 when there were four hurricanes which hit the south. The highways were closing behind us for the 1,550-mile trip from Texas to Miami. The summer heat was oppressive, and the hurricane warnings were troubling. When we finally reached my father's place, I cried all night. He was living in a dump in Hialeah. It was terrible, just like living in Cuba. He had left Cuba only to come to another Cuba. I had all my books and things from Cuba sent to the USA. The conditions were horrifying. There were five people living in the house across that street from my father that let us move in with them. They had me clean house for them while I was eight months pregnant.

Penelope's mother sold her apartment in Cuba to get money sent to Miami through a friend. With nearly $50,000, Penelope and Cesar used this money as a downpayment for a house in 2005. Her son Leo was born at a Miami hospital on October 29, 2004, and the expenses were paid by Medicaid. One month later, Penelope's mother came from Mexico City to visit Penelope shared, "Mother was very unhappy that we were not living together with my father. The day that Leo was born, she told me that she had kidney cancer. She died eighteen months later."

When Leo was nine months old, Penelope started working as a dog groomer. She was employed by the salon to drive to the homes of clients and groom their dogs in the backyards or porches. She drove the dog van and did the bathing and assisted the groomers for three months. Soon she had scissors and a clipper in her hands.

She purchased her own grooming tools and books to start grooming on her own. She encouraged Cesar to stay and drive the van for her first salon to the homes where they could groom in the backyards and porches. Her mother had just died. When Cesar left to go back to Mexico, she was left with a baby, no mother, and a mortgage. She had just left the salon where she had been working and started her own business called Orange Grooming at the age of twenty-nine. She worked diligently on her English by listening to radio, television, and the telephone. This business was the same type of grooming from house to house. She was paid forty to forty-five dollars for each grooming, but she had to provide her own transportation. Cesar had helped her in the beginning; however, when he returned to Mexico, she was left high and dry.

She became depressed and sought help from therapists to help her through the pain. "I was very traumatized because Mother had died on the floor. I will remember that scene for the rest of my life. No husband, no mother, and no daycare for Leo," Penelope shared. This young single mother's entrepreneurial life was about to change. She never felt sorry for herself for long. When she met a girl and her husband wanting to start a grooming business, she jumped at the opportunity. They started with an office space where Penelope could focus on her talent for grooming. This was her second business, and it was also called Orange Grooming. She had nearly two hundred of her own clients at the time to be brought into this new office.

Penelope smiled, and shared:

> After one week, I knew that this was not going to work. I
> was doing all the work, and the lady tried to answer the
> phone and make appointments. She didn't even know the
> breeds and would mispronounce the names. She had no
> clue of running a business. I said either you buy me out or I
> will buy you out. After we settled on the agreed buyout, I
> left this business as well. Luckily, I had the two-hundred-
> client list that was still mine. I had just kissed the steps and
> I was again having to go "door to door."

Following this elusive journey toward being self-employed, she met an Italian investor who needed a business visa and offered to invest with Penelope. Just one month after leaving Orange Grooming, with a loan from the Italian for $130,000 for ten years at a very low interest rate, she opened her third business down the street called Pet Mode. In 2023, she proudly shared, "It was the most beautiful place. I did not spend all the loan money. With $20,000 of this money, a retail area and supplies were attached to the salon. Three years after opening, it was awarded the Best of Miami Grooming." In her eight years of ownership of Pet Mode, she had up to seven employees. She was working ten-hour days for six to seven days a week. Penelope said:

> I got employer burnout and business burnout. The building
> had been sold and the rent on the space went from $1,800
> in 2010 to $7,000 per month in the next seven years. I also
> paid a triple-net which was even more than the rent. I
> went back to the Italian and said I could not continue. I
> sold the business to another Italian couple.

Penelope's business acumen and knowledge of the clientele, along with demand for her services, spawned yet another, fourth business called Penelopets, which exists today (in 2023). It has a small office with a portable grooming van parked in front. She said, "It was crazy how I had started and sold the other two business salons just up the street. And now on Miami Shores, I have a unique Penelopets."

In 2013, through a surfer boyfriend, Penelope bought a surfboard for herself and Leo. Since the Atlantic has limited wake for surfing, she then bought an inflatable paddle board. She now goes miles and miles each day out into the ocean. She is known to disappear for three hours by herself out of sight of land by herself. Penelope learned to skateboard even before the paddle board. "I used to walk Leo to school each day while he was riding his board. Then I was returning home and going to work carrying his skateboard. This was crazy, so I started skateboarding home," she recalled. Obviously, her ballet talent, equestrian balance, and athletic ability was useful.

Epilogue

Leo was enrolled in ballet, much as Penelope had been as a child. He took ballet lessons for five years and performed in *The Nutcracker* at the Adrienne Arsht Center.

His talents were noticed, and he received a scholarship to the arts school called the Miami Arts Charter School. He graduated from high school in 2023. Penelope worked toward getting her General Educational Development (GED) so that she graduated from high school at the same time as Leo.

This dynamic young immigrant is an incredible example of how one can persevere and overcome many obstacles with hard work. She has become an American, a successful leader, and businesswoman. She has achieved success in ballet, equestrian jumping, surfing, skateboarding, and her business ventures. Today, this forty-five-year-old immigrant is an incredible example of how one can persevere and overcome many obstacles with hard work. She has an ear for languages and speaks Italian, Spanish, French, and English. She said, "The greatest success is in raising, as a single mother, a very talented son, Leo."

Penelope has a goal to attend college. With her drive and resolve, this goal will also be reached.

Peter L. and Bengta Anderson

After moving with his young family to America in pursuit of its opportunities, a Swedish man with carpentry skills became a pillar of his community of Swedish immigrants in Swedesburg, Iowa.

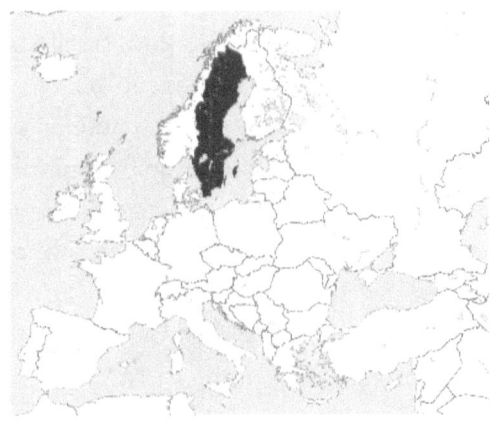

Peter and Bengta

In the late fourteenth century, Sweden, Denmark, and Norway formed the Kalmar Union. Ties to this union lessened leading up to the election of a Swedish king. The end of the Kalmar Union occurred in 1523, when Gustav Vasa led a Swedish rebellion, deposed King Christian II from the throne, and declared Sweden's independence.

Sweden became a great military power, and its involvement in the Thirty Years' War (1618-1648) determined the political and religious balance of power in Europe. Sweden's power extended into modern Estonia, Latvia, and Northern Germany. In the seventeenth century, Sweden's wars with Denmark, Norway, Russia, and the Polish-Lithuanian Commonwealth allowed Sweden to directly control the Baltic Region. This Swedish Empire was crippled in 1721 from The Great Northern War, which ended with the treaty of Nystad. This resulted in Russia's annexation of Estonia, Livonia, Ingria, and Karelia. By 1809, Finland was also lost to Russia. In 1817, Finland declared its independence.

The last war Sweden fought in was the Swedish-Norwegian War of 1814, which forced Norway into a personal union with Sweden. This union continued for nearly one hundred years until 1905, when Norway once again broke away from Sweden.

In 1850, ninety percent of Sweden's population lived in the countryside. Cholera, dysentery, typhus, and smallpox were frequent health problems in the area. However, from 1850 to 1910, what had been a stagnant rural society was changing into a vibrant industrial society. As a result, the agricultural economy gradually changed from communal villages to a more efficient private farm-based agriculture. This resulted in less manual labor, and many citizens moved to the cities.

Emigration out of Sweden became a hope for a better life. Over 1.3 million Swedes came to America from 1840 to 1930. They came for social and economic opportunities. Among other causes for leaving Sweden: the population of the lower classes was growing, the enclosure movement was regrouping the peasant farms, and a religious awakening movement was reforming the state church.

Sweden's current land size of 170,068 sq. mi. is the same size as the states of Minnesota, Iowa, and Wisconsin combined. Their knowledge of traveling for eight to ten weeks across the Atlantic by ship was limited. The voyage from the Baltic Sea into the North Sea, and around the British Isles to America, was much longer than those leaving from Western European countries.

Peter Anderson was born on January 25, 1838, in Stoby Kristianstad, Sweden. He married Bengta Persdotter in 1859. They were living on a small farm with many rocks, surrounded by trees and lakes. Making a living from farming was difficult in those times. Peter came to America in 1866. The next year, Bengta and their three young daughters—Hannah, age 8; Nilla, age 6; and Ellen, age 4—came to America to join him. They first came to Monmouth, Illinois. In 1869, they went west about sixty miles, crossing the frozen Mississippi River to settle in Freeport, Iowa, which was later renamed Swedesburg. Nothing is recorded about that journey to Iowa, such as whether they had come in a wagon or on foot.

The land around Swedesburg in Henry County, Iowa, was poorly drained and was not deemed the best land for farming. The new immigrants knew from their life in Sweden that the land could be drained to make it much more productive for crops. They trenched the farms and laid wooden, ten-foot tiles end to end using their woodworking skills. Those tiles were from the oak trees in the area. They were four inches, square-shaped, and hollowed out either by drilling a bore down the middle or burned out with hot rods.

In Sweden, the family surnames were determined by the father's first name. A man would pass on his name to his son—thus, for instance, the name Peterson. To his daughter, it would be Petersdotter until she was married. This family naming was also traditional in the other Scandinavian countries, Norway and Denmark. The families in Swedesburg had surnames such as Carlson, Olson, Johnson, and Larson.

Peter Anderson was a carpenter. Since he was one of three Peter Anderson's in Swedesburg, he became known as Peter L. to the community. He helped build many of the pioneer homes and farm buildings, and he designed and built the steeple of the second church in Swedesburg after the first church had been destroyed by fire.

During their first year in Swedesburg, Peter and Bengta's infant son died. Peter made a wooden coffin for him, which led him to become the community undertaker. He made metal emblems which were used to decorate the coffin. Early settlers did not embalm. The body was first placed in a cooling basket. Such cooling coffins were used for the first few hours or days after death until the body was placed in a coffin. One of Peter's cooling coffins and his metal casket ornaments are on display at the Heritage Museum in Swedesburg. Peter also was the Justice of the Peace in Swedesburg for fifty-six years, from 1870 to 1926. He was the last one in town to wear wooden shoes.

Neither Peter nor Bengta returned to Sweden to visit their relatives left behind when they immigrated to America. Their great-granddaughter, Louise Tolander Unkrich, has traveled to Sweden ten times. At the age of ninety-eight in 2022, she shared, "I have visited Sweden and met with many relatives and cousins who were descendants of my great-grandparents. I was only two years old when Great-Grandfather Peter L. died, so I cannot remember him."

Peter L. would have loved his great-granddaughter, Louise. She graduated from Olds High School just north of Swedesburg, the spring after Pearl Harbor in 1942. She went directly to drafting school in Des Moines for four weeks and was soon employed at Glenn L. Martin Bomber Plant in Omaha, where she riveted the ailerons on the B29 airplanes. In 2023, she visited Hawaii as "Rosie the Riveter" for a Pearl Harbor memorial service. Louise passed in April of 2024.

More than 200 thousand of the Swedish immigrants to America eventually re-emigrated back to Sweden. Over ninety percent of the Swedish immigrants to the US came to Illinois, Minnesota, Iowa, and western Wisconsin. The 1900 US census showed Chicago as the city with the second largest Swedish population in the world, behind Stockholm.

Ruth L. Jameson

Born to a father who traveled for work, a young Bolivian girl moved around the world with her family before getting her degree at Oxford and finding fulfillment through her family, social work, and the arts.

". . . This was a program funded by Medicaid. I worked in schools and homes with families, helping them with their daily needs, education, and nutritional necessities. I loved that job, more than anything in my whole life." —Ruth

Ruth

In 1958, Alan Jameson was an officer in the Royal Navy of Britain and was stationed at an outpost in the Andes Mountains of Central Bolivia. He was experiencing a tooth problem and was directed to a village clinic. His French friend, Jacques, accompanied him as his interpreter, as Alan's Spanish was limited. At the clinic, a strikingly attractive woman in a white uniform met him. He presented his problem, thinking that the lady in white was a nurse. He mistakenly insulted her by saying that he did not want to see a nurse but a dentist. She shortly affirmed that she was the dentist, and asked if he would accept treatment from her. This dentist was Myriam Ondarza. Her father was a college professor, and she was doing her service year following dental school at this distant village. Myriam did treat the abscessed tooth but was adamant and thought, "I will get even with this gringo for thinking that I was just a nurse!" Alan, however, was smitten and infatuated with Myriam's beauty and pursued her. Her parents were not impressed and tried to dissuade her from this handsome Brit. Her father warned that Alan probably had a wife back in England and would just love and leave Myriam. Alan and Myriam were married in 1959. Myriam was a devout Catholic and Alan converted to her faith.

Ruth L. Jameson was born on August 31, 1960, in Cochabamba, Bolivia, a city at 8,000 ft. elevation. When Ruth was nine months old, her father was reassigned to England and worked for a defense contractor, Bristo Helicopters. Alan, Myriam, and baby Ruth moved to Andover, England, near Southampton and Stonehenge. Ruth remembered, "As a kid, we climbed all over the Stonehenge rocks. Today there is a retaining fence forbidding anyone from using the ancient edifice as a playground."

Myriam and the baby were left alone as Alan was reassigned to Iran with the helicopter company. Myriam had never seen snow and nearly froze from discomfort in this new climate. Her English was limited. She was welcomed by a few neighbors who were amazed that she wore shoes since she was from Bolivia.

Ruth began kindergarten in Andover. The next year she and her mother joined her father in Iran. She continued her elementary schooling at a British school in Tehran. She completed high school at Rustam Abadian, a private school in Tehran for expatriates. She graduated in 1975 at the age of fifteen. As a woman in Iran, of course, her mother could not work. This was during the time when Iran was ruled by Mohammad Reza Shah Pahlavi (Shah of Iran). The British and United States were aiding in trying to modernize Iran. Ruth explained, "When American or British women would go to the open bazaar and wore Western clothes, the Iranian men would urinate on them. After such incidents all the women and girls wore the 'chador' to cover their head and face."

Alan had two-year contracts which he regularly re-signed to stay with the company in Iran. A side benefit was that he was able to get airline tickets at a deep discount. Myriam, Ruth, and her little brother John went every summer to Bolivia, Ireland, Chicago, and Rome, where Myriam's family lived. Her brother was Bolivia's ambassador to Italy in Rome.

After high school in Iran, Ruth attended Malvern St. James Girls' College in England. She was bored and wanted something more stimulating. With the help of her parents, Ruth was accepted at Oxford University. She was a very smart student, but was intimidated because she had to wear a colored necktie designating that she was a very young student. She suffered from depression and anorexia. She graduated in two years at the age of eighteen with a bachelor's degree in political science and a minor in education in 1978. She spoke five languages: English, Spanish, French, Italian, and Farsi.

Ruth moved to Rome in the summer of 1978 to live with her uncle Franz, the Bolivian ambassador. The political environment was becoming tense for foreigners. Ruth became a translator for the food and agriculture division of the United Nations. She took a one-year short course to become a simultaneous translator and interpreter. She worked in all the embassies in Rome until 1981. "It was good money—very good money," she shared. At the American Embassy, she was shocked by a six-foot three United States marine who was assigned as a sentry at the embassy. He flirted with her and begged to have her phone number and address. Ruth rebuffed his aggressiveness and moved on about her business. A month later, while going up the steps at the Campidoglio in Rome, she met this same marine again. He greeted her and said he would like to meet her for dinner and socialize. This seemed much like her mother's experience in Bolivia and her happenstance meeting with the British naval officer. Ruth gave in to the marine's pleading for a date. Seven months later, Ruth married Ken Becker at a civil ceremony in Rome. Ruth's mother was in Lagos, Nigeria, at the time, as Alan had been assigned there. He had been one the of the very last westerners to be evacuated from the revolution in Iran in 1979. Myriam warned Ruth, "You are not going to marry that guerilla. You will live poor." Again, there was a difference of religions. Ken was a Baptist.

The Marine Corps did not take kindly to a marine marrying a local while on active duty. Ken was busted from staff sergeant to corporal, and was reassigned back to the States to the desert at Twentynine Palms, California. On the way, the newlyweds stopped in Andover, England, to meet Ruth's parents for Christmas. Myriam had never met Ken and could not believe they were married. She was quite upset that they were going to sleep together.

The newlyweds next landed at Ken's parents' in Peabody, Kansas, for a month while all the paperwork on the transfer was completed. Ken's mother was extremely rude, cruel, and cold to this new foreign and Catholic girl. Ken's father and relatives told her to ignore the mother-in-law, and they tried to welcome Ruth with open arms. Ruth started cooking for all the meals, as the mother-in-law worked in Hesston and the father-in-law ran a body shop.

Ruth told of her experience with the in-laws in Peabody:

> My mother was a gourmet cook, and I was nearly as good.
> Nothing I ever prepared for the meals was ever good
> enough for this spiteful woman. I once made Scotch eggs
> which are hard cooked, covered with sausage, covered

with breadcrumbs, anc deep fat fried. Again, this woman turned up her nose and put it in the waste can. Maybe it was also because at the time I was cutting my hair like Princess Diana And if I may say, I was nearly as pert as Di. Ken left for Twentynine Palms and arranged for government housing.

Ken sent for Ruth to join him in California. After only two days together, he was sent to maneuvers for six months. He returned only two days before their first daughter, Kelly, was born at the military hospital after a twelve-hour labor. "Ken called me 'My High Desert Queen,'" Ruth said with a smile.

That December 1982, Ken got out of the marines and headed back to Peabody, Kansas. Ken's father had promised him a job at the body shop which did not materialize. He found a job as a cop in Ottawa, Kansas, in the fire and police department.

For the next fifteen years, many job changes and moves occurred:

- 1983: Ken took a position as a cop in Ottawa, Kansas.
- 1986: Patrick was born in a hospital in Lawrence, Kansas.
- 1988: Ken found a job in Gilbert, Arizona, as a cop. Ruth became an interpreter for the Arizona Court System. She became a friend of many of the judges.
- 1988: Jessica was born in Mesa, Arizona.
- 1989: Ken, Ruth, and the children moved back to Cassoday, Kansas, into a tiny farmhouse which was Ken's grandmother's place. Ken did construction; Ruth was now a mother of four and could not find a job.
- 1991: The family moved to Marion, Kansas. They bought a house, and Ken was doing construction again.
- 1992: Ken became a cop in Hesston, Kansas, and Ruth taught grades one through five.

In 1998, Ken was airlifted to Wichita with a case of pancreatitis. He was hospitalized for one month. Ruth often made the one-hour trip to his bedside with the four kids in tow. He was making a slow recovery and progressing well. Ruth received a call at school that Ken had a heart attack. She was told it was a staphylococcus infection from a possible dirty needle. Ken died shortly after Ruth arrived at the hospital in Wichita. Ruth shared with tears in her eyes, "I remember it like it was yesterday. It broke my heart." Ruth and the children moved back to Bolivia to be with family.

Ruth was not a US citizen and only had a green card. She was required to come back to the States every two years to maintain this status. Her parents had a beautiful home in Bolivia and helped Ruth find a house three doors away. She started teaching in a non-denominational school, grades one through five. She noticed a boy with bruises and saw his mother in church with black eyes and bruises. Ruth made a house call to assist the lady and son to get help from an abusive man in their home. This man, in a drunken state, returned home while she was there. He pushed Ruth out a window where she landed on both feet. "I could feel the crunch and looked to see the bones coming out of both of my heels and feet," she said. The mother and son were placed in a safe house. The man was sent to jail.

Ruth underwent surgery where the ball from her hip was removed to reconstruct the fractured tarsal joint. Upon regaining consciousness, Ruth was informed that a nerve in the hip had been damaged and she would never walk again. After six months in a wheelchair and walker, a determined Ruth waited for a recovery. One morning, she felt a tingling in her left thigh, and she slowly wiggled the foot. Elated by this movement, she did not mention it to her mother and family. A few days later the same sensation penetrated down the right leg. She stood and placed weight on both legs. That day, she used crutches and opened the French doors to the veranda. She pushed away the crutches and greeted the family around the breakfast table. Four months later, she was walking.

Ruth and the children moved back to the States to maintain her green card status. Back in Marion, Kansas, she resumed teaching. "It was the only thing I knew," she lamented. After completing a one-year course, she earned yet another degree which made it possible to apply and become a social worker for the State of Kansas in social rehabilitation services. Ruth said:

> This was a program funded by Medicaid. I worked in schools and homes with families, helping them with their daily needs, education, and nutritional necessities. I loved that job, more than anything in my whole life. My mother had always been so involved in service to the community in Bolivia. I just felt it was an extension of her love and concern for others—and I was getting paid for it.

Ruth was known to her friends as Ruthie. Her extraordinary passion for helping others drew the attention of her boss, who encouraged her to follow him to the Kansas City, Kansas, office in the Social Rehabilitation Services program. In 2010 Ruthie moved to Kansas City, where she was a program consultant working in schools. She reached out with her many language skills. She spent half-days in the schools and half-days in the clinic. This was the Kansas Department for Children and Families. It dealt with food stamps, cash assistance, and medical care for families. "I was out in the community and became so disgusted with the office personnel because they were so ignorant of the needs in the community. Some were cruel and considered it their duty as if it was their money," said Ruthie.

She shared a quote she loves of Thomas Jefferson: "In matters of style, swim with the current; in matters of principle, stand like a rock."

"Though this quote is well over two hundred years old, it was my feeling in helping families. They loved me because I cared, and helped them with their needs," Ruthie beamed.

Epilogue

In 2013 another dream for Ruthie, who also loved art, was fostered at Crossroads 504 E. 18th Street in Kansas City, Missouri. Her showroom became an opportunity for young artists to display their work. She started the Free Art First Friday program for artists. It was one of twelve such programs in the country. The requirement was to distribute art literally on the first Friday of each month throughout the community and outlying towns and area. The only requirement to show art at Gallery 504 was for the artist to first give away ten art pieces through the First Friday program.

There were three planned monthly events at Gallery 504. The first was Free Art Friday. Second, a monthly jam session for musicians to gather and share their music with others. The third event was Poet Night, held monthly. There were six walls at the studio for the artists to display their work.

With the Covid pandemic, social distancing, and the national dilemma of unknown circumstances, Gallery 504 closed. Ruthie looks back on all the wonderful artists and the contributions that they have made to America, her new country. First Friday Art is still an active and viable event in greater Kansas City.

I do have things about America that are troubling to my soul. The upheaval of the 45th President's administration and the divisiveness made me yearn for the safe highlands of Bolivia. I still have a home there, though my family is all here in America. A recent experience at the grocery store made me know that there are elements here that are not welcoming, and rather hateful and ignorantly intolerant of others. I was wearing an old *Planet Earth* t-shirt, when a gruff man in the checkout line spoke to me. He said, "So you are one of those earthy hugger people?" I was taken by surprise but was able to respond with a smile and said, "Well if that means that I do have a warm love for this planet and hope for more centuries of mankind and my family, well yes, I guess I am one of those kind. You have a nice day."

Ruthie lives with her new husband of two years, her ninety-four-year-old father, Alan, (Daidí, as she calls him,) and a ten-year-old grandson in a suburban Kansas City home. The walls are decorated with a living gallery showcasing beautiful art from around the world. While in Kansas City on the First Friday of each month, one will see this lady's work—bringing her contribution of service to America.

From the Bolivian Highlands, to England—to Iran—to Rome—to Kansas, California, and back to Kansas, a life of ups and downs and contributions made to her new country, Ruthie L. Jameson helps others and her personality beams with love.

On a visit to Genersich family church
pew in Hungary, circa 2015

Sandor Genersich

A Hungarian boy navigated his home country in WWII before
immigrating to the US to escape communism. His work ethic and
family led him to a successful career in business.

*"When the Americans liberated us, the chaos and immediate danger
lessened. We were freed, but over 150 miles from our home back in
Hungary. Bela was a prisoner of war and worked in the kitchen as a cook.
He was able to smuggle food out for mother, sister, and me to survive . . ."*

—Sandor

Sandor

The Habsburgs governed the Austro-Hungarian Empire as a monarchy for three hundred years until 1918. This vast empire included present-day Croatia, Bosnia, Herzegovina, western Romania, Hungary, Austria, Czech Republic, Slovakia, southern Poland, and Slovenia.

In the summer of 1914, Austria-Hungary citizens, along with most Europeans, suddenly found themselves at war. They were no strangers to the scars of armed conflict like the one following the annexation of Bosnia-Herzegovina in 1908.

The assassination of the heir to the throne—Archduke Franz Ferdinand and his wife, Sophie, at Sarajevo, Bosnia, on June 28, 1914—sparked the beginning of World War I. Seven young Serbian anarchists had planned the plot in Belgrade, Serbia. Just weeks later in July 1914, Austria-Hungary declared war on Serbia with Germany's help.

In statistical terms, the empire mobilized close to eight million for military service between August 1914 and November 1918. Nearly 1.5 million were killed, either in combat or while in captivity. Wounded totaled 620 thousand, and over two million were captured by enemy forces. The war left few families or communities unaffected.

World War I officially ended with the Treaty of Versailles on June 28, 1919. For weeks before the signing, negotiations were being had and agreements were drafted as quickly as possible, as the warring countries tried to find a solution for the Austria-Hungary territory. The Treaty of Trianon in 1920 carved up the Austro-Hungarian territory, and the Habsburg Empire officially dissolved. Hungary lost two thirds of its territory and two thirds of its inhabitants, primarily along language lines. In the east, Romania was given Transylvania and Bukovina. To the north, Poland was given the Galicia region. Austria's new borders included the German-speaking regions of Bohemia, Moravia, and most of Burgenland (western Hungary). A new country took a vast area to the northwest and became Czechoslovakia, which was given Slovakia, Subcarpathian Ruthenia, the region of Pressburg (German: *Bratislava*), and other minor sites. The Kingdom of Serbs, Croats, and Slovenes (Yugoslavia) took Croatia, Slavonia, and part of Banat. The Fiume region was absorbed into Italy. Present-day borders are all that remain of Hungary, with Budapest as the capital.

Kalman Genersich served in the Hungarian Army during WWI. He was a lawyer. After the armistice in November 1918, Kalman returned to his home. His family were now refugees in the newly-defined border area to the north in now-renamed Czechoslovakia. They were deported, or forced to relocate, further south into Hungary. Kalman became a police chief in his new community. His son, Bela, was now fourteen years old and he enrolled in a military school. Bela entered the army and served until 1933. Bela became a worker for the city of Esztergom.

Sandor Genersich was born on May 4, 1933, in Esztergom, Hungary. His parents were Bela and Esther Genersich.

When Germany invaded Poland on September 1, 1939, Hungary refused to allow German troops to cross the border they shared with Poland. The Polish refugees and Jews fled south from Poland into Hungary. With Regent Nicholas Horthy and Prime Minister Pál Teleki, Hungary stayed out of the conflict until June 1940, when the Soviet Union (USSR) occupied Bessarabia. The Hungarian leaders compelled a reluctant Germany to cede to Hungary's northern Transylvania. They then allowed German troops to cross Hungarian territory into southern Romania, and in November 1940, signed the Tripartite Pact, joining the Axis Powers.

In this 2021 interview, Sandor remembered, "Romania had started fighting the Russians first, hoping to bring Hungary along. They [Romania] bombed Hungary using Russian planes at Kassa on the Slovak border. Others blamed the Germans for the bombing."

On June 22, 1941, Hitler's operation Barbarossa, the invasion of Russia along a 1,600-km (1,000 mi) front, began at 3:00 AM. Hungary declared war on the USSR five days later and was sucked into the ill-fated conflict. Sandor recalled, "I was eight years old at the time. My father, Bela, went off with the army."

Hungary sent a token force to help the Germans in what everyone thought it would be a short battle. The Germans were being bogged down by a brutal winter, poor roads, poor reinforcements, and a better-equipped Russian defense. Hitler forced Hungary to mobilize all its available manpower and sent them to battle the Soviet Union.

By January 1943, the Hungarian forces were crushed by the USSR and lost nearly everything at Voronezh in western Russia. Bela fought for the Axis Forces. After three years of fighting along the eastern front, the Germans retreated west through the same one thousand-mile front they had invaded in the summer of 1941, with the Soviets in pursuit. The rape and pillage of the countryside first by the Germans going east, and then by the pursuing Russians moving over the same countryside, was horrific.

Sandor remembered the times:

> My dad, Bela, was a motor pool officer. He organized the retreat effort to move motorized vehicles west into Austria. As the Soviets neared the Carpathians, Hitler decided he could not leave his vital communications at the mercy of untrustworthy regimes. In May 1944, he offered [Nicholas] Horthy [Hungary's leader] the choice between full, undisguised occupation with treatment like an enemy or full cooperation with German supervision. While Horthy was in Berlin, the occupation of Hungary began by Germany.

As the USSR rolled through Hungary, they raped tens of thousands and sent many to Gulags—forced labor camps—for ten to twenty-five years. These were all violations of the Geneva Convention.

Sandor continued:

> On Christmas Day, 1944, with Bela the commander of the motor pool, they tried moving vehicles west. It was the Christians against the Communists. The Russians

surrounded Budapest. was eleven years old. With mother Esther and my sister, also named Esther, who was now eighteen years old, we all evacuated Hungary. By Easter Sunday—April 1, 1945—we were in Linz, Germany, just five weeks before the war ended. I remember the Germans celebrating Roosevelt's death on April 12. We all were sent into military camps. There were Austrian soldiers dressed in German uniforms who robbed us of all our money and jewelry. When the Americans liberated us, the chaos and immediate danger lessened. We were freed, but over 150 miles from our home back in Hungary. Bela was a prisoner of war and worked in the kitchen as a cook. He was able to smuggle food out for mother, sister, and me to survive. By October 1, 1945, we started heading back to Hungary. Just like the soldiers, we bought food from the farmers along the way. At one farm, a crippled old woman greeted us. Father noticed in an adjoining shed a tarp was pulled over a vehicle. It was one of the trucks that dad tried to evacuate from Hungary the year before. The woman said, "The Americans let me have (truck) because they 'made nice' to me!"

Bela was separated from the family for interrogation to determine if he was a Nazi. Sandor found himself the head of the family at age thirteen. By the spring of 1946, Sandor, Esther, and his sister made it back to Hungary from Germany. He enrolled at St. Benedicts Catholic School. At the time there were forty such Catholic schools in Hungary. Just three years later, with the Communists in control, there were only eight schools remaining. When Bela was released by the Russians, he made his way back to Esztergom. He found work in a factory.

In 1949, Bela and sister Esther, now twenty-three years old, were arrested by the Communists because of their military background. Sandor was kicked out of school because he was the son of Bela. The Russians confiscated everything. Some people were able to keep their homes, but the Genersich's were all forced to live in a small, one-room flat with six people.

By late summer 1949, a new constitution was promulgated by the USSR on August 20, which was Hungary's traditional St. Stephen's Day. It specifically had the goal of transforming the national holiday connected to Hungary's Christianization into the politically inspired Constitution Day with this new constitution (Hungary had been a republic since February 1, 1946). It now became a "people's" republic.

In May and June 1951, 12,700 upper and middle-class people were driven out of their apartments in Budapest and deported to small villages on the Great Alfold or scattered to labor camps on mud flats. Churches were forced to close their schools and the schools were nationalized. The Calvinist and Lutheran churches accepted financial arrangements imposed by the State. The head of the Roman Catholic Church, Cardinal Jozsef Mindszenty, had refused to follow their example and was arrested in December 1948. He was condemned to life imprisonment. Monastic orders were dissolved until finally the Roman Catholics accepted financial terms.

A friend of Esther's informed her that it might be possible to get Bela and sister Esther out of prison if she appealed their case to a judge and begged forgiveness. When Esther went before the Jewish judge with Sandor at her side, the judge's wife cried out, "Esther is that you?" Yes indeed, she recognized her even this many years later after they had been kindergarten classmates thirty years before. The judge's wife promptly started nursing a baby in front of them while Esther was pleading forgiveness from the judge. While the interrogation was proceeding, another child, about five years old, started nursing after the baby was full. The appeal for Bela and young Esther's release was promised after Esther gave the judge a gold watch. Sandor remembered, "On the way back to our flat, mother tried to explain the nursing incident to me. Her words still resonate to me, 'Dear, that is what the Jewish people do, and they do not think anything about it.'"

Bela's friend, Nadar, was a Communist organizer. At the age of seventy, Nadar had been a Communist since 1914. He hired Sandor as a mechanic without pay for eighteen months. He also repaired cash registers. One day a man came for his cash register. Nadar quickly grabbed an oversized screwdriver and acted like he was working on it. He told the man, come back in one week with fifty pounds of potatoes and it will be fixed. He ardently and frequently told Sandor how great the Communist system was. He always touted his pocket Communist red book. After many months of working for Nadar, the Communists nationalized everything. Sandor shared, "They took Nadar's car, house, and business. In front of me, he tore up his red book and threw it in the fire, and blurted, 'Communism is like a nice red apple—take a bite, and it is rotten!' I could not wait to get home to tell my mother what he had said."

Esther, Sandor's mother, had a cousin who was a Czech communist. She contacted him to see if he could help get Sandor a job. This cousin had lost his wife in the war. He told Esther to have Sandor meet him at the front gate of the company and he would let him in. He introduced himself and gave Sandor a job milling machinery at a tool and die company for the next four years.

On October 23, 1956, a student protest march in Budapest incited the police to fire into the crowd. Cardinal Mindszenty was released, the prisons were opened, and peasants went back to their farms. The communists seemed to melt away. On November 1, the government, now with Imre Nagy back in power, announced withdrawal from the Warsaw Pact. They asked the United Nations to recognize Hungary as a neutral state. Within three days, Soviet tanks entered Budapest and began liquidating the revolution. Casualties greater than 20 thousand and more than 2,500 deaths were recorded in the next few weeks. More than 200 thousand refugees fled to the borders, of which 38 thousand of them came to North America.

Sandor continued to work at the milling company. In this interview, sixty-five years later, Sandor told:

> I was under suspicion of activities which I do not care to
> share. I had contact with a Polish driver who was working
> for the Russians. I asked if he could make me papers to

get out of the country. He tells me that he had the commanders' keys in his pocket. He came back within an hour with a typed letter which allowed me to get to the border. I gave my key to my mother and left the same day by foot. I met up with four other men who were escaping, too. We hitchhiked and were picked up by a Russian Army truck and rode on the top.

We were stopped several times and the incredibly young Russian guards looked at our papers like they really knew what they were doing. Back at home, mother told me that the Russians knocked on our door the night that I left looking for me. All five of us escapees then boarded a train and took it to the Austrian border. We asked a farmer if he could get us across the border. He located a mailman who took us across and got us to Vienna. I was sitting in a train on a sidetrack heading west, when I spotted a guy who recognized me standing on the platform below the window. I was looking out. I yelled to him "Have you seen my parents?" He pointed across to the other side track and shouted, "Look who is waving at you!" There were both Esther and Bela waving frantically with excitement.

Sandor, Bela, and Esther boarded the USS *Haan*, a troop ship, on Christmas Day, 1956. They landed at Ellis Island, New Jersey, on January 7. They were told since it was a Sunday that the Red Cross had taken the day off. All the refugees had to spend another night on the cold troop ship. After being processed at Ellis Island, they were taken to Camp Kilmer, New Jersey. They were fortunate to identify a sponsor who was a surgeon in Chicago. His name was Janika Ertl. His father was also a Hungarian doctor and had taken Sandor's tonsils out in Hungary when he was five years old. During the First World War, the senior Dr. Ertl discovered on the battlefield the "Ertl Procedure" for saving battered and injured limbs of soldiers.

The threesome—Sandor, Bella, and Esther—left for Grand Central Station in New York and boarded a train headed west to another big city they had never seen. Sandor said:

> We each had a sign around our necks saying our names
> and that we were headed to Chicago, as none of us knew a
> word of English. We just sat there like a piece of luggage
> and when we were told we were in Chicago, we were
> escorted off the train. Disembarking at Union Station, we
> were directed to a waiting area and met a cousin, William
> Genersich, who was Bela's brother's son.

Using the yellow pages, William was able to find Dr. Ertl's name and telephone number and called him to come get the three Genersich's. He came to the train station and met them. Upon joining the Ertl's at their home, they were welcomed and had the first comfortable bed since fleeing Hungary some two months before.

Bela was too old (fifty at the time) and was unable to find a job because he was a liability at his age. He became a gardener. In a short time, he became involved with a business that shipped flowers across the country. Esther became a cleaning lady. They had moved into an apartment in Hillsdale on the western edge of Chicago.

On the first day in Chicago, William had lined up a job for Sandor at Idola Rubber Company in Chicago. For the next two years, he took the train to Western Avenue, where his job entailed replacing the rubbers on printers. He was next assigned to the plant where the rubber nipples for milking machines were made. They were processed in large vats which had to be cleaned with chlorine bleach. Sandor recalled:

> I was the only Hungarian in the crew and was often given
> the grunt jobs. Cleaning those vats was now my job.
> Whether the foreman was picking on me, I do not know.
> But he told me that I had not cleaned the vat well enough
> and that I would have to do it again the next morning. As

far as I know that vat may still be dirty—because I quit
and did not come back the next day.

On the first day without a job, Sandor drove his Mercury to a VW
garage to have the oil changed. He told the owner, "I need a job." The
owner said, "What can you do?" To which Sandor confidently replied,
"I am a mechanic," which he later admits was a slight exaggeration. He
told the garage owner, "I will work without pay for three days, and if I
prove myself, you can either hire me or tell me goodbye." Sandor was
told to come back tomorrow. After the first day, he was hired for the
next eleven years as a mechanic. He worked for two dollars per hour.

And work he did, indeed! Volkswagens at the time did not have air
conditioning installed at the factory. An air conditioner system was
being manufactured in California and was shipped across the country
to be installed in cars. The installation job was to take sixteen hours
for a typical mechanic. Sandor could do the job in six hours but was
paid for sixteen hours of work. The owner gave Sandor the keys so
that he would be able to come to work at 5:00 AM. He worked on
Saturdays and Sundays. Sandor recalled:

> Mother told me, "Sandor, you are bringing home money in
> wheelbarrows." I did not like unions from my Hungarian
> days and my work output far surpassed a quota system. I
> soon had enough money to buy a duplex building. I did not
> smoke. I did not drink coffee, and I had no wife.

In 1964, Sandor married Olga, having met her seven years earlier
at a Hungarian club in Chicago. She was forty years old when they
married. As a teenager in Hungary, she had been a beauty queen when
the war broke out. She married a handsome lieutenant in December
1944 while he was back in Hungary on leave from the war. After a
brief ceremony, he was back with his unit on the front lines. He was
killed in action two months later. When the Russians overran Hungary,
Olga fled as a refugee west toward Germany.

Sandor and Olga honeymooned in Miami. At the Miami hotel where they stayed, it rained for two solid days. When a man came through the lobby with a scarlet sunburn, Sandor asked where he had been in that kind of sun. The man said, "At Key West." The next day the newlyweds were off to Key West. On that trip they bought three undeveloped bare lots.

A son, Peter, was born in 1968 in Chicago. Sandor had his eyes and dreams set on buying a VW dealership in Florida. Sandor shared:

> The dealership was sold out from under me, in an overnight backroom office deal. I had flown to Florida to make the transaction and was staying at a motel when I got the news. Stewing to myself and walking around the parking lot of the motel, I asked a maintenance guy, "Who owns this place?" He quipped that it was owned by the bank because it was in bankruptcy.

Sandor set out to find the bank in Sarasota, having no idea which bank or who to look for. On his second stop at Ellis Bank, he lucked out to find the trust officer that had knowledge of the motel property and was overseeing the operation. Sandor told him, "I would like to buy it from you."

The bank's trust officer said, "I am asking 100 thousand dollars for the property. What kind of collateral do you have?"

Sandor confidently replied, "Ah, I have a duplex in Chicago clear, and three lots in Key West."

That spring, Sandor, Olga, Esther, and baby Peter drove down to Key West from Chicago. Sandor was swimming in the ocean when a call from the trust officer came to the motel where they were staying. Taking the call, he was instructed to go to Sarasota to meet with him as soon as possible. "But I am in my swimming trunks," Sandor protested.

The voice on the other end of the phone said, "That is okay, but please come immediately."

Sandor and Esther drove their car to the meeting place. On a handshake, the deal was completed. "One condition is that I do need a down payment," the officer added. Esther had a ten-dollar bill in her purse, and it was left with the man for the down payment on the Sunset Terrace Motel in Bradenton, Florida.

Upon getting back to Chicago, Sandor contacted his lawyer, who had agreed to be a partner on the motel venture. They met at the lawyer's plane on Easter Sunday, 1969, and flew to Sarasota with 100 thousand dollars to buy the motel. Just thirteen years after fleeing Hungary as a refugee, Sandor and Olga set off on the business venture at 4644 Tamiami Drive, Bradenton, Florida. From being a mechanic to owning and operating a fifty-five-unit motel with five villas attached on a five-acre property, this became their life for the next thirty-three years. Sandor proudly said in 2021:

> We had a great clientele. The main bookkeeper for Sears in Chicago sent many of their executives to stay with us. The repeat business made us successful. I was able to do all of the maintenance, electrical, plumbing, painting, and the repair work. I built the beautiful swimming pool for our guests which was a great draw for the motel. Olga managed the personnel and hiring of the staff.

Epilogue

In retirement, Sandor and Olga sold their property and moved to southern Sarasota in a Spanish-style veranda. Their son Peter had been sent back to Budapest, Hungary, for high school. When he returned to Florida, he had a career in banking.

In 1991, with the collapse of the Soviet Union, The Genersich's were able to reclaim their house and property in Hungary. They spend summer months back in their native country. "Ah! Budapest is the most beautiful city in the world. You must go there and see someday," Sandor beamed as he shared.

Authors note: Taking Sandor's advice, I did make the trip to Budapest in 2023. Indeed, I have to agree, it is a beautiful city.

Snezana Radnovic

A young woman fled Serbia during the Bosnian War, but ran into trouble in the US. After overcoming obstacles, she became a highly-educated, accomplished nurse practitioner.

". . . My friend said I could stay with him and his mother if I preferred. So, I did . . . His mother was wearing the exact same special necklace that my mother had worn when I was a little girl back in Serbia. I thought this must be a special sign that I was loved again and that my life could indeed change." —Snezana

Snezana

Describing the country of Serbia in a few paragraphs from the sixth century onward is very complex and nearly impossible. Here is a snapshot of Serbia in the twentieth century:

- Serbia is a country on the west central part of the Balkan Peninsula. It is the size of Ohio in the United States.
- It is of Slavic heritage and Eastern Orthodox religion.
- Serbia has experienced many wars throughout its history.
- Serbia was ruled by the Ottomans until the First Balkan War of 1912-13, when it came under Austro-Hungarian rule until 1918.
- Serbia was renamed Yugoslavia (Land of the South Slavs) after 1929.

A brief history of Serbia for the past one hundred years begins with the formation of Yugoslavia at the end of World War I. This was commonly referred to as the "Versailles State," or as the Kingdom of Serbs, Croats, and Slovenes. The government renamed the country Yugoslavia in 1929. This lasted until the end of World War II, when the Communists renamed it the Socialist Federal Republic of Yugoslavia. This included six republics and two provinces: The republics of Serbia, Bosnia-Herzegovina, Montenegro, Croatia, Macedonia, Slovenia; and the provinces of Kosovo and Vojvodina.

A third twentieth century version of Yugoslavia was formed in 1991 with the dissolution of the Soviet Union. First to declare secession were Slovenia and Croatia on June 25, 1991. This was soon followed by Macedonia in September 1991, and the Bosniaks (Muslims) in March 1992. Serbia and Montenegro creating a federation in April 1992.

To most of the Western world, the ensuing civil wars in Bosnia and Kosovo were little understood. What was primarily known was the fact that the countries of the former Yugoslavia were choosing sides based on religious and ethnic differences. To further complicate the understanding, there were minorities in each country because of intermarriage and business relocations.

The terms of ethnic cleansing and genocide were used to describe the horrific images from this conflict. Deaths, assassinations, mass burials, massacres, and mutilations were commonplace, described in pictures and documentaries from media exposure. Without further describing the blame, over one million refugees were relocated. It is within this world that innocent civilians lived.

On December 12, 1981, a baby girl, Snezana Radnovic, was born in Belgrade, Yugoslavia, as it was known at the time (Serbia). Her parents were well-educated. Her father was an engineer. Her mother had a degree in economics and business and worked in the construction material supply business.

Snezana means "Snow White" in the Serbian language. She attended school at a preparatory high school through the ninth grade. Like her mother, she excelled in economics and business classes. She had studied English since elementary school. When her mother died in October 1999, her father wanted to protect her during the impending civil war. He was able to connect with a distant cousin in Los Angeles, California, who promised to take Snezana for one month in November 1999. This sixteen-year-old girl was placed on a bus to Budapest and on a plane headed to America all by herself. Following a sixteen-hour flight overseas with one stop, she was met at the Los Angeles International Airport by this cousin whom she had never seen before. Snezana said:

> It had always been a dream of mine to visit the United States. After my mother passed away, my dad arranged for me to go as a distraction. This cousin was like a mom to me, my only family in Los Angeles. I had intended only staying for one month, but the war started in Serbia right after I arrived, and it became impossible to fly back home. It was impossible to fly to the airports in Belgrade, as they were closed because of the daily bombing. My father and brother were hiding daily in shelters.

The cousin agreed that I could stay with her and that she would process my papers. My dad sent money for me to attend a good private school.

Complications were soon revealed and things gradually changed. The cousin and her husband did not have jobs and were always short of money. During that time, Snezana attended five different high schools. She was pulled out of high school when she was about to graduate because she was told that she had to work to start earning money. She learned that the money her father was sending was being taken by the cousin. She continued:

> My teachers did not understand. I think they knew something was off. The school wanted to help me because I was a good student. Even though I did not graduate with my class in May 2003, it was arranged for me to get my diploma in November, which was unheard of, but I am tremendously grateful to them. This was the fifth high school that I had attended in Los Angeles because my cousin and husband were continually on the move.

> From then on, the cousin forced me to work two jobs and took all the money. She had taken my passport early on, and I found out she had never processed my papers, so basically, I was an illegal immigrant. I was trapped. She told me that my dad had remarried, and that he had a new family and had forgotten about me. She told me he never even tried to call. I was young and brainwashed into believing he really didn't care whether he would ever see me again.

It didn't seem like things could get much worse, but they did. The cousin and her husband moved numerous times. They had several different IDs and passports. They appeared to always be fleeing from someone. The three of them moved to Miami where, again, Snezana found work in two different restaurants, working morning and afternoon to evening shifts back-to-back. Under the control of the cousin, Snezana said:

> This went on for the next six years. When the cousin thought I was not making enough money, she would take me to IVF [clinics] and forced me to donate my eggs for money.

Snezana had made friends at work and started to share her story with them. A colleague's boyfriend took her and introduced her to the Florida Immigrant Advocacy Center (FIAC). She remembered:

> They said I should contact LUCHA, which is an organization that provides free legal help for immigrant women that are victims of trafficking and domestic abuse. A close friend at the restaurant advised me that I had to get away from the control and slave-like treatment of my cousin. He invited me to stay with him and his mother. So, one day, I left work with all my things and moved to his house. The cousin actually tried to get me arrested.

Hearing her testimony, FIAC wanted to sue her dad's cousin, but she had already moved again and most likely taken on a different name; they could not find her. Snezana wanted to forget that period of her life. She never saw the cousin again. They recommended that she move into a shelter for protection. Snezana's father in Serbia had heard she was in Miami. He had come once to find her but was unable to locate her. He had tried numerous times to call, but the cousin lied about their whereabouts. Three months after moving out from the cousin's control, Snezana wrote to him, and he came back to Miami to look for her, but the cousin had moved yet again. It would be seventeen years before they would be reunited. She shared:

With LUCHA's advice, I quit my jobs. I did not move into a shelter, as my friend said I could stay with him and his mother if I preferred. So, I did. They were so nice to me. His mother was wearing the exact same special necklace that my mother had worn when I was a little girl back in Serbia. I thought this must be a special sign that I was loved again and that my life could indeed change.

I was depressed and confused about what to do with myself. I rested and went to counseling and therapy sessions through Medicaid. I didn't want to go back to Serbia because I had built my life in Miami. All my friends back home had gotten their college degrees, and I hadn't. I felt bad about that. My dad had his life too. I felt like there was nothing left for me in Serbia, so I decided to stay here in Miami. My mother used to look after my dad. He didn't even know how to cook. He didn't know how to look after himself after she died. The war was raging, and he soon remarried. But he never stopped missing me or thinking of me. There are many regrets, but I am so glad I have a relationship with my dad back in Serbia again, even though he lives so far away.

With the counseling advice, Snezana explored some other career opportunities. She explained:

I wanted to do something to help people. I love being able to serve and give to others. My counselor thought my choice of nursing seemed like a good idea because it was a short study which would allow me to make some money quickly. I wrote an essay about freedom, and I used it to apply for a scholarship. At the same time, a friend of a friend offered me a job in a dental office.

Snezana's college experience had just begun. She enrolled at Miami Dade College and earned an associate's degree in nursing in 2009. Her first job was in a nursing home. She kept writing essays and applied for several more scholarships. She said, "Many organizations gave me money, often just small amounts, but together it was enough for me to continue my studies. While studying, I worked night shifts at a hospital to get by."

Snezana was able to get a visa with the help of FIAC because of the trafficking background that she had endured. She then applied for a green card. With this she was able to work legally. She then applied for United States citizenship and was accepted in 2013. "This whole process took like eight years," she shared proudly.

Epilogue

Snezana Radnovic, a beautiful 5' 4" blonde, blue-eyed immigrant now works at the nationally renowned Bascom Palmer Eye Institute in Miami as a nurse practitioner. With her infectious smile, she assists in anesthesia for surgery, and in ambulatory care from newborns to older adults.

America's arms have opened to this immigrant. Though the path had many roadblocks, she received help from LUCHA, FIAC, Medicaid, food stamps, counseling, and friends who have enabled this exceedingly talented lady. She is now giving of herself as a nurse practitioner and serving others.

With her strength, determination, and dedication, she climbed many educational ladders. The list of her accomplishments is many. She received a bachelor's degree in nursing (BSN) from Miami Dade College (MDC) in 2012. She graduated with the highest honors and was an MDC Wall Plaque Recipient. Her first master's degree was as a Family Nurse Practitioner, earned at Florida International University. She received the Excellence in Civic Engagement Medallion Award and graduated with a 4.0 GPA. She completed her second master's degree in leadership and management at University of Miami Business School, again with a 4.0 GPA.

Snezana's honors and awards continue to accumulate:

- 2006 ESA Foundation Scholarship Recipient 2007 Blue Shield Blue Cross Scholarship Recipient
- 2008 Municipalities of Cuba in Exile Scholarship Recipient
- 2009 Possible Women Foundation International Scholarship and Possible Women Enterprises Twelfth Annual Leadership Conference Honorable Guest: Power, Promise, and Possibilities with Dee Dee Myers (First woman White House Press Secretary).
- 2009 Dr. Padron's Student Leadership Retreat Workshop Honored Guest
- 2009 International Scholar Laureate Program Delegation of Nursing Recipient
- 2010 All-USA Community College Academic Team Recipient and member of 1st Team for 2010 All-Florida Academic Team
- 2010 MDC Board of Trustees' Scholarship Recipient
- 2010-2011 Florida International University Honors College Scholarship
- 2010 Florida Nurse Foundation, Agnes Naughton Scholarship in Nursing
- 2010 November Employee of the Month at Unity Health-Rehab Center
- 2011 Florman Family Foundation Endowment Scholarship in Nursing
- 2012 Association Cubana De Mujeres Universitario Scholarship
- 2013 The DAISY award; Extraordinary Nurse Nominee U. of Miami Hospital
- 2013 Florida Nurses Foundation District 14 Marcy Klosterman Scholarship
- 2013 Health Foundation South Florida Scholarship
- 2014 Lena Pearl Curtiss Wheeler Miami Springs Women's Club Nursing

- Award and Scholarship
- 2014 FIU University Wide Scholarship Recipient
- 2014 Florida Nurses Foundation Connie Dorry Memorial Fund Scholarship
- 2014 Excellence in Civic Engagement FIU Medallion of Distinction
- 2018 ARNP of the Year at University Health Bascom Palmer
- 2019 National Nurse Practitioner Symposium Scholarship Recipient

In April 2023, Snezana was a presenter at the American Society of PeriAnesthesia Nurses' second national conference titled, *The Heart: A Science of Caring.* The title of the scientific paper was, "Bringing the World into Focus; Identifying Red Flags in Eye Surgery," by Snezana Radnovic, APRN, FNP-BC, CAPA.

Many days after work, she can be found kite surfing and sailing along Miami's Atlantic shores. With her husband, she visits Cabarete, a small town in the Dominican Republic. They kite surf and stay in a small apartment on the beach. She exclaimed, "This is my happy place!"

Tamene "Tom" Gelashe
and Shuna Tosa

A teacher and an entrepreneur from rural Ethiopia won the
immigration lottery to bring their family to the US.
Their work ethic and attitude allowed them to build a
beautiful life for themselves and their large family.

"Remember, I said I was born to work." —Shuna

Tom and Shuna

Ethiopia is in the Horn of Africa, or the nose of the continent that protrudes on the eastern side of Africa where the mouth of the Red Sea opens from the Indian Ocean. The country is landlocked with Sudan and South Sudan to the west, Eritrea to the north, Djibouti to the northeast, Somalia to the east, and Kenya to the south.

Ethiopia is the tenth largest country in Africa and has a population of eighty million. It is one of the oldest countries in the world. Ethiopia has been under Ottoman, Portuguese, and Italian rule. It became prominent in world affairs in 1896 when they defeated colonial Italians. Italy invaded again in 1935 and was in control of the government until 1941.

It was one of the first countries to sign the United Nations Charter on June 26, 1945. Ethiopia played a leading role in the decolonization of Africa. The forming of the Organization of African Unity brought former colonies together for cooperation on economic and education issues. This organization became known as the African Union in 2002.

Ethiopia is ethnically diverse, with over one hundred languages. Amharic is the language of the federal government. The religious makeup is also very diverse, with two fifths of the people Eastern Orthodox, two fifths other Christian faiths with the majority Protestant, and one fifth Muslim. There is a perception that Ethiopia is an "island of Christianity in a sea of Islam."

The growth rate is among the largest in Africa, with many refugees fleeing famine from Somalia, Sudan, South Sudan, and Eritrea.

From 1930 to 1974, the country was ruled by Emperor Haile Selassie I. He was known as a descendant of the biblical King Solomon and Queen of Sheba. He attempted to modernize Ethiopia through a series of political and social reforms. He was overthrown by a military coup led by a Marxist-Leninist junta. This military group was aided by Cubans and Soviets and became known as the Derg. It was under the leadership of the Derg that land was appropriated back to individual farmers. In 1991, a severe famine in the country led to the fall of the Derg.

Tamene Gelashe (shortened to Tom in America) was born in 1961. Shuna Tosa was born in 1967. They were both from farming families, near the village of Afranoromo in the state of Oromia (Oromo: *Oromiyaa*) in southeastern part of Ethiopia. Oromo refers to a tribe of this area. Their families raised barley, wheat, cows, sheep, horses, and milk cows. They farmed with horses.

Tom and Shuna both attended school from the first through the twelfth grade in the big city of Dodola. There was a six-year difference in their ages. They knew each other even though they attended different schools. Tom continued his education at an institute to become a teacher, where he majored in Ethiopian history. He rode a horse to a very remote rural area for his first teaching job. Tom recalled:

> As a teacher, I was treated with the utmost respect. I was like a father figure to the students and was honored as a professional. The distance from Shuna strained our relationship. We waited until she finished her schooling and were married in 1984 when she was seventeen years old. We lived in a hut where I was teaching school.

Tom taught school there for ten years. He worked his way back to being closer to the city with his years of experience. He taught a total of nineteen years, and spent twelve of those years as a principal. A principal was also required to teach at least one course, which in his case was language arts and history. Transportation was by bicycle or horse.

Shuna had a business which she ran both out of her house and in a store. She took coffee to the city, traveling by bus. She proudly shared, "The name of coffee in Ethiopia is Kafa, and it is the first place in history that coffee is known. I became a community volunteer, and our family was rewarded with farmland being given to us. We had milk cows, donkeys, chickens, and horses." Shuna milked the cows and had a contract with a hotel to provide them with milk With this money, she was able to buy food for the family. Tom shared,

"We had to run around in the surrounding farming area to find roughage for the animals."

Shuna's business also included selling soap and sugar from their home. She bought coffee in town and resold it in the cities. Shuna said, "I started working when I was born." Tom included, "Shuna is a queen. She always prepared a nice dinner and breakfast for our family, which grew to six children."

Tom and Shuna had applied to the National Visa Center in the United States. One hundred thousand had applied and fifty-five thousand were granted immigration to the States. In the last month of 2001, the family name was drawn from the lottery to come to America. What a celebration they had, and yet, the unknown was at times overwhelming. The packing was daunting. The trepidation of flying with six children was a huge concern. They boarded a plane in the capital of Addis Ababa for an eighteen-hour flight to a country halfway around the world where they would make a new home. Tom's accented English was the conduit to communication with the airplane personnel and customs authorities in Minneapolis. The food offered to them on the flight was an adventure. Foreign flavors and different options were challenging for all eight family members. After four days in Minneapolis, the family shuttled to Cedar Rapids, Iowa. They were met by a friend who acted as a sponsor. Shuna smiled and said, "We started life from scratch, again."

Within eleven days of being in the United States, Tom had a job in a hotel as a houseman. He cooked at another hotel at the same time. That cooking job would last for twelve years. "My specialty was lasagna. Maybe I had learned some of the Italian cooking from some of the wives back in Ethiopia. I surprised my middle daughter, Sadia, when I brought lasagna to her school classroom when they were studying Ethiopia and Africa," remembered Tom.

Tom inquired at a Cedar Rapids school about a possible teaching position. He was informed that his credentials were not satisfactory. He would have to get a four-year degree and a teaching certificate.

Authors note: Rigid hoops for a teacher with nineteen years of experience. How many students would have benefited from his history and language arts lessons?

An attentive janitor in the hallway had overheard the discussion about Tom's lack of adequate education to teach. He pulled him aside and suggested that he was hiring three people for various jobs in the district. By 2006, Tom was the head custodian at Washington High School. In 2008, he applied and was hired as the second-shift custodial engineer at McKinley Junior High School. Keep in mind that his second job was as a cook at the hotel.

Tom is an avid gardener. "Back home we had never farmed with a tractor, so I am very adept with a hoe and shovel. I had never driven a car. After our purchase of a car, I taught Shuna to drive. All the children learned to drive in driver's education at school," Tom reflected.

Lemi, the oldest son, graduated from Coe College in Cedar Rapids with a degree in political science. He spent four years in Washington DC as an intern and later worked in the Obama administration. Tom grinned and shared, "Lemi said he was going to invite President Obama and Michelle to his wedding—though I do not know if he actually did." Lemi married an Australian and they presently reside in Melbourne.

Shuna, in addition to directing the adjustment of the children into a new culture and schooling, soon had a job at a hotel as a housekeeper. She walked ten minutes to and from work each day. Her winning smile and bounding work ethic made her a treasure at the Crowne Plaza Hotel. After three years and seven months, she moved to the Clarion Hotel. Now that she was driving, she accepted a job a half hour away at the University of Iowa hospital in Iowa City in the surgery area where she worked for fifteen years. When Shuna's sister died from cancer back in Ethiopia, they brought her five children to live with them in Cedar Rapids. These two nieces and three nephews were then welcomed to the family's home as daughters and sons. To afford to bring these five children to America, Shuna took a second full-time job at St. Luke's Hospital in Cedar Rapids. After an eight-to-four job in Iowa City, she started at 4:30 PM at St. Luke's for the next two years. She grinned. "Remember, I said I was born to work."

As a writer, I was extremely fortunate to be introduced to this family by a fellow writer, Kathy Ulch. She had met the family eight years before when Tom brought Sadia to enroll her at Kennedy High School. Kathy was the secretary to the Associate Principal. She overflows with love and admiration for Tom and Shuna and their eleven children and says, "they are my second family". Sadia calls Kathy her "second mother."

Upon arriving at the Gelashe home in a very modern suburban neighborhood, I was struck by the attractive four-to-five-bedroom home, the two-car garage, three cars in the driveway, the basketball hoop in the front and the beautiful lawn. Upon being invited into the home by Tom, my eyes were first drawn to the large dining room table where the wooden chairs were adorned with a knitted yellow and brown headrest coverlet. I inquired if Shuna had made these. She informed me that, "no," indeed they were very typical to the chairs around the tables back in the homes in Ethiopia. The youngest daughter, Dureti, a fifteen-year-old with a gleam in her eyes sat very attentively and glowed when listening to the interview with her parents. She prided herself when later explaining about the *injera,* or a type of pancake that was offered for the evening meal. When Tom asked, "You will stay for supper," it was more of a directive than a question. I responded that I had a six o'clock appointment which was about an hour's drive away. He quietly and quickly quipped, "Well since it is now 6:05, it looks like you can just be a little more later. But would you please excuse me for just a few minutes while I run to pick up our son, Abdisa, from basketball practice?"

So, it was for supper that I was treated with hospitality and *injera,* greens, and a turmeric-spiced potato, carrot, and vegetable dish. It was one for the books! *Injera* is made from Teff flour which is brought to the States from Ethiopia and can be bought in Minneapolis and Chicago. Sometimes barley and rice are added. It is cooked on a stovetop much like a pancake, but the velvety texture is much softer.

Shuna instructed how to tear off a small portion and fold it around the other offerings and eat it like a traditional wrap. She warned that my fingers might turn yellow from the turmeric, but that they would easily wash clean. When Tom returned with the basketball player, he suggested that I come down to the lower level to see the "coffee ceremony." This was a miniature table with decorative bone china cups and saucers, with a coffee vessel which was heated by an electric heating iron. When resting on the floor, the coffee would be served in a seated position.

Epilogue

From a farm and a remote school in Ethiopia, to a new land and culture, this beautiful family with now eleven children has come to America as the pioneers and immigrants who bring their hopes of wonderful new beginnings even today in the twenty-first century. I assure you that their work ethic is a testament to their assimilation and love for their new country. Whenever in Cedar Rapids, Iowa, there is a "coffee ceremony" waiting for you with this incredible family.

Vasil Ianakiev

A Bulgarian man fled from communism to Mexico
before seeking asylum in the US, where he
became a successful businessman in Florida.

*"We were warned about ten times to stay on the plane. Every flight had a
KGB agent on board. In Miami, we all got off and left the plane and
headed for a hallway where we sat down with our backs against the wall. I
had heard that the officials would not touch us if we were sitting . . ."*

—Vasil

Vasil

Bulgaria is bordered on the north by Romania, the east by the Black Sea, the south by Greece and Turkey, and the west by North Macedonia and Serbia. It is one of only two countries in Europe (the other being Denmark) that refused to send its fifty thousand Jews to concentration camps during World War II. Its 43,240 sq. mi. (110,994 sq. km.) makes it approximately the size of Pennsylvania in the United States and the sixteenth largest country in Europe.

Bulgarian history dates back to the eighth century BC with traces of its civilization found there that are older than those of Mesopotamia and Egypt. Bulgaria was ruled by the Greeks—Macedonia was led by Phillip II and his son, Alexander the Great—as well as Romans, Byzantines, Slavs, and Ottomans. After World War II, Bulgaria became part of the ex-Soviet bloc. From 1946-1990, the Communist government ruled the country. The land was collectivized and industry was nationalized. In 1990, Bulgaria was transformed into a democratic country and part of the European family. It is picturesque, with beautiful mountains and golden beaches along the Black Sea. The national literacy rate is ninety-eight percent, compared to sixty-five to eighty-five percent in the United States.

Plovdiv is the second largest city in Bulgaria. It is 170 miles from the Black Sea to the east and ninety miles east of the capital, Sofia. For many centuries Bulgarians, Turks, Armenians, Jews, Greeks, and Romans lived together in the city. It has houses of worship including those of Orthodox, Catholics, Protestants, Armenians, Jews, and Muslims.

Vasil Ianakiev was born on October 26, 1964, in Plovdiv. Gregor, his father, was Greek. Donita, his mother, was Bulgarian. Ultimately, Vasil married Elena. Vasil was a merchant and sold earrings, necklaces, and belts. He declared:

> I refused to sell anything made in China. My city was the
> most ancient city in Europe. When building a new

building, you could dig down and find foundations below.
History got buried. The history we learn in books is all
fake.

He was studying psychiatry but did not finish because he was trying to go to America. In 1991, after the wall fell and the Iron Curtain was lifted in Eastern Europe, Vasil went to the Bulgarian Embassy and told them he wanted to visit the United States. His passport was stamped black which meant that he could not ask for another passport for ten years.

Vasil then went to the Mexican Embassy in Bulgaria and met an agent who was able to set up vacations for people to Mexico City. For some reason, the embassy lady took the passports of the eight adults and four children traveling with Vasil. She set up the travel arrangements to Mexico City. Vasil, Elena, and the other six adults and four children flew from Sofia, Bulgaria, to Moscow, Russia, to Shannon, Ireland, to Miami, Florida, and finally to Mexico City, Mexico, all on a Russian airline.

The dozen travelers stayed one night in Mexico City and then boarded a bus for a two-day trip, headed nine hundred miles north to Neuvo Laredo. The morning of the second day, a man got on the bus with a badge turned over backward, no ticket, and sat in the first row of seats. Elena was the only one who could speak English. Vasil mumbled under his breath, "I think that guy must be an immigration agent." He said of the day:

> When the bus stopped, the man said, "Come with me."
> He asked for our passports, and we said they were lost.
> We told him that we were Armenians. How stupid we
> were. I had heartburn and always traveled with baking
> soda to help my stomach. When they opened my
> suitcase, they found the baking soda and thought it was
> cocaine. The man's name was Pepe. I had about twenty-
> five thousand dollars in my pocket and thought I could

offer a bribe to Pepe. I had Elena ask him how much
money, but Pepe said, "I can't do it." We were all taken to
jail and they took good care of us. We gave them money
to get us food. All our luggage came to the jail with us.
We were separated from the other inmates. It was like a
1920s jail in America where there were no windows, just
metal bars over the openings. We were there about a
week.

When there seemed to be an impasse in getting their release, the
group next told the jailer they were Greek. After some time, a Greek
translator came to interview them. "Oops! We were screwed, as none
of us knew any Greek," chuckled Vasil. The eight adults and four
children were put on a bus headed back to Mexico City, and were sent
to another jail. This time they were not separated from the other
inmates. Vasil remembered, "There was an eighty-year-old man laying
on a dirty mattress who had been there for eight years. Our future
looked bleak. Elena suggested that we call the Bulgarian Embassy."
She got on the phone and pleaded their case. Three days later, the
embassy employee came to the jail to rescue them.

The twelve travelers were taken to the Mexico City Airport and
placed again on a Russian airline. They told the flight attendant their
passports were in Moscow. The plane took off and first landed in
Miami. Vasil relived the day:

We were warned about ten times to stay on the plane.
Every flight had a KGB agent on board. In Miami, we all
got off and left the plane and headed for a hallway where
we sat down with our backs against the wall. I had heard
that the officials would not touch us if we were sitting.

A United States immigration officer approached the group and
escorted the twelve of them to a nearby airport hotel. They were given
rooms on the fourth floor and were warned not to leave the hotel.
Vasil had an urge for a cigarette and bought some in the lobby and

went out on the sidewalk of the hotel to smoke. "An authority yelled at me to get back in the hotel and to never leave it again," said Vasil.

After the two-month stay at the hotel, they were taken before a judge and represented by an attorney. They were given asylum and told they could fly to Chicago where Vasil had a friend who could vouch for them. All their money had been spent on food in the two months at the hotel and the attorney. Vasil and Elena took their gold bracelets and nearly two pounds of gold jewelry and hocked it at a jewelry store. They were given three hundred dollars in cash for their gold which was worth nearly seven thousand dollars. This cash was used for airline tickets for Vasil and Elena to Chicago.

On the second day in Chicago, Vasil had a construction job which paid ten dollars per hour. After ten days in Chicago, the couple left for Janesville, Wisconsin, where they both got jobs cleaning restaurants. "We cleaned restaurants like Chi-Chi's with over seven hundred seats from 11:00 PM until 3:00 AM," recalled Vasil.

At one of the cleaning sites, he met a man from Milwaukee who had two restaurants there. He offered Vasil and Elena jobs in his restaurants. They were in the cleaning area again because of their language barrier. "This was a much better job for us," Vasil remembered. After one year in this business with his friend, Vasil and Elena both received a letter in the mail from Immigration Services. The letters read: "You have been selected by the Bulgarian lottery and have won the lottery to immigrate to America and be awarded a green card." With this news and the letter in hand, Elena flew back to Bulgaria to retrieve their son, Anton, to bring him back to Wisconsin with her.

The couple found a two-bedroom home north of Milwaukee on two acres. They rented it for eight hundred dollars a month. They saw an advertisement in the Milwaukee paper for a cleaning service. After answering the ad, Vasil and Elena bought the cleaning franchise. Within a year, Vasil and Elena had thirty-eight employees working for them. They cleaned factories and offices in Appleton, Oshkosh, Green Bay, and Milwaukee. Vasil bought a Ford Expedition truck and put 320 thousand miles on the truck. "I never touched a thing on the truck except new tires and changing the oil in the five years of owning it. I was learning English from my employees and television," he proudly shared.

Vasil had seen an empty building where the store had gone out of business. He called the number on the sign in the window. He bought the shelving and converted the building into a liquor store. At a cost of sixty thousand dollars, he had stocked the shelves and was open for business. Vasil proudly said, "I never took anything from a bank. I always paid cash and had no mortgage on anything."

Vasil then opened his own restaurant in Milwaukee called Fresh. He was very handy in all areas of construction. The only contractors he used were electricians and plumbers. Five years later, he opened a second Fresh restaurant.

A friend who had moved to Punta Gorda, Florida, had begged Vasil to come see him there and experience the business opportunities in the area. After about five years of putting off the visit, Vasil and Elena drove to Florida. Their last experience in the state had not been a very happy time while confined to the airport hotel in Miami. They drove to Sarasota and fell in love with the city. "It was like a pretty woman—I fell in love," he laughed. They had seen a restaurant on St. Armands Circle while sitting on a park bench. Little did they know at the time that this would be another door to their life in America.

They returned to Wisconsin, but four months later Elena and their second son, Ivan, were once again in Florida. On St. Armands Circle, they found a store for lease. It only had 1,200 square feet and the lease was for twelve thousand dollars a month. Elena called Vasil back in Wisconsin to report what she had found. Vasil told her the lease for that amount was crazy, but directed her to call the owner that they would like to buy the store front. Within the next two months, Vasil and Elena sold the Wisconsin cleaning business and their two restaurants and moved to Florida.

Vasil and Elena opened the Green Zebra restaurant on St. Armands Circle. In the first sixteen months, they had two days off. They worked from seven o'clock in the morning until ten at night.

Epilogue

While sitting in Vasil's office in 2023 (actually, on two benches behind the second Green Zebra restaurant on Main Street in Sarasota), Vasil shared the rest of his story:

> I am sixty-nine years old. I became a citizen just two months ago and Elena two months before that. Our three sons, Anton, Ivan, and Alexander, are all here. The first two went to school in Wisconsin and Alexander to Sarasota High School. Anton is in the restaurant business. Ivan is in real estate. Alexander is in the computer software business.
>
> Thinking back on my life, it has been a great adventure. My happiness is my family. They are all here—what else do I need? There has never been a fight in our family. The boys live a happy life. I think we taught them well. I never had to punish them. If I kick the bucket one day, I think they will all continue to work and do well.
>
> There is a joke about a younger lady who married an eighty-year-old man. He asked her if she married him for his money. She made him a promise to put all his money in his coffin when he died. When that day came and when the coffin was about to close, she slipped a check inside for thirty-five million dollars.
>
> You see, my happiness is my family, and that is worth all the money in the world.

From their native country, Bulgaria, living under a Communist regime, Vasil and Elena's journey to America took many turns. Their drive for success in business brought the family to Florida in their city on Sarasota Bay.

Vicky Vengoecha-Beter

Born into the midst of violent political conflict involving cartels, a girl and her family fled to Florida to escape their dangerous circumstances. It was there that she got her education and discovered her passion for teaching.

"My mother only had an eighth-grade education but saw that I was a very good student. She felt that education was a ticket to freedom. She encouraged me to go on to school. I was going to work my rear off so that I could be independent." —Vicky

Vicky

This story begins when a baby is born in Colombia, along the Caribbean Sea, in the important port city of Barranquilla. Although she would become a United States citizen twenty-three years later in Miami, Florida, let us learn about her native country and its early history first. The city's name refers to the canyons in the area where the Magdalena River forms a delta flowing northward to the sea. Waves of European immigrants made this area a haven to escape the ravages of the two world wars.

The country of Colombia is twice the size of France. The Andes Mountains are along the western edge of the country. This mountain range starts at the southern tip of South America and continues northward through Chile, Peru, Ecuador, Colombia, and Panama. The lofty, snow-tipped peaks of the Colombian interior Cordilleras features the highest peaks of Pico Cristóbal Colón and Simón Bolívar at 18,947 ft. Colombia is bordered by Panama on the north; Venezuela, and Brazil to the east; and Ecuador and Peru to the south. The Pacific coastline extends eight hundred miles, while the Caribbean coast line, which includes Barranquilla north of Bogotá, is one thousand miles in length. Steep and articulated bays, inlets, capes, and promontories accentuate the shoreline on the Pacific side, interspersed with sandy beaches. The country is an archaeologist's dream, as cultural artifacts date back to the last ice age—more than twenty thousand years ago. Indigenous people were brought to Colombia by the land bridge which exists today between North and South America through Panama.

The Spanish came to the northern Caribbean coast in 1499, near today's Cabo de la Vela. They found settlements and societies of Indigenous peoples, most notably the Muisca Confederation, Quimbaya, and Tairona chiefdoms. The Spanish made several attempts to settle along the coasts in the early sixteenth century, and the first permanent settlement at Santa Marta, Colombia, dates from 1525. Cartagena was founded in 1533 in the former location of the Indigenous Caribbean Calamari village. Cartagena grew rapidly, fueled by gold found in tombs of the Sinú culture. Thirst for gold lured Spanish explorers to visit the Chibchan nations of Muisca and Tairona, who still inhabit present-day Colombia. The Spanish came independently from three different directions under Jiménez de Quesada, Sebastián de Belalcázar, and Nikolaus Federmann. Although all three were drawn by Indian treasures, none intended to reach Muisca territory, where they finally met. In August, 1538, Quesada founded Santa Fe de Bogotá on the site of the Muisca village of Bacatá. The Spanish colonization created the Viceroyalty of New Granada. In 1549, the Spanish Royal Audiencia in Bogotá gave the city the status of capital of New Granada, which was comprised of, in large part, what is now the territory of Colombia.

Independence from Spain was declared in 1819, but by 1830, Gran Colombia was dissolved. Throughout the 1800s, the new nation experimented with federations. In 1863, the name was officially changed to the "United States of Colombia." In 1886, the country adopted its present name: Republic of Colombia. Constant political violence continued within the country. Two political parties grew out of conflicts, as the Conservatives and Liberals dominated Colombian politics. The Conservative Party sought strong central government, alliance with the Roman Catholic Church, and limited franchise. The forerunner of the Liberals wanted a decentralized government state rather than having the church with control over education and other civil matters, along with broadened suffrage. Throughout the nineteenth and twentieth centuries, each party held a presidency for roughly equal periods of time.

Even with the country's commitment to democratic institutions, Colombia's history has also been characterized by widespread, violent conflicts. Civil wars were frequent, with bilateral confrontation and assassinations of leaders. The influence of the United States in the area, especially from its construction and control of the Panama Canal, led to a military uprising in the "Isthmus Department" in 1903. This ultimately led to the secession and independence of Panama. From 1958 to 1974, the Conservatives and Liberals governed jointly. The presidency would be determined by an alternating conservative and liberal presidency every four years. The two parties would have parity in all elective offices. Despite this arrangement, many social and political injustices continued.

A guerrilla movement, *Movimiento 19 de abril*—also known as the 19th of April Movement or M-19—grew in 1970 when the dictator, President Gustavo Rojas Pinilla, was defeated in a questionably fraudulent election. Another guerrilla group, *Ejército de Liberación Nacional*—also known as the National Liberation Army or ELN—rejected any negotiations and continued to cover itself using extortions and threats, particularly against foreign oil companies of American and European origins. The illegal drug trade was widespread among these guerrillas and wealthy drug lords, who had mutually uneven relations leading to numerous incidents between them. Kidnappings by drug cartel members were rampant. The violent Medellín Cartel hitmen bribed or murdered numerous public officials and politicians who stood in their way by supporting the implementation of extradition of Colombian nationals to the United States. The violence came to a head on November 6, 1985, when M-19 stormed the Colombian Palace of Justice. M-19 held hostage the Supreme Court magistrates who were intending to put President Belisario Betancur on trial.

It was into this historical time that Vicky Vengoecha-Beter was born on June 16, 1976, in Barranquilla, Colombia. Vicky's father was Heriberto (Eddie) Vengoecha. Heriberto's mother was French. She had come to Colombia from war-ravaged France during World War II. Vicky's mother, Maria Sophia Beter, was Heriberto's second "wife," though they were never married. Maria's father had come to Colombia from Holland, having fled Europe during World War II.

Heriberto was involved in the Colombian Cartel. He attempted to come to the United States with his family in the 1970s. In New York City, he tried to get a green card. Vicky said:

> He paid a lady in a black fur coat, who promised to get
> him the green card. She stole his money, and he was left

with no green card. My mother was Eddie's second wife, though he still had his first wife. His first wife was German and did not like my mother, Maria, and us kids. He was a good man and did his best that he could. He got all our family out of Colombia because of the Cartel. After the green card incident in New York City, he brought us, his second family, to Pinecrest, Florida. It was a very ritzy neighborhood. It was during Ronald Reagan's time, so we were able to get out of Colombia. It was the so-called "war on drugs" that got us to Florida.

The whole family waited outside a government building in Miami to get a green card. Vicky recalled, "We were desperate, and it was very cold, but all we wanted was a chance in this 'land of opportunity.'" After two hours of standing in line in the cold, Heriberto showed up when they were just inside the building. Maria, Vicky, and little brother Eddie all got their green cards that day.

Vicky attended Coral Reef Elementary School in Pinecrest. In 1990, at the age of fifteen, her mother asked Vicky if she wanted to go back to Colombia to live with her godmother for a month. She did so reluctantly for a short time, but was able to safely return to the States. In 1992, Hurricane Andrew hit Pinecrest, and their house was destroyed. The insurance reimbursement was not very good. Vicky's mother said, "That's it!" She had a Cuban friend and she moved Vicky and her brother Eddie in with a lady. "The lady agreed to let us live there until my mother sold the house," Vicky said with a smile. An older next-door neighbor, an American from Ohio, became Maria's boyfriend, helping her out with projects while Maria made ends meet by cleaning houses.

Vicky attended public high school at Palmetto Senior High, where then-Governor Jeb Bush's daughter attended as well. "I looked up to my American friends. They were very driven. I saw what my friends' parents had, and I wanted it too," she reflected. Her high school job was in retail. She soon had enough money saved to buy a 1986 maroon Chevy Celebrity for eight hundred dollars, which she named the "Vamp Mobile." Vicky explained:

> My mother only had an eighth-grade education but saw
> that I was a very good student. She felt that education
> was a ticket to freedom. She encouraged me to go on to
> school. I was going to work my rear off so that I could be
> independent.

She enrolled at Miami-Dade Community College (MCC), which was a junior college at the time. She moved out of her mother's home, as there was trouble with her younger brother, Eddie, at the time. She lived with a boyfriend while attending college. She had two jobs for the next four years, which helped pay for tuition and expenses. The first job was at Miami-Dade Public Schools, where she tutored children to become English speakers. She had learned English at the age of seven and became a natural at teaching English to children. Her second job was as a receptionist at an accounting firm.

She received an associate's degree from MCC. She then received a Coca-Cola scholarship and a Pell Grant, which enabled her to enroll at Barry University in Miami. Vicky had inquired at Florida International University (FIU) but was told by the registrar that they would not allow a work program at the time. "With the help of the scholarship and loan, I was able to enter a program called 2+2. This scholarship meant that I could go to school in the daytime and work at night," she explained. She earned her Bachelor of Science degree from Barry University in 2005.

Vicky started teaching as an intern in the fifth grade. She told of her teaching experiences:

> As a first-year teacher, it was such a struggle for me.
> Everything I had learned in college went out the windows.
> My next job was teaching fifth grade at St. Thomas the
> Apostle Catholic School. This was a private school. I had
> started to doubt that teaching was for me. I then

transferred to a public school instead and started
teaching ETO [Educational Transformation Offices], which
in Miami are schools that are at risk. Most of the students
are African American and Latino. This school was Van E.
Blanton at 103rd Street in Miami. I taught second grade.
My principal, Dr. Hall, became my mentor for many years.
I had met my calling and loved teaching. I taught
kindergarten for four years, where I had to teach the
fundamentals and phonics. This training from
kindergarten through second grade is "training to read."
Then from the third grade on it is "reading to learn." I love
teaching, I really do.

Vicky continued in her passion for teaching:

Many teachers are leaving the profession. But these kids
really need to earn. Just keep politics out of the teaching
classrooms and hopefully provide more pay to keep the
good teachers. These kids can learn. I taught EBD
[Emotional/Behavioral Disability] kids for ten years. I had
up to forty-five students in the morning and afternoon
classrooms. Most of them were boys.

She taught for ten years at these "at risk" schools. Vicky now
teaches at David Lawrence Jr., a K-8 Center in North Miami. It is a
Title I school, meaning it has a high rate of students on free and
reduced lunch. It is a multicultural school with Caucasian, African
American, Hispanic, Arabic, and Central American children. She
teaches English for Speakers of Other Languages (ESOL). She
reflected:

I find that children who come from these other countries
who have had some schooling and good educational
training can learn and read English much better and
quicker by the time they are seven years old. Cognitively,

they can so much better absorb and observe by the time they are in the third grade.

Vicky (front) with her fellow teachers

Vicky's mother, Maria, became a United States citizen in 1995. At the age of twenty-seven, Vicky became a citizen in 1997. "It was a proud moment for me. It was during the Clinton administration. I received a letter signed by President Clinton congratulating me and welcoming me as a new citizen," Vicky remembered.

Vicky married a man from Cape Cod, Massachusetts. He had problems with the law and spent time incarcerated in Montgomery, Alabama. For the next four years, she traveled the seven hundred miles from Miami to visit her husband in prison each weekend. They are reunited today and live along the Miami north shores.

Vicky has always loved the water, from her childhood spent on the beaches of the Colombian Caribbean shores and now the north shores of Miami's Atlantic Ocean. She shared, "I always loved the ocean. In Miami, like how can you not be around water." In high school she was on the track and field team. She ran distance events. At the age of thirty, a friend suggested that she might want to start running as a means of stress relief from her day of teaching. Short training runs led to half marathons and eventually twenty-six-mile marathons. She ran at least one marathon a year all throughout Florida. When a painful hip threatened her running, she consulted with a doctor. The doctor suggested surgery. Three doctors later and a stem cell treatment, the therapist told her all this treatment would not help if she did not cut out the running.

Vicky and her husband are scuba divers. She is a Scuba Schools International-rated advanced diver. While on a dive trip to Costa Rica in 2013 with her husband, she was introduced to surfing. She now owns a surfboard and catches the north swells along the Atlantic coast at least three times every week during the winter months. "This is quite a surfing community. Everyone wants to be the 'Queen of the Surf,'" she said with a grin.

Epilogue

Vicky knew no English when she arrived in Miami at the age of seven. This dynamic girl assimilated into her new surroundings and excelled in public school classrooms. She learned English at the age of seven, aspiring to be like her American friends. She worked, graduated from high school, and put herself through college while obtaining two degrees. Passion is her hallmark as she helps students through adversity. Whatever she attempts, whether it be teaching, surfing, skateboarding, or scuba diving, she pushes herself to be the best.

"I don't think I am anything special," Vicky says. What a great asset to America she is!

Epilogue

Ever since the first Europeans came to the new world, those coming to America came to an unknown land. Some were fleeing religious persecution and others from political unrest, war, and poverty. They all came with hope for a better life.

With each generation, immigrants from around the globe assimilated into the patchwork of people in their new country. They brought their language, customs, and celebrations to share. In many cases their children learned English in school and brought this language home to their parents.

The Immigrant Next Door is meant to educate the reader to the world and history of the countries from where the new immigrants came. It is not intended as a political statement about current American immigration and border issues where millions of uninvited illegals are coming with their hope of a better life. Paraphrasing 1 Corinthians 13:13, I believe that "faith, hope, and love abide," but without empathy for people, we are nothing.

The underlying theme for all the stories in *The Immigrant Next Door* is that people came for freedom. As America professes, we are the "land of the free, and home of the brave." May all Americans always choose and believe this noble premise.

Acknowledgments

A heartfelt thank you to all the people who shared their stories which made *The Immigrant Next Door* possible. What a journey this book represents.

I have been asked, "So, how did you find these people and how did they open their doors and hearts to you and share their memories?" I was not trained as a journalistic reporter, but I thrive on meeting people. As a veterinarian by trade, I had to follow leads in diagnosing puzzles and problems without verbal cues. My wife and I were traveling in Paris with Anna, our fourteen-year-old granddaughter. While they were waiting on the street for me to catch up with them, Anna asked my wife, "Does Papa always talk to everyone?" Her grandmother replied, "Yes, now you are getting to know your grandfather better."

Finding these people came randomly. I often commented to friends or acquaintances my purpose and mission for immigrant stories. They enthusiastically shared, "Oh, I know a person you should contact." They would either make the connection for me or give me the contact information and send me on my "Sherlock Holmes" journey. I had no litmus test or preconceived requirements for these individuals and their stories. I found that after a few questions these people poured out their life stories to me.

I am indebted to the following who were the sources for the names of these immigrants: Gini Berg, Robert Diedrichs, Gwen Good, Willard Jenkins, Marijke Klahn, Charlie and Betty Kirkwood, Marty Port, Jean Richardson, Tom Strub, Karen Ramey Torres, Kathy Ulch, Brenda Vemich, Will Volskis, Dianna Warren, Pat Woepking, and Anne Woodrick.

Finally, a huge thank you goes to my dear friend, Dr. Judith Harrington. Her unselfish editing and "Miss Grammarly" input and proofreading has given me such an appreciation of word order, narration, description, and dialogue.

About the Author

James Kenyon is a thirteenth-generation American immigrant. His family left Exeter, England, to come to Rhode Island in the 1600s. His grandparents migrated and homesteaded on the prairie of Western Kansas.

James is a veterinarian, historian, and public speaker. Following retirement from his mixed animal veterinary practice in Iowa, he has enjoyed writing, interviewing for stories, and presenting at events in four midwestern states.

With his wife of fifty-three years, Cynthia, he enjoys traveling, gardening, community boards, and volunteering. Their adult children and spouses, and seven grandchildren are all special in their lives. Most holidays, birthdays, and school events are family occasions.

OTHER MEADOWLARK BOOKS
BY JAMES KENYON

This is a book for ailurophiles (people who love cats). From the award-winning author of *A Cow for College and Other Short Stories of 1950s Farm Life*, comes 23 stories dedicated to those who adore their feline friends. From a three-legged barn cat to a Siamese that loved showers, from the best cat a fisherman could ever have to a veterinary clinic's greeter, these cat stories will warm the heart, bring laughter, and perhaps a tear or two.

ISBN: 978-1-956578-05-8 (paperback)
ISBN: 978-1-956578-06-5 (hardback)

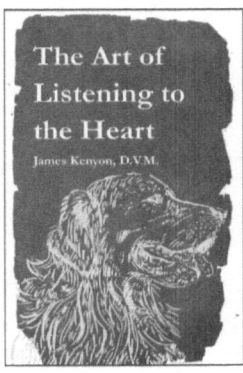

In this memoir collection, retired veterinarian James Kenyon recalls his days in veterinary practice. From heartwarming to heartbreaking and everything in between, Kenyon writes of his care for beloved family pets, livestock, and their human caretakers. Each chapter relates a specific memory of working with a quirky, loyal, and loveable animal, as well as the quirky, loyal, and lovable humans who owned them. The work offers not just insight into the work of a veterinarian, but to human nature and the manner in which people relate to and care for each other, as well as their animals.

ISBN 978-1-956578-16-4 (paperback)
ISBN 978-1-956578-17-1 (ebook)

James Kenyon writes an account of growing up in 1950s rural America that will make a reader laugh, smile, and occasionally shed a tear. Raised on the high plains of western Kansas, James shares memories of learning to care for cattle, ride (and fall from) a horse, nurse a piglet, and drive a tractor. Whether selling eggs from the back of his red wagon to the women in the nearest town of Bogue (population then approximately 300) or saving the family cow from death by bloat, readers will enjoy these pleasant reminiscings from a simpler a time in America, post-depression, post-war. ★

ISBN 978-1-956578-16-4 (paperback)
ISBN 978-1-956578-17-1 (ebook)

James Kenyon's series of books exploring the histories of closed high schools in the Midwest:

ISBN: 978-1-7342477-9-4

This collection of stories, often told in the voice of the alumni of 102 closed Iowa high schools, documents institutions from Iowa's 99 counties.

ISBN: 978-1-7322410-4-6

James Kenyon, a native of Bogue, Kansas, collected stories from student alumni of closed Kansas high schools as he traveled through every county in the state, documenting 109 institutions. ★

In both of these books, Kenyon consulted county historical records as well as interviewing former students and teachers, culminating in unique school profiles that include information ranging from the growth of school classes and programs to songs and traditions.

★ Recipient of the Martin Kansas History Book Award

If you loved this book, leave a review!

Follow Meadowlark Press
on Facebook & Instagram:

(f) facebook.com/ReadAMeadowlarkBook

(O) @meadowlarkbooks

Books are a way to explore, connect, and
discover. Reading gives us the gift of living lives
and gaining experiences beyond our own.
Publishing books is our way of saying—

We love these words,
we want to play a role in preserving them,
and we want to help share them with the world.

Meadowlark

PRESS
Emporia, Kansas, USA

MeadowlarkBookstore.com